Having Jesus for Dinner:
Community or Cannibalism

Having Jesus for Dinner: Community or Cannibalism

Can Christians Reset the Table for a New Expression of Jesus' "Holy" Meal?

CHRISTOPHER LEVAN

WIPF & STOCK · Eugene, Oregon

HAVING JESUS FOR DINNER: COMMUNITY OR CANNIBALISM
Can Christians Reset the Table for a New Expression of Jesus' "Holy" Meal?

Wipf & Stock
An Imprint of Wipf and Stock Publishers
199 W. 8th Ave., Suite 3
Eugene, OR 97401

www.wipfandstock.com

PAPERBACK ISBN: 978-1-6667-6566-3
HARDCOVER ISBN: 978-1-6667-6567-0
EBOOK ISBN: 978-1-6667-6568-7

05/03/23

For Marjory Edna Levan (Cunningham)
Ellen Signe Vesterdal

Contents

Acknowledgments

When I was fourteen, I was left alone at the family cottage for seven weeks. I now have had three sons who have, in their own unique ways, gone through that early-tween time in life, and I cannot imagine having given any of them the kind of freedom my mother and father gave me. What were they thinking? They were off to Uppsala, Oslo, Copenhagen, and God knows where else. I was consigned to Maple Leaf, Ontario, and Papineau Lake.

Ask me if I was happy? Closer to ecstatic! What a gift. My parents trusted me to run the operation of the cottage, keep the boats and docks in order and find work around the lake to pay for my own expenses. Brilliant!

My mom expected me to clean and cook for myself. The latter being top of her list of expectations. We went over menus, discussed the preparation of my favorite meals: meatloaf, spaghetti—simple fare. (I stuck mostly to roast hotdogs.) I recall asking her about making pastry. I was particularly interested in baking a cherry pie. She was busy at the time, but she rattled off her never-fail pastry recipe: 1 cup of flour and 1 lb of lard. Any bakers in the audience? You'll know immediately that this is an impossible mixture. You need six times the amount of flour to absorb that much lard. Nevertheless, surprisingly, I did get a pastry from Mom's recipe, rolled it out and put it in a pie pan. Then I filled it with a canned cherry pie mixture and crimped a topper crust to complete the picture. With that finished product, I popped the whole thing into the small oven we had in our "Bunkie," where I was staying. No sooner did my pie hit the heat than the pastry turned to a white soup, boiling over onto the electrical element and starting a minor fire, requiring the immediate application of my dad's brand-new fire extinguisher. (He later told me he was happy it worked so well.)

So, I can't say that I learned to cook from Mom—one cup of flour?!!?

To be fair, she was preoccupied, and I was being a pest. And, truth be told, when I was young, her focus was on quantity, wanting to keep her children feeling full and satisfied. Quality could wait. In later years, she progressed on to more graceful, qualitative refinements. Mom had her "party pieces" that I still enjoy as comfort food: roast beef dinners with apple pie, Christmas Eve oyster soup, hot chili by the fire (there's a pot down on the stove right now). But my own cooking skills came from a haphazard series of trials by fire, some quite literal, others more metaphorical. Since that first pie, I have been mostly on my own in the kitchen. Over time, I grew proficient—some would say even "good" at pastries. So now in later life, bake ovens and I—we're now a matched set.

Small kitchen fires notwithstanding, I am endlessly thankful to my mom. While she didn't teach me how to cook, she taught me *why* to cook. At her side, I learned the many important lessons and benefits of the dinner table: physical delight, shared love, empowering trust, soul safety, honest exchanges of opinion, and sheer joy. When trouble brewed, Mom would head to the kitchen to prepare a meal. Tears and laughter were best met with the delight of rich flavors on your tongue and satisfaction of good food in your belly.

So, I begin this text with deep gratitude, acknowledging the gifts of my mother's table. Her first and lasting language was food. Through preparing and serving it, she spoke volumes. At her table, I saw miracles unfold. And it is with her whispers in my ear that I write this book. It is only now that she is gone that I can recognize and acknowledge the depth of wisdom she shared with me.

With similar affection, I would like to thank my circle of friends in Cuba, who have allowed me to cook for them, exploring the social solidarity characteristic of Cuban culture that has become an endangered species in my homeland: Ary, Beidy, Joel, Nashla, Sergio, Nacyra, Sarah, Manuel, Ester, Papo, Tulia, Osmani, Orestes, Wanda, Stan, Dianelys, Kim, Carlos, María Victoria, Beny, Dopico, Adianes, Moisés, Chuchi, Mamita, Eric, Elaine, Yivi, Ingrid, Esther Lila, Ana María, Angie, Patricia, Reinerio, Moraima, Justo, Rosita, Estercita, Flor, Luis, Alexandra, Milagros, Lázaro, Tamara, Servando, Orquídea, Yaquelín, and Harry. Now, you will tell me that no one goes to Cuba for the food. And, you would be right, if you are referring to the menus served at all-inclusive resorts. But sit down to a home-cooked Cuban meal of congri[1] and roast pork . . . and it is a spectacular delight. And, while

---

1. A uniquely Cuban dish of rice, black beans, green peppers, garlic, and onions. I've tried to make it, but I am convinced you need to start with a pot that has been used to make congri for a few generations. Substitute red beans and the recipe becomes:

teaching in Cuba, I was introduced to a curious twist of culinary fate. The first generation of revolutionary leaders realized they needed to supply the population with a tasty, cheap street snack. Hence, pizza became a staple of the Cuban diet. State bureaucrats devised a cheap six-inch cheese pizza that could be folded and sold on the side of a plate of tomato sauce-soaked spaghetti. Called "pizza-getti," it was an instant hit and was made available on every street corner. The twist? People do not make pizza at home. Never. However, if you walk down a commercial street around five in the after-noon, you'll see folks walking and eating pizza. And so, any offer to bake pizza is met with laughter and applause. I have lost track of the number of varieties I have baked in Cuba, but it was certainly in the delight of a freshly baked pizza that I have come to understand again the meaning of shared food. And I would be remiss, if I did not acknowledge how much more I have learned than I have taught by the sharing of this special Cuban meal.

As I write this book, my "brother" in crime in Cuba, Orestes Roca, a Baptist pastor and New Testament professor, is writing his doctorate on the theme of the common meal portrayed in Luke's gospel. What better companion could I need? I am so grateful to him for our weekly chats on food and the early Christian community.

Closer to home in Canada, there are also so many patient people, who joined in my "Jesus Feasts," to whom I owe my thanks. Over the course of twenty years, the materials of this book were presented as a three-hour, nine-course "feast." It was informal education linked to table delights. No question, the insights of this text would have been impossible without the dialogue those feasts engendered.

Sticking with the themes of Canada and Cuba, I owe a great deal to the solidarity group: CUBAbility. Together we have sponsored pastoral care in local Cuban congregations, provided neighborhood clean water pumps, funded social justice programming for ministry students, and shipped musical instruments for use by conservatory classes and aspiring individuals. Teatro Sauto, the great hall in Matanzas, has a new concert grand piano because of CUBAbility. The list of members has changed and grown over the years, but I want to thank André, Bronwyn, John, Margot, Janet, Ralph C., Barb, Nancy, Deborah, Silke, Marjorie, Iris, Bill, Monica, Tony, Jamie, Ellen, Anne, Lisa, Sally, Susanna, and Ralph W.

In a strange way, I need to thank fate or circumstance that had my household pass through the COVID-19 pandemic, on a small island off the coast of Vancouver. Unable to travel, we decided to set up a bake stand—a

"Moros and Cristianos," similar to the dish Gallo Pinto in Latin America. Here's a good recipe: https://food52.com/recipes/83081-congri-cuban-black-beans-and-rice

modest affair at the bottom of our driveway. It quickly grew into what is a now a thriving, weekly bakery: "The Piper's Buns." And through many late Friday nights, I have had time to refine my bread making skills and reflect on how bread is a central part of the Jesus story. To enhance your understanding of my text, I have included a bread recipe, before each chapter. So, as you read, you can try your hand at baking and perhaps appreciate, in a tangible way, how bread is a miracle working marvel.

Everyone knows I can't spell. Modern inventions like autocorrect have only marginally helped me. So, I owe a great deal to my editor, Bronwyn Best. Her attention to detail and her goodwill have been my salvation. Thank you, Bron.

I would be remiss if I didn't thank you, my reader, for your interest in this subject and my insights on it. Please note that the biblical references in this book are taken from the "New International Version" unless otherwise noted.

Finally, I thank the powers that reign over our universe that brought Ellen into my life. It's been a wild ride. Apart from companionship, Ellen is a constant source of support and goodwill—listening attentively to my theories on food. Not only is Ellen a companion in great adventures, it is her willingness to host and help prepare so many meals of all sorts at our many homes that has made the joy of cooking and eating come alive. It is because of her energy and faith that I am able to dedicate quality time to this project and complete it with grace. With deep gratitude, I dedicate this book to her.

. . . Both Christian feminist theology and biblical interpretation are in the process of rediscovering that the Christian gospel cannot be proclaimed if women disciples and what they have done are not remembered. They are in the process of reclaiming the supper in Bethany as women's Christian heritage in order to correct symbols and ritualization of an all-male Last Supper that is a betrayal of true Christian discipleship and ministry . . .[1]

1. Schüssler Fiorenza, *In Memory of Her*, 86–87.

Introduction

IT BEGINS WITH DAILY BREAD

Jesus begins with bread, ordinary bread. Not spiritual bread, not bread from heaven, not even bread of everlasting life. Not the bread of the Last Supper, certainly not the bread of redemption. If you must give it any theological adjective, you might call it "sabbath" bread. But as you will see, this is as much a political qualifier as it is a transcendent one. All our spiritual qualifiers notwithstanding, the story of Jesus starts with just a few commonplace loaves—daily bread.

Consequently, the Christian fellowship also begins with daily bread. That is my first and most important assertion about the Kingdom movement of Jesus. The seed that Jesus of Nazareth planted in the hearts of an unlikely band of fishers and forgotten folk was a loaf of bread. Nothing more and nothing less! And it is from that modest offering that a whole universe of meanings and rituals—some extravagantly relevant and derivative of Jesus' daily bread and others dangerously irrelevant and deluded—has been born, as far from real bread as one could imagine.

And while scholars might make a claim that Jesus' sermons or his parables are seminal and necessary for understanding him, it's only the real, simple bit of shared bread that can claim historical and theological truth.

To the Christian ear, this assertion may sound ridiculously crude or one-dimensional. This can't be all. Surely, there must be more. After all, we have a two-thousand-year-old religion under our belts, rich in imagery and spiritual depth. Is it credible that all that we see and recognize as "Christian" began with a fistful of flour, a splash of oil and a pinch of yeast? Like explorers seeking the source of the Nile, who stare down at a trickle of water sprouting from the ground, we question our bearings and doubt the evidence of our eyes. "Surely, this can't be it!" Just a loaf of shared bread? That's too simple!

3

A great and majestic movement like Christianity must arise from an equally monumental mystery. Where is its noble beginning? Show us the shock and awe of an impressive, earth-shattering start. Yesterday, I picked up a street evangelist's flyer, which boldly stated "Jesus came down from heaven to die on the cross." Doesn't that sound more providential, more impressive, than a loaf of bread? Most Christians expect a show. Paul saw a blinding light. Can't we get an earthquake, a mighty shift in creation? Matthew speaks of a natal star leading us to the Christ child. Luke has an angelic choir announcing Jesus' arrival. John's Jesus feeds a multitude to give glory to God and to make a testimony of his personal power to shape creation. Isn't it quite natural that we would imagine something equally dramatic as the source and beginning of the Jesus movement? After all, Moses saw a burning bush. Zachariah was struck silent.

According to Mark's account, Jesus did face fierce winds on the water and calmed the storm. Surely, such a miracle worker would begin his mission with a serious departure from the ordinary. We are told Jesus received some pivotal insights coming from his sojourns in the wilderness. Are they not the source of our movement? All the gospels speak of a moment at Jesus' baptism, when a voice from heaven announced heaven's approval of his vocation as a prophet/pilgrim. Surely, one or all of these dramatic events makes sense as the spiritual well from which flows the living water of Christianity.

But a crust of bread—passed from hand to hand? It seems hardly credible to imagine that is where our movement began.

Nevertheless, it is the main argument of this book that all we know of Christian faith, worship, and action finds its origins in bread. When we have Jesus for dinner, the menu is simple. First course: bread without condition—food for the hungry body. Second course: healing acceptance—made clear, concrete, and unequivocal, when a crust of bread passes from hand to hand—food for the starving soul. Third course: bread served up for all who are hungry . . . no restrictions or qualifications—everyone has access to what they need.

Jesus' bread is a three-course, complete meal: extravagantly and foolishly free! There can be no other explanation for how it began. Jesus did not preach "church," nor did he organize what he was doing as a new religious movement. His mission was the promotion of what he called the "Kingdom of God,"[2] a very Jewish idea, which was tangibly and clearly distinct from

2. For this text, I will capitalize Kingdom of God, when I am making reference to the specific idea and model Jesus was promoting. Described further in this Introduction, it is the key message of the Jesus in Mark's gospel. His meal fellowship of shared bread is the embodiment of the Kingdom of God.

the Kingdom of Caesar. And it was shared bread that made this distinction both real and transformative.

Later, church leaders and Christian theologians have turned the phrase Kingdom of God into a code phrase for a Christian heaven or a global government founded on Christian principles.[3] Conservative evangelists use it interchangeably with the time when all people have accepted Jesus as their "Savior and Lord." In many instances, it is described as a realm above and beyond human history. Makes for great preaching.

All these homiletical advantages notwithstanding, it is much more realistic to assume that Jesus intended a simple meaning for his mission statement. The Kingdom of God is a time and place, when the God of Israel rules the people. Move over Caesar; God is in charge. Not just in theory, but in real life. Can you picture God as the head of our household, right here and right now? And Jesus embodied that radical idea of God ruling over the earth as our king, with a broken bit of bread passed among a circle of social rejects and spiritual cast-offs. In that sense, we can fix the seminal aspects of God's reign among us as a "holy meal."

I use the world "holy" with care. We have mistakenly associated it with many "religious" circumstances. It is not what we imagine. Jesus' meal is not "holy" because it provides spiritual insight—though that may happen. Nor does its sacred quality stem from a specific geographic location—like a temple or cathedral. Likewise, holiness is not dependent on the priestly figure, who holds the bread and wine, or what unique words are uttered over this meal. Nor does the bread convey "holiness" like that associated with an altered psychic state—a spiritual LSD, so to speak. Alas, true holiness does not come from religious assignation or ritual concentration.

According to the Hebraic mind, the "holiness" of God is based on justice. Liturgically speaking, a meal is "holy," when people pray over their food, offer thanksgiving to their God and fellow creatures, who had a hand in making it. But such piety is useless and, in some ways, counterproductive, if it is not matched by the basic materialistic necessity that everyone is fed without restriction or penalty. In short: *holy* bread is only holy, because it is *shared* bread.

It goes without saying that Christianity is now much more than this common meal. A great deal has grown from Jesus' bread—an entire religious structure, in fact. But let us not be fooled. Theological principles and liturgical rituals did not fall from the sky. They are not eternal, immutable

3. While this may seem like an archaic and outdated notion—a "holy" empire founded on Christian values and ideas, we still hold on to such extravagant evangelical aspirations. Did we not call the twentieth "The Christian Century," because we believed we would "convert the world to Christ" in those 100 years?

necessities. They are human constructs: guideposts or signs that point to the mystery that first became evident in a shared loaf of bread.

At the start of my classes on Christian theology, I would say that "theology is secondary." It comes after, not before, faith. To use a distinction made clear by Harvey Cox,[4] "belief"—the articulation of creedal statements and doctrinal principles—is not the same as "faith"—the trusting in a mystery that cannot be totally explained. Our journey with Jesus begins with the relationship of trust, trust built in large part because when we are with him, we are fed. It is only after we are satisfied and, yes, transformed, by this offering of bread, that we try to explain it to ourselves and codify our experiences of faith into principles of belief.

Clearly, we have added a great deal more to our mission and ministry as Christians than shared bread. We didn't stick with a simple loaf passed from hand to hand around the circle. We added music, prayers, buildings, organizational structures, spiritual disciplines, and, finally, political power.

No doubt, you noticed that there is a play on words in the title of this text, "Having Jesus for Dinner." Our tradition began as an actual meal for the first followers, and Jesus was literally our host—or a real guest in our homes. We reserved a place in our circle for him. After the cross/empty tomb event, he was still our guest, albeit his presence was more "spiritual" than material. We still might have reserved a special spot for him—much like the cup for Elijah in the current Seder meal ritual.[5] Part of the Easter message is the miracle of Jesus "still with us" in our community. "He is risen" began as an affirmation of who was reclining to eat beside us. So, Jesus continued to share our food, even when he was absent, because it was the way the bread was shared that made his presence real. Thus, in the phrase of our title, one puts the emphasis on the eating: "Having Jesus for *dinner*."

Nevertheless, with time, Jesus was no longer just the unseen guest of our fellowship. In a curious twist of ecclesiastical thinking, he *became* the dinner. We consumed him—as we might eat a grape or cracker. And for close to 1800 years, we have been "Having Jesus for *dinner*," meaning that he was our meal—whether symbolically, as is the case with Protestants, or literally, as is the case with the Orthodox and Roman churches. Our understanding of the central ritual of our community changed dramatically. To be blunt, in a very short space of time, we moved from community to cannibalism, from radical hospitality to exclusivist exceptionalism. And

4. Cox, *Future of Faith*, 3–8.

5. In the Passover meal, the cup of Elijah is the fifth ceremonial cup of wine poured and left untouched, as a symbol of hope. Tradition has it that Elijah will join in the Seder meal, unrecognized, but as a herald of the coming of the messiah.

that is a significant theological and spiritual shift—one that I will argue needs to be "reset."

Once Jesus became the sacrificial elements, any number of priestly functions were added to the basic meal. Bread was made holy and untouchable because of priestly prerogatives. The two aspects, bread and wine, were reserved exclusively for the deserving. A shared dinner became a sacrament that was fenced off for the righteous. And the previously ordinary daily practice of eating together in Jesus' name was transmuted into a reverent, once a week, or, in some cases, once in a lifetime, exercise, controlled by "beliefulness" (Cox) and restricted by external spiritual authorities. The crust of bread we broke and ate with Jesus became a wafer-thin bit of heaven, so sacred you dare not even touch it—except to let it melt on your tongue!

Such a development from simplicity to extravagance may seem exaggerated, but if one looks at the development of church buildings, you can see the gradual development of ornamentation and excess. A mundane kitchen table became a public, sacred piece of furniture. It moved from being used by a circle of friends to an altar presided over by priests. Everyday, cobbled-together utensils were replaced by the finest silk. Only the best tableware was then made and reserved for this meal. The elements were themselves soon objects of devotion and artistic extravagance.

If you visit Rome, you can see this architectural and spiritual progression written in stone. Hidden away around the corner from the famous tourist site, Santa Maria Maggiore, is a smaller, older chapel, San Martino ai Monti (Viale del Monte Oppio 28)[6]. Christians have been worshipping here since the third century. They first gathered in the house of a man named Equitius. At the turn of the sixth century, Pope Symmacus built a church on the site. This church was replaced two hundred years later by a bigger chapel, which itself was renovated and rebuilt in the ninth century, only to be totally transformed by a Baroque renovation completed in 1650. If you find the custodian, you can be taken back down to the original house, stand around a crude block table, where common meals were shared, and then walk your way up through the many refits and restorations. And as you rise, the building materials become more precious and the furniture more specifically priestly and pious, until you reach the frescos of the seventeenth century, which speak of the glories and the triumphs of Christ's church. It's a walk between a rough rock kitchen table to a carved marble alter; from humble bread to holy sacrifice; from community to cannibalism.

---

6. For a good video tour along with commentary from a current American perspective try: https://thecatholictraveler.com/lenten-station-churches-of-rome/san-martino -ai-monti/

It goes without saying that these developments of our tradition—what some might call "additions"—are worthy of respect, even reverence. A quick walk through any art gallery or cathedral will point to the beauty of human imagination, how it develops and builds on a simple fact and blossoms into a majestic garden of delight and color. For instance, just down the street from San Martino ai Monti is the more well-known church, San Pietro in Vincoli, in which Michelangelo's sculpture of Moses is located. There's no question that Christianity would be a much poorer movement, if such expressions of faith had not been produced.

Rome is the living example that Christianity has furnished the mythology, symbols, and ethical ideals that have fueled an entire civilization. And the fact that a prayer, or a ritual, or a saint day, or even a theological precept is merely a derivative of the simple shared loaf of bread does not make it wrong. And it does not follow that the only authentic form of Christianity is the most primitive or that new innovations are necessarily incorrect, because they are a long distance from the original plan and program of Jesus.

Nonetheless, when we are lost[7]—and some would argue that historic expressions of Christianity in the U.S. and Canada in the twenty-first century are suffering from precisely that problem[8]—then there is merit in returning to our roots in order to rediscover the simple richness that lies at the heart of our faith. Not to replicate it exactly—for that would be impossible and largely counter-productive—but perhaps in examining our origins we will uncover the dynamics of faith that can be reinterpreted and contextualized to address our current challenges.

And that is what this book seeks to do. Why don't we travel back into the world of the first few generations of Jesus followers? Join them for supper, so to speak. Did they know something we "post-enlightenment" believers have forgotten? Let's ask what they heard and saw, what inspired them, and what frightened them. When they had Jesus for dinner, what happened?

The religious fervor that surrounded Jesus and spread like wildfire (some historians even equated it to a pandemic)[9] must have had tremendous appeal. How did it move people, and why did it outlast the other expressions of Jewish devotion? For instance, what made the Jesus Kingdom of God more appealing and long-lasting than John's "Baptism of Repentance"

---

7. I will outline this "lostness" in more detail in chapter 1 of this text.

8. Hall, *What Christianity is Not*.

9. Tacitus, a first century Roman historian in his work, *Annals*, (4.282–83), describes Christianity as "the pernicious superstition . . . checked for the moment, only to break out once more, not merely in Judea, the home of the disease, but in the capital (i.e., Rome) itself, where all things horrible or shameful in the world collect and find a vogue." 604.

campaigns? What allowed Christianity to breach the confines of Hebraic piety and move into the Roman world? And since the movement began as a Kingdom of God, we must ask how did this Kingdom, which Jesus described, fit with or fight against the Kingdom of Caesar[10] in which he lived?

Without trying to answer all these questions immediately, let me, nonetheless, state my operating thesis at this point. It is my assumption that Jesus' Kingdom of God began as an empire-resisting reform of temple Judaism, starting as non-violent opposition to both the guiding principles and the theology of the Kingdom of Caesar. In as much as Second Temple Judaism collaborated with and even promoted these "imperial" principles and theology, Jesus and his movement found itself in opposition to both grass roots[11] and aristocratic[12] religious authorities. Jesus' Kingdom of God was a positive and concrete alternative to imperial rule. However, in less than 100 years, forsaking many of its Hebraic roots, this alternate, empire-resisting Kingdom became an empire-embracing church. So, the questions arise. How did this happen? How did the Kingdom movement spread throughout the Roman world, and why did it eventually accommodate itself to it? And did our meal fellowship resist, assist, or enhance the shift from an anti-imperial to pro-imperial religious movement?

To explore these questions, I will focus almost entirely on the early gospels of the early Christian community: the three synoptic gospels of Mark, Matthew, and Luke. I will also make references to the letters of Paul and some early books, not found in the Christian canon, that claim to be gospels, church manuals, and teachings of early fellowship leaders. What do these documents say about how the movement began and why it lasted, its key elements, and chief opponents? Specifically, what role did bread play in building the first generations of Jesus followers?

In brief, through this book, I am going to invite you to bring your questions to the table, as we invite Jesus for dinner. What will it look like, and what will happen when we recline together to share bread?

---

10. Crossan, *Render unto Caesar*. Crossan writes on precisely this relationship between the Kingdom of God and Kingdom of Caesar, and I will touch on some of its conclusions in chapters 5 and 6.

11. In Mark's gospel, Jesus regularly interacts with local Pharisees, who are mildly sympathetic, sometimes critical, and always presumed to be on the edges of the crowd—a kind of Greek chorus that frames the questions from which Jesus draws inspiration. In Matthew, Luke, and John, these same local religious authorities are portrayed as more antagonistic—even belligerent.

12. In all the synoptic gospels, there appears to be a unanimous assessment of the temple elites: chief priests and scribes. They are intent, initially, on undermining and then finally destroying Jesus and his credibility with the crowds.

I realize that many of the responses or answers to the questions I have raised are more conjecture than verifiable fact. We are reading backwards through the written texts into the social and religious context of the Kingdom movement of Jesus. A guiding question in this educated guesswork is: "What is the social condition or personal circumstance to which our gospels are a response?" And while to some my musings may look like nothing more than baseless speculation, it is in the murky waters before and behind the written word that we find some of the best material upon which to build our common practice as twenty-first-century Christians. Perhaps . . . and this is a long stretch . . . perhaps we may even find greater clarity for our own path.

But before we claim too much, let us return to the bread and state our premise again. Jesus begins with bread. In his simple meal and the fellowship, Jesus performed three miracles[13] that have sufficient power and appeal to explain how the Christian world view and movement both grew and thrived. They are:

- *abundance: in the Jesus circle, real food was always plentiful*

- *acceptance: in the sharing of bread, everyone, especially the spiritually and socially undesirable, was expected and welcome and not merely tolerated or patronized*

- *access: in the circle of Jesus, there was no head table, no patron's position, but an actual reversal of power practices and principles*

These three miracles will be described in greater detail, below. I believe they were cornerstones of the Kingdom of God movement that Jesus proclaimed. And while he didn't invent the principles that performed these miracles— for Jesus was thoroughly Jewish and dependent on the justice or "sabbath" traditions of Judaism—he, nonetheless, was the genius behind bringing them together to inspire a radical and revolutionary spiritual renaissance of his faith tradition.

At this point, let's be clear about the terminology and fix in our minds what the audience of Jesus[14] would have understood by the idea of the Kingdom of God.

---

13. I have written extensively on these miracles in a previous book: Levan, *Prayer*.

14. It would be too much to ask to get into the mind of Jesus and what his intentions might have been for his movement. We have no record of his personal ideas or ideals. But we do know a great deal about the religious and social context of first-century Palestine, and so we can make some fairly accurate assumptions about how a peasant audience in northern Galilee would have heard and understood his message of the Kingdom of God.

THE KINGDOM MOVEMENT OF JESUS

Originally, Christianity had no name. Jesus didn't give it one—not officially. The gospels portray him as an itinerant preacher and healer—not unlike the prophets before him. Jesus was a Jew[15]and seemed intent on addressing the failings of Second Temple Judaism. It is only later, in the first century, that devotees of Jesus retroject back into his time the sense of separateness from Judaism and the vilification of Jewish religious leaders. Examined without these later interpolations, the gospels portray a Jesus who did not promote the creation of a distinctly separate community of faith from the one he knew as Judaism.

To be fair, in Mark's gospel, Jesus was decidedly anti-establishment. And from that stance, one could infer that he was promoting the destruction or rejection of Jewish authority. One might even argue Jesus wanted to tear down the old and build something brand new—religiously speaking. But these seem to be distortions of the original story. There is one instance when Jesus is reported to say that he would tear down the temple only to rebuild it in three days,[16] but apart from that one apocryphal example, when Jesus does address religious structures or practices, it is almost always as a means to reforming them.

No matter how much we might want him to be our archetypal "Christian," Jesus doesn't help his cause much. He regularly refuses to be made into a saint or to be held down to a specific geographic location, which could, therefore, be venerated. Achieving "holy" status is an anathema. From the very beginning (Mark 1:38), Jesus resisted the temptation to settle down. So, he was speaking to an audience, when there was no understanding of "church," no ecclesiastical organization, not even a building to which he returned. If anything, when thinking of a spiritual structure for their faith, his first followers would be drawn either to the Synagogue, which might have been a building, but, in more destitute regions, was nothing more than a designated, open-air meeting space, or they would imagine the grand, established Second Temple in Jerusalem.

To add further confusion to the modern mind, Jesus seemed to have no interest in calling himself or his followers by a specific name. They were not ascetics like the Essenes down by the Dead Sea. They weren't "Jesuites."

---

15. Funk, *Honest to Jesus*, 42. Funk points out that Jesus was not the founder of a distinct religion, called "Christianity," but remained a devout Jew his entire life. ". . . in short, very little of what we associate with traditional Christianity, originated with him [Jesus]."

16. This assertion is made in John 2:19 and reported as an accusation against Jesus during his Maundy Thursday trial before the Sanhedrin in Mark 14:58.

Jesus didn't accept labels like zealot, or scribe, or priest. He didn't seem to object to being called a "rabbi" or teacher (Luke 10:25), though Jesus was careful to point out that some people used that title to exaggerate or flatter as a means to achieving a favor from him as a spiritual "superstar" (Mark 10:18). Not for Jesus! No false flattery, please! He rejected adjectives like "good" and, in Mark's gospel at least, dismissed the accolades of both the grateful recipients of his healing touch and the evil spirits expulsed by his other-worldly power. Jesus chose humility over grandeur, and his followers were a rag-tag band of followers without a common name beyond "disciple."

In Mark's gospel, which most scholars believe was the first text written between 65 and 70 CE, Jesus never spoke of his movement as being "Christian" and might well have blushed at the suggestion of a religion named after the title of "Christ," which is a Greek translation of the Hebraic notion of "the anointed one" or king. As stated above, Jesus didn't call his movement anything. If there was any word or phrase that Jesus employed to clarify his ministry, it was the Kingdom of God. Wherever he went, Jesus simply proclaimed that God's Kingdom was close (Mark 1:15), or coming soon (Matthew 25:1), or already here (Luke 19:9). It is this Kingdom of God which came first and finally to his lips, when he spoke his "good news." So, what was it? What did his first listeners hear, when he spoke to them of a Kingdom of God?

Perhaps it would be best to begin with what a Kingdom of God is not. There are four general misconceptions of this idea.

First, in the social and political context of Jesus, a Kingdom of God is not a place beyond time: a paradise to which ones goes when you die. Of course, it could be construed that way. There would be nothing unorthodox or unusual if Jesus promoted an utterly unique meaning of Kingdom, but before we invent these novel connotations, can we not ask initially what his followers would imagine when he initially mentioned the phrase? Why would a first-century audience think of a Kingdom as an ahistorical, spiritual realm? It would be similar to assuming that when a modern preacher speaks of the "legislature," she or he means a heavenly courtroom. For the people listening to Jesus, a Kingdom was a real, concrete structure. It's what you needed to get things done here on earth. It had legitimacy as a governing principle, despite the many ways it was corrupted.

Second, a Kingdom was not a location above the earth, from which the angels and saints look down on creation. Yes, in Matthew's gospel, Jesus speaks of a "Kingdom of Heaven," but this is a polite allusion to God. In the same way that journalists today refer to the president of the United States by saying,"the White House." So, Matthew avoids referring directly to God out of reverence for the holiness of God's name and inserts the word "Heaven," where Mark has the word "God." But it means the same thing.

Third, on first hearing, the Kingdom of God would not be construed as a spiritual principle or mythological concept, as opposed to a material one. There is no question that Jesus had some spiritual, other-worldly undertones in mind, when he coined the phrase, but these would not and could not be separated from the daily, and very pedestrian, concerns of life on this planet. How do we survive in the here and now, in Capernaum, 30 CE, the occupied territory under the rule of Rome, personified in Herod Antipas—the local puppet "quarter king?"[17] There was no split between body and spirit, earth and heaven. They were one. In the world of Jesus, no one would hear an idea like Kingdom and give it a meaning separate from its concrete connotation as a structure of governance and political control. After all, that's what the first audience knew. They knew kingdoms and kings.

Finally, the Kingdom of God was not understood as the elevation of male dominance and control. Of course, that was how kingdoms functioned, but one must be careful not to assign eternal validation to this unfortunate aspect of kingdoms. It is not that Jesus wanted to lift up monarchies and males, or elevate hierarchical power as a principle to admire. Let us not apply our twenty-first-century concerns for political and gender equality as a measuring stick for first-century rhetoric. Our modern ideas of democracy, individualism, human rights, due process of law, etc., had not yet been imagined in the first century. Jesus was pointing to a simple, yet startling, idea. What if God was really in charge? In our world, we might need a longer phrase. Could we say that Jesus is announcing the arrival of a realm in which God has been elected our prime minister or president? What would our world look like, if God was the legitimate ruler of our lives? Cabinets would not be shaped according to partisan politics or economic favoritism. Imagine if God named the Minister of Finance or the Secretary of State. From first to last, the Kingdom of God was not a distant spiritual principle, a fiction of our imagination, or a mystical creation of our faith. To use North American ideas, we'd say, "Picture it: God is sitting in the Oval Office, or has taken up residence at 24 Sussex Drive, in Ottawa, or Los Pinos, in Mexico City."

Even more surprisingly, Jesus invited his followers to live in that Kingdom now. Don't wait for it to happen as a distant, utopian ideal. No permission needed—not from the temple priests or the Roman authorities. Live in God's household this very day! Stop scrounging around in Caesar's world

---

17. Herod the Great's son, Antipas, was not a full "king," much though he wished for that title. He was given the title of "tetrarch" or partial king. As a political position, it was not nothing, but it was far from the majesty and power his father enjoyed.

and build your homes in God's Kingdom. And Jesus used bread freely given and shared as his primary evangelistic tool in spreading this Kingdom.

The idea of the Kingdom of God was provocative, even inspirational—particularly to a people living under the grinding conditions of occupation; but it became transformative, because Jesus made it happen. He built and inspired households of God's Kingdom—right here in our own home town . . . next door. When his followers gathered, they met in God's Kingdom and lived out their days in that world. Caesar's realm had no influence on them.

I can say it no more clearly. When Jesus spoke of the Kingdom of God, it wasn't wishful thinking. It was a statement of present fact and a lived reality[18] —as real as the loaf in your hands. God rules.

This raises very interesting, transformative, and frightening possibilities. First, if God is my king, then Caesar isn't. That's a treasonous idea—one that could get you in deep trouble, if you made it real. Second, if I live in God's world, then the principles of Caesar's world don't apply. I can begin to orient the expending of my resources, my taxes, and the benefits of my work life toward the principles of God. Finally, if I live in God's world, I must build it each day in contradistinction to Caesar's world all around me. What will be the outward signs that I live in God's Kingdom and not Caesar's?

We must be careful not to intrude on the mission of Jesus with a modern question like: Is a Kingdom with God on the throne a credible concept? Would people believe Jesus? Could such a thing be accepted as historical? Let's remember that, in the Mediterranean mind of the first century, Caesar was a god. He ruled from Rome. The idea of a Kingdom of God was not outlandish. The Roman empire was already a Kingdom reigned by God, i.e., Caesar. People, who heard the phrase Kingdom of God, would not be asking if it was a legitimate idea, worthy of faith. More than likely, they would want to see how it differed from the Kingdom of Caesar. Everyone can see what Augustus has done in his Kingdom—temples to his veneration and architectural wonders dedicated to his prowess were scattered around the known world. We see what Caesar did and is doing. So, people would naturally ask, "What has your God done, Jesus?" "How does your Kingdom differ or distinguish itself?"

And it is in the three miracles mentioned above that Jesus' movement first distinguished itself as an alternative, positive Kingdom. These miracles have largely been lost in the current expression of Christianity, and in chapter 1, I will offer a lament for what has been forgotten by Christians and their church.

---

18. In the book on prayer which I mention in footnote 9, I make the argument that the Lord's Prayer really begins with the statement: "Thy Kingdom Come"—a statement of realized fact not speculative aspiration.

THE CONTEXT OF THE MIRACLES OF JESUS' MEAL FELLOWSHIP

"You want to know about Jesus' Kingdom of God? Why don't you come to dinner?" That's how I imagine the apostle Paul worked the crowds. "Come . . . have Jesus for dinner." His evangelism was invitational and concrete. I doubt if he would get too far in the Hellenistic world with appeals to the divinity of Jesus, his resurrection from the dead, or his healing power to raise the dying from their beds. There were countless religious traditions, mystery cults, and venerated magicians who could claim as much—not the least of which was Caesar himself. Christian apologetics and creeds proclaiming Jesus' divine power come later.

With Paul, it begins with a meal. I don't imagine a sermon on the unique power of Jesus would get very far with a gentile audience—unless it could be made concrete and real. The proof is in the pudding, so to speak, and first-century citizens were no less intelligent and no more gullible than twenty-first-century individuals. "Show me," is what they would say—either out loud or in the quiet of their own hearts.

Paul was a brilliant thinker and activist. He knew what he had to do to spread the mission of Jesus. He had to recreate the miracles that were at the foundation of the movement in the first place.

Imagine the first ten or twenty people, who joined in the Jesus following. For them, it wasn't about the veneration of Jesus. They didn't come to worship a majestic god/man. They came because something marvelously wondrous happened in his presence. It was those first Jesus miracles that built the movement that eventually bore his name. In time, the followers of Jesus switched their focus away from the miracles onto the man. *Having* Jesus for dinner became having Jesus for *dinner*. In chapters 4 and 5 of this text, we'll examine how this shift arose and why the church has been impoverished by that shift in emphasis.

At this point, it is not sufficient simply to name the miracles of Jesus' meal fellowship: abundance, acceptance, and access. These three things changed lives forever, and they all began with a meal; and we will not understand them in their social context without some careful qualifications.

When speaking about the miracles of shared bread, let us just get the right picture in our minds. Having dinner . . . what does it look like?

While in chapter 3 I will go into greater detail, a brief summary here will underline the main ethical and social currents associated with having Jesus for dinner. First, Leonardo Da Vinci notwithstanding, there was no table in the meal fellowship of Jesus. In first-century Palestine, there were chairs and tables of course, but they were not used for eating. A meal, in

Jesus' context, was served on the floor, on a rug or special meal cloth. You reclined to eat. It was the polite thing to do. In rich environments, there might be couches provided for eating and perhaps a cadre of servants or slaves to bring the common dish to your couch, but most ordinary people, when they ate at a public meal, reclined on their left elbows (perhaps supported by a pillow) around the central "tablecloth," and they expected to dip their hand into a common dish. Most commonly, at a formal feast or public meal, men lay down to eat in a circle or horseshoe formation. The food was placed in the middle of the guests on platters.

Once blessed, everyone helped themselves to a mouthful-portion at a time. Right hands, fingers, and bread scoops were used as both dishes and utensils. Again, there were spoons and knives in first-century Palestine, but they were for the kitchen. In the first century, no one would host a dinner and offer utensils for each person to select and separate out their own food. How selfish!

Food was common. It was a joint venture, a show of trust and a test of cooperation, in which no one had their own portion separated from the others. Food was a way to honor the importance of all who reclined together. The order in which guests took their portion from the common dish was determined by their respective level of righteousness. It would be boorish and rude to break from tradition and offer a guest's meal separated from the others! Only lepers and women having their period were subjected to that kind of segregation. Of course, one's place in the circle—proximity to the host being a preferred place[19]—was a sign of importance.

At this point, given the need for close cooperation and the vulnerability implied by sharing a common dish, we can imagine that the meal fellowship of first-century Palestine was peppered with social expectations and spiritual connotations. In that world, food was communal and mutual. It created social bonds among neighbors, established family alliances, and proved itself to be, above all else, the place where trust was built as the food was consumed. Joint needs and shared vulnerability were always on the menu.

On a simple level, the meal established and perpetuated social structures. For instance, men ate together. Women and children got what was left over. Usually, men ate separately, when the meal was public. Women served and then left the men in peace; children waited further down the food chain. They were nobodies, lower than women, since they had not yet become productive!

19. See Mark 10:37, as John and James ask for proximity to Jesus in the final banquet, because they wanted the honorable place. You can see how Jesus reversed the common assumptions about taking the place of honor in the eating circle in his story of the wedding banquet: Luke 14:7–14.

The meal table was made sacred because of the dynamics of a shared meal. The food itself was not holy (unless of course it had been sacrificed at the temple)[20]. It was the sharing that was a vehicle to establish righteousness. One's spiritual health and religious purity were at stake, when you dined with your friends. Their hands were going to be in your soup, as it were. You could catch their impurity and sin . . . quite literally. (Think of modern sensitivity to the SARS or COVID-19 virus.) The danger of unrighteousness being passed through the meal fellowship was obvious and accepted by all as a reasonable assumption. When your neighbor's fingers play with your food, you look very carefully at those to your left and right. What does she have by way of sicknesses? Is he suffering from anything that might be construed as evidence of God's disfavor? Is that leprosy or only a blemish on her thumb? Where has his hand been lately? What has she touched that I will now be eating?

In that world, serious physical ailments were construed as evidence of God's disfavor over some past sin. And sin was contagious. So, eating was a precarious moment, when one could "catch" impurity. Here's how it worked. Through sharing a common dish, it was not uncommon that one could catch the disease of a meal partner. And given that sickness was equivalent to God's judgment, it appeared that one had contracted the other person's sin. You can see how easily the questions of purity arise, when we share a common dish.

It was these kinds of concerns around purity that meant that the walls around the dinner table were high. In some cases, very high. Not just anyone was allowed to eat from the common platter. We'll elaborate the details of this sin-meal relationship in chapter 4, when I explore the complaints leveled at Jesus and his meal fellowship.

As we move up the levels of significance, at the pinnacle, the ancient meal fellowship was more than social and political safety. When strangers came to your meal, it was not just your purity, it was also your honor that was in question. Your role as the host was to lavish hospitality upon your guests. Their job was to return gratitude in equal measure. Superlatives on both sides. In such a way, the governing principles of social hierarchy were established and reinforced. The patron served his guests with the best he had, and in exchange, they offered praise and obedience. Everyone is happy, and society rests on a stable, though strictly hierarchical, foundation.

---

20. In chapter 3, we will explore in more detail how an animal sacrifice in a temple functioned within temple Judaism—what it looked like and how it operated. But at this point, we can simply state that the animal that was sacrificed was not wasted. It was either consumed by priests or returned to the one making the sacrifice. In either case, the sacrificed animal was the basis for a meal shared with God by sharing it with others.

In the context of Palestine during Jesus' time, honor is the primary means of conferring value. And since a public meal is all about conferring and reinforcing honor, a good dinner party is money in the bank. Patrons are, therefore, very careful whom they invite to dinner. Dinner guests are likewise watching carefully not to cross the carefully constructed lines of honor and authority.

Of course, not all meals were public and formal. Nevertheless, in more informal settings, some of the same dynamics were at issue, even though the setting might have been rougher or cruder. Men, crouching rather than reclining, would eat from a common pot or bowl with their right hands. And they would eat first. Women didn't intrude. Children got the scraps.

One last point. We know that life in Galilee, at the time of Jesus, was not easy. The circle of Jesus lived in occupied territory. They were not free. Twenty-five years before his ministry began, the Roman legions had scourged the land as punishment for a minor revolt.[21] Hence, within Jesus' generation there was the memory of a militarily-induced famine. More recently and regularly, the people of Jesus' time knew privation. A local crop failure, a minor drought, an infestation of locusts or noble rot could quickly tip living conditions from marginal to impossible. People starved to death.

So, when you think of the mealtime during the time of Jesus, think small portions: mouse size. "*Lean cuisine*" was not a fashionable fast-food diet. It was a fact of living and dying. And while you're at it, think plain! There was scarcity of actual food, and there was scarcity of variety. Dinner would consist of a starch/bread product or portion, an olive derivative, perhaps some greens, and watered-down wine. There might be an egg. Perhaps you had fish, rarely chicken, almost never red meat. Cover the whole thing in yogurt, and you have a first-century menu. What you had for breakfast, you had for dinner, and it rarely varied. Eating wasn't often about taste and pleasure. It was a function of survival.

It is in this context that we must appreciate the miracles of Jesus' bread. There are two other factors to keep in mind, as we invite Jesus for dinner: the role of women and the importance of Jesus' meal fellowship as resistance.

---

21. This was the uprising that broke out in Sepphoris—a few kilometers from Nazareth—soon after Herod the Great died (4 BCE). It was significant enough that it required the legions stationed in Damascus to crush it. For a more fictional but dramatic portrayal of these events, see Crossan, *God and Empire*, 108–110.

WOMEN, THEIR ROLE IN THE KINGDOM OF GOD

There were many expressions of Judaism that lived side by side under the over-arching umbrella of Second Temple Judaism. Some renounced the temple as corrupt. For instance, the Essenes created isolated communities, featuring an ascetic approach to faith, free from what they perceived to be the contamination of the Jerusalem temple cult. Others focused their religious fervor against empire. The zealots advocated violent resistance to Roman occupation. Some were non-violent reform movements, trying to bring the people and the temple authorities back into a more "acceptable" attitude toward God's justice. John's baptizing movement was of this latter type of Judaism. Jesus was similarly a prophetic reformer. He advocated a non-violent resistance to Rome by creating a new, alternate, and positive community of faith.

If we can read backwards from what his critics say about Jesus, it seems possible to construct some of the unique features of the Kingdom movement of Jesus. His meal fellowship was certainly one outstanding aspect of God's Kingdom. A second would be the profound implications of free healing. A third would be the inclusion of women in his circle. Unlike some of the more orthodox expressions of temple Judaism, Jesus seems to allow a greater, if not central, place to women. We have several accounts of women being present when he taught. They were present when he was crucified and were the first to proclaim that the tomb was empty and he was "risen."

Moreover, women are portrayed in both Mark and Luke as the key characters that bankrolled the Kingdom movement of Jesus.[22] Without their help, there would have been no itinerant preachers.

The influence of women continued after the death of Jesus, and it was their central leadership role that caused considerable friction with the emerging communities in Corinth, for instance. Paul felt constrained to address how women embraced leadership in the Jesus circles. In the modern world, we may accept women's spiritual authority as self-evident and a basic right. But this was not so in first-century Palestine. The Kingdom movement of Jesus distinguished itself by the inclusion of women in their spiritual practices and the important role they were given in the unfolding of the gospel story.

I can't separate the role of bread in that nascent Jesus circle and the role women played. They are one and the same story. As Elisabeth Schüssler

---

22. See Luke 8: 1–4 . . . a passage in which Mary of Magdala is listed among other women who supplied the resources for Jesus' mission in Galilee. See Mark 14:41. in which the women who are at the cross were those "who cared for his needs."

Fiorenza pointed out in her book *Bread not Stone*,[23] simple bread was the work of women. It was only when it was turned "holy" that it was seen as the sole preserve of men. Previously, at the beginning of the ministry of Jesus, in making bread, women transformed a religion, based on two tablets of stone, into a faith sustained by shared bread.

At the heart of this book, there is a simple, some might say "crude," question. Initially, Jesus was the host of the meal that we recognize is happening throughout the gospel record—regularly in Mark and Matthew and more often in Luke—a meal that included rejects and unsavory types. After the crucifixion/resurrection event, Jesus was present as *the* guest, an essential part of the real, and the spiritual, community of followers who shared their bread freely. "Having Jesus for dinner" was a question of hospitality. Over time, this changed. Jesus ceased being a guest and started to become *the* meal itself, as the elements of bread and wine were ritualized and sacralized. Having Jesus for dinner became an issue of sanctification. How and why did that happen?

My first hypothesis: when women, who are the guardians of household spirituality and equilibrium, are excluded from the Jesus meal, it loses its basis in reality and shifts to spiritualized ritual. As we watch the shifting and deteriorating "authority" given to women, we witness a change in the bread of life offered to those living the Kingdom movement. If Jesus made it open for women, especially unsavory women (prostitutes, women with bleeding, etc.), what does it mean when the Christian church excludes them? As we restrict women with ecclesiastical barriers and burden them with theological shame, are we moving away from the original intention of Jesus? Is this the source of the key conundrum of this text: how the followers of Jesus moved from community to cannibalism in its central expression of faith and identity, and what are the consequences of this shift in practice and thinking? These are questions to be addressed in chapters 5 and 6.

POWER CORRUPTS?

Another way to explore the shifting importance of shared bread and food in the Kingdom of God and the changing role that Jesus played in the common meal is to examine the opposition. Who opposes Jesus and why? As I will illustrate in chapter 4, there is substantial push back against Jesus and his eating practices. A quick read of the four canonical gospels reveals that there are a number of identifiable groups who oppose Jesus. Clearly, the religious elite and temple authorities had a great deal to lose as his Kingdom of God

23. See footnote 1, above.

movement spread. Their opposition makes sense. Jesus was tearing through some carefully constructed religious safety nets. So, it's a question of power; but of equal importance are the "what" and "who" of their complaints. Not only does Jesus associate with the repugnant, sinful, and contagious side of society, he eats with them as well. Can you imagine!

For different reasons, Jesus attracted the attention of political opponents. The Romans were experts at both economic exploitation and political intrigue, and they could read the writing on the wall. Jesus was an easy target for their suspicion, if not animosity. Someone, who proclaims he is founding a new Kingdom (especially when the Roman-appointed king is very much in evidence), will not last long. He would be eliminated as a small threat, but a threat nonetheless. The Romans were not devils or satanic monsters. We don't need to vilify Pilate in order to explain the crucifixion of Jesus. Anyone who resists empire, even non-violently, will pay the price for that resistance.

It is more difficult to explain other people, who are identified as resisting Jesus. Peter, for instance, both denies and refutes what Jesus preaches. The other disciples are portrayed in a similar light . . . especially in Mark's gospel: unthinking, often wrong, resistant to Jesus' truth, and argumentative among themselves. Why? What do we make of their unreflective resistance to the one they called their "teacher" and "messiah?" While we cannot be assured of the historicity of the gospels as reflection of what actually happened during the meals of Jesus, they are the record of how the circle of Jesus understood itself at the time the gospel was written, i.e., in the latter third of the first century. What is that community of followers saying about itself, when its chief spokesman (Peter) and other eminent leaders (disciples) seem to be perpetually confused by or in opposition to Jesus' ideas, and how they are out of step when it comes to his meal fellowship?

In a similar fashion, the gospels' portrait of the Pharisees, especially as we move from the earlier gospels into the later ones, raises some good questions. The Pharisees were not initially his enemies. In Mark's gospel, Jesus eats with them more than with other named groups. They had very similar objectives and sensibilities. Why are they eventually portrayed in Matthew's gospel as villainous and in John's gospel as the chief opponents of Jesus?

And finally, there is Pontius Pilate, the proconsul governing Judea during the time Jesus was crucified. Why does the portrait of Pilate, as the manipulated ruler, become clearer and crisper as we move from early to later gospels? Was he as weak as the gospel of Matthew would have us believe? Could he be so easily intimidated by the growing crowds demanding Jesus' execution? Why was it necessary to make the Roman authorities look less and less responsible for the death of Jesus? Apart from the obvious implications of Christian anti-Judaism, do we have evidence of a creeping tolerance, if not acceptance, of imperial values and standards surrounding meal practice?

These questions lead to a second hypothesis surrounding the shift from common meal to exclusive ritual: the gospels give testimony to a capitulation to imperial values of elitism and control. Is it possible that the Kingdom of God movement of Jesus, which initially resisted Caesar's rule, based on the theology of power, slowly but relentlessly came to embrace these self-same values? In the process, it turned a real meal into a sacred rite and took the power of the gathered people and vested it in a select and privileged priesthood.

Unraveling this second hypothesis will be the subject of chapter 6, which offers some hints of how we can reset the table for the twenty-first century, which is the subject of chapter 7.

KNOWN IN THE BREAKING OF THE BREAD

Let's conclude these introductory remarks with a story that remains for me the quintessential story of the followers of Jesus. Of course, it revolves around a shared meal. No doubt, you have heard the story before. We call it the road to Emmaus,[24] and it's found only in Luke's gospel.

On Easter morning, when all is in doubt, with rumors swirling about the rising of Jesus, two disciples are leaving Jerusalem for a town called Emmaus, about 60 stadia (seven miles) outside the city. Our best archeological evidence cannot identify with certainty which small village might have been intended by Luke. The point is that this journey is not undertaken on a whim or to fill time. It's an intentional journey. We can picture these two companions settling in for a serious road trip.

And, according to Luke, they spend the long miles debating what had just happened. Their dreams of a new realm were in tatters. Their beliefs in the picture of new world order, prophesied by their leader, Jesus, demolished with his crucifixion. All hope was gone. All they had were questions: How could it happen? Were they fools? Did Jesus get it wrong? Was he tricked by his own dreams? And then there's the guilt and recrimination. I can imagine them trying to lay blame, pointing fingers at the hated Romans, dissing the religious leaders, and even reprimanding themselves for not being more careful.

---

24. Emmaus is a Hellenized version of a common place name in Palestine. In Hebrew the word for "warm" or warm spring is *hamma* or *hammat* (חמת). So, the two travellers are going to a "warm" town, Emmaus. To the modern ear, it sounds like special location, but it might be more accurate if we imagine that Luke was using a generic place name like "Centreville" — an acceptable and seemingly real location that gives the story a sense of accuracy and historicity.

Since Christians have been told for two thousand years how the good news triumphs in the end, it is difficult for us to understand the dismay of these two disciples. Let us remind ourselves that, in the space of a week, their best intentions and plans fell to the ground, returned to dust.

If we read the story without the assumption of resurrection, then one can feel a big dream building among the followers of Jesus. His Kingdom project was gathering momentum. Perhaps it wouldn't be realized immediately, and certainly not without work and perhaps a little intrigue. But the disciples could almost taste victory: the triumph of their hopes. Perhaps this would be the moment that God would intervene, the long-awaited time when the Romans would be sent packing, and a true Kingdom of God would be finally established in the promised land. It was so close. How many late nights had they spent debating how he (Jesus) would do it? They were not certain about the "how," or "when," but a "what if" was never entertained. Didn't Jesus himself say often that the Kingdom is right here, right now?

And when they arrived at the eastern outskirts of Jerusalem, the people had welcomed them with rejoicing. A glorious moment, when their little street theatre parody of Pilate's triumphal parade, taking place at the opposite side of the city, had enjoyed universal approval. They were the talk of the town, celebrities of the Passover celebrations. Then in four short days, with astounding ruthlessness, the soldiers came, took Jesus away, and, before any intervention could even be imagined let alone organized, he was crucified. Nothing left. That sabbath was the darkest they had ever known.

Then on the day after the sabbath, these two followers decide to go on their journey. Seems like a strange choice, given what we now see as the shining glory of the first Easter morning in Jerusalem. Perhaps it was too painful to stay in the holy city. Or was it too dangerous? Was it fear for new hope? Had the rumors of his rising begun to circulate, and they had no stomach for more false hopes? It could well be that this journey was part of a future plan of Jesus. Luke doesn't tell us. There is no reason given for the trip to Emmaus.

Their debate must have been lively, for they didn't even notice a stranger coming up from behind. He matched their pace and listened for a time to their recriminations, finally asking what was vexing them. They were astounded, so absorbed in their grief and pain they couldn't imagine someone else would not be aware of the tumult in Jerusalem.

The readers of the gospel are told from the beginning that this stranger is actually the risen Lord. And he spends the rest of their journey explaining how it could be possible that a "dead and crucified" messiah could fulfill the prophecies of the scriptures.

At this point, one should take a brief pause and be reminded of a simple fact. At the time of the gospels, the death of Jesus was an incredible stumbling block to the Jewish mind, as Paul puts it in his first letter to the church in Corinth (1 Corinthians 1:23). The messiah was a savior, a leader, who would rule the land of Israel. And having expelled the hated, occupying Roman forces, this leader would receive spiritual authority from God, purify the people and usher in a reign of light and justice. Of course, these dreams require any candidate for the position of messiahship to be alive. A dead messiah is non-starter. More, it was a ridiculous suggestion, a sick joke.

So, the first evangelists are facing a serious problem: a dead messiah. But then add to the undeniable fact of his death the fact that Jesus was crucified, and you are seriously handicapped as a preacher. Crucifixion adds considerable shame to the already impossible proposal that Jesus is the long awaited "anointed one." Crucifixion was a punishment reserved only for runaway slaves and rebels, and while that might be construed as a badge of courage to the zealous anti-Roman Judean, it spells humiliation to the ordinary citizen of the empire. The cross is proof of guilt and ignominy. Bad people get themselves crucified.

In that light, these two travelers are walking the route, listening to the risen Lord's explanations. One can only suppose that Jesus made reference to the passages from Isaiah that speak of a wounded servant of God. Perhaps he quoted Psalm 22 or other hymns of lament, which allow for the possibility of disappointment and dismay being part of God's plan. Did he recite the poem we call the "Book of Job?" They are so engrossed that they don't realize they have arrived at their destination. And while the stranger (Jesus) makes as if to continue on his way, they entreat him to stay with them. Here is one who makes sense of their grief.

They recline for a dinner, and Jesus breaks bread with them. At this precise moment, their eyes are opened, and they see Jesus for who he is. The story concludes, as if they didn't even finish their meal. Jesus is no longer there, but they are so enflamed by the passion Jesus awoke in them, that they run all the way back to Jerusalem to report what they have seen and heard. Their tale of Jesus' appearance is corroborated by others, and the community of "the Way" is given its commission by Jesus himself. And that is how the good news in the gospel of Luke concludes. It's Luke's chief resurrection story. Did it actually happen? Likely not. Emmaus is a faith statement turned into history. And yet, Emmaus becomes real every time disciples gather to share a meal. And that's Luke's point! And while modern ears might hear it as a once-upon-a-time mysterious or magical moment, when Jesus is finally revealed to the blind and unseeing, I hear it as a self-authenticating awakening of the first church. Here is a third-generation community of faith explaining, through Luke, that they come alive when they break bread together.

To be devout, a follower on "the Way" with Jesus, one must divide up one's food with strangers. Like a slogan or mission statement, the phrase is: "He was known to them in the breaking of the bread" (Luke 24:35). In the shared bread, Jesus rises again. Can there be any clearer statement of both identity and purpose for the ancient church? Could it also act as a new direction for the modern community of faith?

It is to the state of the twenty-first-century church that we turn now.

Daily Bread: A No-Fail Food

This recipe is the heart of my bakery. At The Piper's Buns, we base our recipes on this foundational bread . . . whether one uses sourdough, or a mixture of other grains, the proportions stay consistent.

MIX:

8 cups white flour
½ cup sugar
¼ cup oil
1 Tablespoon salt
2 Tablespoons dry instant yeast
2 ½ cups warm water

STEPS:

1. Mix flour mixture until gluten begins to form and the dough turns into a slightly sticky, spongy mix.

2. Roll dough onto a floured surface and knead for 10 minutes (sing "Amazing Grace" 10 times).

3. Place the dough in a slightly greased bowl and let it rise for 2 hours.

4. Divide the dough into 3 equal parts and place in 3 greased 8 inch by 4 inch bread pans. Beat one egg and use it to paint the 3 loaves with a pastry brush. Let stand in a warm place for 1 ½ hours.

5. Bake at 350 degrees F. for 30–35 minutes.

6. Remove from pans and allow loaves to cool for ½—1 hour before cutting.

7. Enjoy!

NOTES:

This bread can be shaped in a multitude of ways. You can roll the dough into 21 separate balls and place them in a circle on a greased 8 inch pie plate to make dinner rolls. You can roll the dough into 18 balls and flatten them to make hamburger buns or make them into tubes to do hotdog buns.

1

Lament for a Church

Not only have many people left church, but a growing number have never been to church. What's more, many have no interest in finding out what church is about . . . There is no fix. That is not to say that some congregations aren't flourishing. Some are, but for reasons particular to them that cross the spectrum in theology, styles of worship, and religious culture. Many more congregations are struggling: some will survive, but many will amalgamate or close.[1]

INTRODUCTION: LISTENING TO A CHILD'S VOICE

I can still recall my daughter's frankness. When she was six and we were seated in our kitchen, Rebecca told me plainly that she could be a preacher just like her daddy. When I pushed her a bit to show me, she immediately hopped up onto a stool, and pointing an accusing finger at an imaginary congregation over by the stove, she shouted in a frighteningly accurate imitation of my angry father's voice, "Why have you been so bad?" How did she get such a perfect rendition of guilt mongering from what we had done in church? I certainly don't remember preaching anything close to it. But she heard it . . . at six!

Alas, this is a telling parable of our modern dilemma as a community of faith. Leaders of historic, liberal churches have been working very hard, expanding our language for decades, so we can move away from the more

1. Clarke and Macdonald, *Leaving Christianity,* 12.

odious and onerous doctrines that inspire guilt or condemnation: original sin, double pre-destination, purgatory, divine punishment, exclusivist salvation through the "born again" experience. You name a dogma, we have dropped it. On any given Sunday, you'll find a clean slate: there's not a single fork-wielding devil in sight. No hints of sulfur in the air. Pits of fire, eternal flames, burning brimstone . . . they are all extinguished. No one has been sent to hell for a generation at least. And yet people still catch whiffs of recrimination. There's a "should" in the air. Never mentioned, not even intended, but people feel it. Who or what makes people culpable?

Perhaps it's just part of the social presumptions of religion. Not just Christianity. It could be that any form of organized religion, with its façade of rules and its obvious valuation of order, is by its very nature guilt-inducing. Established order quite naturally triggers the contrarian reflex within us. As we feel a commandment coming, we respond with resistance, and on a deeper level we tap into what I would call the "naughty" zone—that deeply held, arational swirl of emotions that reminds us how we haven't measured up, that we are wicked and have disobeyed. Is that where the guilt arises?

Even those who were never groomed by a Christian family, and who are therefore not consciously aware of the facts of these past religious "shadows," are still inheritors of Christian values. Though they may have no knowledge of Jesus stories or church dogma, nonetheless, they have been shaped and nurtured by a culture whose roots are essentially Christian. Given centuries of a judgmental and domineering *ecclesia*, it is not surprising that as inheritors of a Christian culture, we all take in a latent sense of culpability and inadequacy. And along with the undeniable sensation that we are all on Santa's "naughty" list, we drink in a suspicion of anything religious. Even when preachers or church leaders try to avoid any reference to "sin" or "guilt," people hear it.

For two years, I wrote and voiced a national radio column on ethics. We removed any theological language and spoke in simple terms about "right" action and "fair" behavior. And yet, regardless, the reviews of the column came back saying, it sounded too "preachy." Any suggestion of "doing the good" was heard as scolding interference in the individualism of our society. And the most obvious example people could use to explain their discomfort was to conjure up the image of a finger pointing preacher.

Is it this latent, unthinking, guilt reflex that accounts for the numerical collapse and social disintegration of the historic, northern[2] Christian

---

2. "Northern" is a reference to liberal Protestant and some Catholic churches found in the U.S., Canada, U.K., and Europe . . . many of which show the same characteristics of decline in membership and social status and irrelevance to the wider secular society in which they exist.

churches? "Who needs it?" the secular world mutters, as it passes our front doors. Maybe back in the dark ages of the last century people found a sick satisfaction in being berated or scolded on a Sunday morning. A public dressing down confession of sins was good for the soul, back then. But no longer. As Rebecca, now an adult, would put it, "It's not my jam!"

Some church leaders have argued that there is another reason church attendance is falling like a stone. They say, with a measure of truth, that it is the church's obscure theological imagery or perverted sacred writings that exclude many sincere souls, who would otherwise be amenable to joining our community.[3] And of this group, the genuine, but disappointed, people—who stay away from church in large numbers because of language and dogma—fall into two types: the faithful seekers and the disillusioned cynics.

The seekers want to join with us in a common mission, so the argument goes, except that Christianity's archaic ideas, obscure symbols, and doctrinaire writings get in the way. They sit in our pews with an open mind, but without intending it, we have cut them out of the conversation and, by extension, bewildered and belittled them through our murky, outdated ideas—making these newcomers feel stupid. They have faith. They seek understanding, and we have denied them both.

And it is true. From an outsider's point of view, notions like substitutionary atonement, triune monotheism, and transubstantiation, to name only a few, are unintelligible mysteries that can act as significant obstacles to participation. And when people "don't get it," they feel ignored or put down. At best, our theological jargon and doctrinal creeds are outmoded notions that highlight the inadequacies of the church's convoluted communication; at worst they hint of a deeper exclusivist self-assurance. If you don't know the code words, you're not really "in."

That's the problem for the seekers, but then there are many who have studied our books. They have actually followed our reasoning—wading through our doctrines—and they remain unconvinced—worse, disillusioned. These cynics claim that there is clearly a great deal of theological nonsense that passes for Christian truth. Having spent my career exploring our theology systemically, I will be the first to admit they are right. For many sensitive people, the church's history of misguided and manipulative doctrinal thinking is a serious obstacle.

Take the idea of original sin as an example. While writing this chapter, I attended a bible study in a poor neighborhood in Havana, Cuba, and I heard it again: shame, self-deprecation, and guilt. A blessed and saintly

---

3. See Spong, *Sins of Scripture*, 4. ". . . in the history of the western world, . . . the bible has also left a trail of pain, horror, blood and death that is undeniable."

woman began her intervention on John the Baptist by stating that she too was a sinner, a hopeless soul needing Jesus' salvation. Across the room, another chimed in that we could do nothing worthy in this world. "Didn't we all know that Adam and Eve ate the apple, discovered they were naked, and human beings have been lost ever since in the jungle of lust and desire? So, we all require Jesus, who washes us clean and offers us God's gift of grace!"

Now I am polite and careful, so I sit quietly, but I wanted to stand up and scream or sit still and weep. What is the matter with us? How did it happen that Christian believers have been duped into such a sick, self-deprecating dead end? How is it possible that Jesus, a teacher and healer whom we call the "prince of peace," got twisted into a scolding parent who wants us to think of ourselves first and foremost as spoiled experiments? Isn't there something fundamentally wrong with a movement that speaks of love and forgiveness, on Sunday, and inspires such misguided self-doubt and culpability during the week?

And you? Do you do guilt and shame? Do you seek them out or hope to see them sit beside you on the commute to the office? Think about this for a moment! If you heard that an association down the street believed that human beings were little more than "worms five feet high" (Luther), would you feel inclined to join them? Not on your life. You'd run the other way. And you'd be right.

And that is just one example of how our language and dogma are both repulsive to those who have had a brush with religion and unintelligible to those who have not. Alas, there are so many misguided or outdated doctrines that act either as unseen barriers to welcoming spiritual seekers or as evidence of the church's duplicity: the hierarchical and patriarchal assumptions of our theological language, homophobic pronouncements, a history of racism, the endorsement of economic and political oppression, the church's suppression of women, the promotion of slavery, the resistance to reason, and animosity to scientific discoveries. How much time do we have? I can count many centuries of misdemeanors. Taken honestly, from the point of view of our inadequacies as a human institution, it's a miracle that anyone takes the church seriously at all.

To be fair, historic American and Canadian churches are not static nor unaware that we have to address the concerns raised by seekers and cynics alike. So, in response to the inadequacies of our language and the church's dark history, some leaders have abandoned all theological language, even dropping any Jesus talk. In this way, they grow a vocabulary of spirituality from the ground up. Fresh and new. It's a very engaging and appealing exercise.[4] Time will tell if these experiments are adequate. Their premise is noble: showing a wider, agnostic world that Christians are not closed to new visions of the Ultimate.

The difficulty of such movements is the inadequacy of the human condition. Symbols and signs that speak to our collective anxiety, caress our souls, and point to that distant shore beyond death cannot be created at will. They evolve from the crucible of searching and suffering. It takes time. In the interim, some of the prayers and creeds that this movement have developed feel artificial and contrived, as if we are trying too hard.

In a less dramatic way, many congregations are devising new ways to "open" the front doors. Churches promote jazz vespers, coffee house devotionals, band choruses, Internet chat rooms, public lectures, the revival of medieval meditation or Gregorian chant. Tremendous creativity has gone into reshaping the "old, old story." We've plastered a welcome message on any surface that will bear it, paid for ads in the subway, designed websites to blow your eyes out, used Twitter and Facebook, until we're buried in spam. Given the demands of the 2020 pandemic, almost all congregations have installed Wi-Fi and regularly stream their services from the sanctuary. One church has redeveloped the back of the sanctuary, turning it into a cappuccino bar, while another opened a bar in the basement.

So, Christian leaders are working hard, using as many languages as we can imagine. How many ways do we have to say it? "We're open for all."

And yet, the "all" whom we imagine are outside, are also passing us by on the other side of the road (Luke 10:31). Very frustrating. Is it possible that people know, on a level of understanding that church folk won't admit to themselves, that we don't really mean it? We want to welcome "all" as long as the "all" who arrive on our doorstep are much like us, respect our traditions (large and small), and join us in the way we want them to belong.

Allow me to be quite clear and personal at this point. I have spent my entire career within the United Church of Canada, the largest Protestant denomination in Canada, and my best energy went into this specific project of making a space for "all" in our congregations and church buildings. And after all those years of shaping and teaching Christianity hospitality, I confess that our "all" is conditional. It is still the case that if you smell, can't keep up a coherent conversation, haven't got a home, come from a country whose name we cannot pronounce, don't have clean clothes—you are tolerated. But *never* confuse that tolerance with inclusion. Patronized perhaps, but included, never. Our hospitality is polite and we may even tell ourselves

---

4. Of particular note in this regard is Gretta Vosper's work in Toronto. Her wisdom and mission are captured in her first book, *With or without God,*.

we are virtuous for letting "those people" into our services and suppers. But they are not really embraced fully. Given a few bumps in the road, they're pushed out.

I admit this failure of hospitality, with deep regret. On countless occasions, I have been healed and saved by churches that have welcomed and embraced me.[5] Alas, my reception was based on some long accepted preconditions: I am white, male, clean, and educated. Others are not afforded such cordiality. The welcome, that takes no notice of social or political bias, is still an endangered species in church circles.

I know there are ministers who feel personal responsibility for the numerical decline of their congregations, but my sorrow is associated with what I see as the growing rigidity and parsimony of our spiritual accommodation. We say we want people to join us, but we don't really mean it, and the smaller we get, the less we can embrace difference. I find myself commiserating with more and more church leaders, using the adage about African drinking holes: "As the watering hole dries up, the animals start looking at each other differently." And that is us as a church organization. We're getting meaner in spirit and much less flexible in heart.

Alas, that is the internal struggle we face as a church; and externally, the reality is even more stark. There is no evidence that the secular world is at all interested in what the church says or does.

Perhaps it is time to face reality without flinching. Most people in Canadian society don't care, don't know, and don't have the time to find out about Christianity. As difficult as it may seem to us who cherish it, the Christian church is largely irrelevant and invisible to the majority of people in our world.

That does not discount the fact that clergy speak of the resurgence of seekers—young people who slip into the back pew to check us out. Not a flood, more like a trickle. And often they don't return. Is it possible that these one-time explorers are reticent to commit to the church community, because they know that nothing is as it seems? Like my daughter, those, who are otherwise sympathetic to things spiritual, sense a latent contingency in our welcoming messages. There's a catch! All our protests to the contrary, the sensitive among a secular audience can detect a "price" in our preaching. What do we really want? Isn't there's a charge buried in the fine print? We don't really mean "all" when we say, "All are welcome." And let us give credit where credit is due. Modern audiences have very keen intuitions. And they are right to sense a hidden agenda, an unspoken message, in our

5. I recall singing over and over again the line from "Song of the Mira," in which the listener is told by a welcoming, east-coast community, "If you come broken, we'll see that you mend."

backpedaling modesty. Around the edges of our welcome sign is a desperation that belies our efforts to appear easygoing and relaxed.

And they are right, aren't they? We do want something! We want people to join our congregations, help us pay the expenses, and take on leadership roles in the church. To be frank, Christians are in the unenviable position of sustaining an expensive, unrealistic institution. The costs are rising, and the revenues are shrinking. We're looking for someone else to pay the bills! Of course, we would never be so single-mindedly crass. We couch our economic concerns in spiritual language and the importance of the good news for the modern world. But in the end, we are hoping to attract people to our institutional way of being spiritual and to invite them into accepting our worldview—so they will eventually help us sustain it.

Perhaps before expecting someone new to join in our mission and adhere to our ethical and holy precepts, and certainly prior to pillaring strangers to pay for our mission, we might examine what we are really called to do and become. Take away the flowery language and the glowing mission statements. What's the point? To paraphrase the prophet Micah:[6] "What does God want from us?"

Is it possible that, as a church, we should work with what we have, rather than yearn for what seems impossible? Can we admit that numerical growth has been an intoxicating distraction? Isn't it possible that the basic model of church, one that evolved in imitation of those structures promoted by the Roman empire, is faulty? Called "the Christendom" church, this model assumed social acceptance, constant growth, and political favor. It was a mass-based organization that needed relatively large buildings and budgets to sustain itself. When membership is growing, the Christendom model works and works well. But as membership declines, the weaknesses of the model become evident. We can no longer sustain the enterprise, and keeping Christendom Christianity afloat leads to a fixation on survival. And there seems no way out. Our best energies are spent shoring up sagging envelop offerings and, quite literally, patching over holes in the roof.

However, if we shift slightly and ask another question, we might make some headway. The "what if" question. What if we didn't have a church building to support? What if our budget was not our downfall? What if we were faithful—suspending the current church model for the moment, what would we do and be?

It is the thesis of this book that the feeding ministry of Jesus can act as a model for this faithfulness. What if we went back to shared bread?

---

6. Micah 6:6a: "With what shall I come before the Lord and bow down before the exalted God?"

Before we can move to elaborate just how a new Jesus movement might arise out of the bread ministry of Jesus, we had better be clear about the current unrealities of our institution that inhibit movement forward. I can see three dimensions to this unreality: real estate, misorientation of mission, and a poverty of spirit. Let's look at each in turn.

THE UNREALITY OF THE CHURCH: REAL ESTATE

There is nothing more concrete than church buildings, nothing more "real." And I begin with the church's considerable investment in real estate as the first obstacle inhibiting the community of faith, because it is so clearly determinative of everything else. We are held back from being a thriving movement, because of the weight and cost of our buildings. It would not be an exaggeration to assert that our original movement has suffered considerable distortion, because of a surplus of church physical structures. Could we say it's at right angles to the original direction Jesus walked?

Historic, U.S. and Canadian Protestant churches are not unique in this regard. Real estate was a problem almost from the beginning. Clearly, the author of the gospel of Luke, who was writing during the last decade of the first century, was distressed by the growing establishment feel of his audience. They were getting too comfortable, and he is constantly inviting them out on the road. Luke's key stories, such as the post-Easter road to Emmaus, champion life "on the Way."[7] So buildings and the permanence they offer are an old problem.

Of course, a sanctuary, by its very name, connotes security and peace. Church buildings promise safety and longevity. They are built right into the bricks and mortar. Who doesn't seek a safe haven, especially when it comes to prayer and meditation?

Then there's the question of convenience. Clearly, the first missions of Jesus followers, while adopting the radical itinerancy of Jesus, still required someone to be "at home" when they came to town. Having a fixed address is not a modern contrivance. A safe place was a necessity for the fledging two by twos preachers. Ergo: holy homes, worship locations, a welcoming and waiting family.

And yet, the very strength of a stable geographic locale, and the protection it provided, is also its weakness. The community of faith embraced what began as an expedient facility for gathering and ended as a suffocating establishment.

---

7. See chapter 2 in this text for a detailed description of Luke's vision.

In our modern context, our church real estate is currently bleeding the life out of many local congregations. The demands of upkeep and repair focus our mission inward and bend our hearts and minds toward the self-serving maintenance of a structure designed for an outdated model of spirituality. Buildings ask questions we can no longer answer. Majestic sanctuaries speak a language of grandeur that does not suit our humble state.

Can you imagine how much good energy might be unleashed, if Christians did not have to pay for the constant repair and renovation of their physical plants? Likewise, would our hearts be freer, if we didn't have to worry so much about building security[8] and we could focus more on the food security of our brothers and sisters on the street?

On a simple economic level, it is an irrefutable fact that we can't afford our buildings any longer. The actual cost of retaining and repairing the current places of worship is beyond most congregations. Shrinking memberships and alternate giving patterns of the few donors who are left make it impossible to sustain the rising costs of paint and plaster. In a recent church where I served, the loss of one very energetic and generous member constituted a drop of 10% in the envelop givings of the congregation. One death and the finances are in peril! We saw it coming. How many times have we told ourselves that the end was near, that a few unfortunate and untimely funerals, and the church finances would be in ruins. And then we sighed and we agreed among ourselves that we'd cross that bridge when we came to it. Well, we are at the bridge. No denying it, now!

Most congregations can hardly attend to minor repairs. As the architectural standards and cultural expectations rise, what was once a state-of-the-art building is now outdated, in some cases deemed unsafe. Modern communities of faith have trouble keeping up with the civic codes, regulations of accessibility, lighting, and fire protection. And these are just the bare bones of the building. The current expectations for technological sophistication require churches to invest heavily in audio-visual aids, musical accompaniment, and accommodation for families and cars.

These expenses made more sense in a time when the church was essentially the chaplain to empire. We were once the town hall, the entertainment center, the school, and hospital all rolled into one. In those times, our buildings kept pace with the culture in very concrete ways. In return, church institutions were the beneficiaries of the society's generosity.

---

8. How many times, in recent years, have I been subjected to the question of putting video cameras on our locked church doors—to protect the building and or the administrative staff. They're costly, largely ineffective and expensive—not just in cost of installation but also in staff time to review video recordings.

And as the church is shuffled more and more to the margins, our real estate looks redundant or out of step. Here's our predicament. In the fifties of the last century, many U.S. and Canadian churches, enjoying the surge of the baby boom, built Christian education wings and gymnasiums for burgeoning youth groups. But the society did the same, with more expertise and better resources. Our Christian education wings enjoyed a few years of frantic activity, a time when we were riding a tide of enthusiasm and high spirits. Then came the rise of secular community groups. Church buildings declined in importance, and we have been trying to fill the vacant spaces ever since. Our own church-sponsored children's programs withered, the hockey leagues, badminton clubs, children's choirs, and reading groups fell away, as non-religious facilities offered better, less cumbersome, events and programs. So, the buildings, that were to be used to promote and enhance Christian education, have devolved into a cheap alternative for not-for-profit agencies and transient projects: everything from hot yoga on demand to opera by request.

The alternate use of church facilities is a parable of our problem. We rent out the building to groups not affiliated with our community of faith, often with aims that are only vaguely related. We do this to preserve the facility, so that one hour a week we can worship the God who asks us to minister to an aching world in need of assistance—assistance we would gladly offer if only we had available resources. We don't have any excess, because we spend all we get to keep the building that is being rented to groups not . . . See the vicious cycle?

To be fair, the crisis of empty real estate has led to a specific, unexpected, and, sometimes, very fruitful ministry. We have become the landlord of last resort. Since the church space is subpar, our prices are usually quite reasonable. Outside groups with marginal means take advantage of our cut-rate prices. So, we "minister" to the world by allowing any number of deserving associations to meet in our space. Take away church halls, and they would be unable to continue. And this worthwhile ministry continues to the present day. Many churches list their renters as part of their community life and outreach. Laudable though this ministry might be, one has to ask if as disciples of Jesus we are called by God to be facilities managers? Is this a particularly Christian vocation?

Surely, we are called to a wider ministry than filling in rental schedules and arbitrating disputes between competing children's programs: "does karate get the gym, or do we let yoga for youngsters have it?" As a disciple of the crucified prince of peace, I am constantly asking myself if we can do more? If we were only freed of the real estate, how much could be accomplished!

Alas, it seems beyond us.

That's the cynical accounting of church real estate. But to give the devil his due, human beings do need some stability in their lives. Having an unchanging, safe, community gathering space is certainly a gift. Maybe a necessity. There is very little that can substitute for a sanctuary—a place that holds our unspoken anguish and reminds us our blessings. Of course, sacred spaces can take any shape, but a church building that has history, that remembers you when you were young and embraces you when you are old . . . that's a living benediction. It can function as a stable influence through life's upheavals, such that lost souls find their way to the church building to be held.

The real estate is a solid, unchanging anchor that offers a tangible sense of the permanence of God's protection and guidance. We keep that old church and rebuild its roof, and paint its pews, because that spells faithfulness. People invest in buildings as a natural and understandable act of faith. Like Peter on the mount of transfiguration (Mark 9:5), our instinctive response to life's marvels and movements is to build a protective space to find comfort and safety.

And yet, all our spiritual and emotional needs for security notwithstanding, the very establishment of the church buildings undermines one of the key aspects of Jesus' Kingdom movement: its radical trust in God's hospitality —itinerancy.

If we look quickly at one of the first stories in the gospel of Mark, we'll see how Jesus deals with the call for establishment. In the first chapter, once Jesus has been baptized (Mark 1:9–13) and has returned to Galilee to call his disciples (Mark 1:16–20), his healing and hospitality mission begins (Mark 1:21–28). Fabulous results! His fame begins to spread. Jesus brings health to Peter's mother-in-law, and they all eat together (Mark 1:29–31). That evening, he continues his healing ministry. Mark paints a tremendous picture. The sick and ill, the shamed and blamed, are streaming to see Jesus. Standing room only. Crowds are growing with his fame. Here is a spiritual leader who speaks with remarkable authority. Never heard before. This man is able to walk his talk.

I can imagine Peter and others seeing their future clearly. They would turn Capernaum into a new Jerusalem; the family house would be transformed into a shining temple. In the minds of Jesus' followers, their future was secure and they went to sleep that night secure in the knowledge that they were on the cusp of a great religious revival—established in their humble fishing village.

Mark tells us that Jesus rose early the next morning and went off to an isolated place to pray (Mark 1:35). His disciples rose later and searched for him, finally encountering him away from the town (Mark 1:36). Obviously,

the crowds have begun to gather at Peter's house again, waiting for the healing touch of the rabbi. I can catch an expectant excitement in the statement
of the disciples, "Everyone is looking for you." (Mark1:37). Are the disciples
rubbing their hands together in anticipation of the good times ahead?

Imagine their disconcerted looks, when Jesus says he is not staying
in Capernaum. "Jesus replied, 'Let us go somewhere else—to the nearby
villages—so I can preach there also. That is why I have come.'"[9]

What? Can you hear their retort? "The show is just starting to take
hold in the little town square! Hopes are rising and people are beginning to
get it. You don't leave now, just when you are riding the wave of being on a
winning roll! This is our time. Now is when you stay and get established."

Clearly, Jesus is unwilling to allow himself or his ministry to be tied
down to a specific location and structure. It is not that he has an animosity
to buildings. His itinerancy is a positive statement about trust in God. Like
the chosen people in the desert, Jesus sees considerable merit in having to
rely on God to provide for his needs. His *modus operandi* of preaching missions, a practice that is reflected in the stories of sending out the disciples
two by two (Mark 6:7–13, Matthew 10:5–15, Luke 9:1–6), was, itself, a message. The people who follow in God's Kingdom do not enjoy security of being established. They rely upon the radical hospitality of God made manifest
in the generosity of human communities.

Having no place "to lay his head" gave his movement a clear incentive
to reach out to those on the road. His message of radical reliance on the
gifts of God, expressed through love and justice, was made real every night,
when the Jesus crowd had to find a place to sleep. And this message came
with a price. People who were devout and willing couldn't go that far. The
story of the one called a "rich young ruler" found at Mark 10:1, repeated in
Matthew 19:16, and Luke 18:18, is a case in point. He had done everything
right, kept faith with the commandments, and apparently, Jesus loved him
at first sight, but in the end, he couldn't go homeless. He needed something
more secure, more lasting. Surely, this was the early community saying to
itself that no one can survive without a tangible and lasting sanctuary by
which to hold and hallow their hopes and fears.

The itinerancy or anti-establishment direction of Jesus' movement was
more than a technique. It has several implicit theological principles. First,
the road to truth never ends. You don't arrive at the end of the journey
into understanding God. There is always another twist in the road, more
to learn. So, we avoid one of the two great pitfalls to discipleship, which
is self-satisfaction. Second, no one has arrived, completed, or ended their

9. Mark 1:38.

search for God. And itinerancy inspires humility. One who never can claim completion or perfection is partially immune to the second pitfall of discipleship: self-righteousness.

Perhaps beyond its personal meaning, itinerancy was and is a clear message about our master's role in the religious journey. Jesus will not be our patron, a go-between with God. Refusing to play the patronage game most common to spiritual enterprises of his time, Jesus set a different standard. In that time and place, there was an unspoken assumption among the priestly caste that ordinary people require an intermediary, someone to communicate with God on their behalf. You don't approach the holy of holies on your own. You use the good graces of a spiritual patron who knows the proper language with which to make petitions to the Almighty for you. Sacrificial rituals and predetermined rites and rituals add to this structured intermediator work. Religious buildings, temples, and altars all act as physical reminders of this patronage system. Jesus regularly refuses to be that kind of gatekeeper to the Almighty. He invites his followers to trust their own resources (Mark 6:10) and to use their own reasoning to come to the truth (Mark 8:14–21).

To be sure, the Jesus in John's gospel is much different. In that text, his invitation and open mission work are almost buried behind his declaration of the centrality of his own person. But in the earlier gospels, Jesus is quite insistent that his disciples join him as equals as they walk in the peace of God. They are invited to meet their God on the road and shape their own salvation. Like wandering in the desert for forty years, the lack of permanence is tough, exacting, and uncontrollable . . . And that is precisely the ground upon which authentic trust is built.

In conclusion, given this biblical background, it is a simple step to recognize that church buildings are a hindrance, an understandable, but regrettable, perversion of the original intention of Jesus. We began as a traveling band of healers, whose message of homelessness was one of the key elements of our miraculous appeal. Without buildings, the disciples of Jesus were forced to build a "sanctuary" in every home where they were hosted. Building a permanent worship site robbed both the host and those who were being hosted of the dual gifts of insecurity and surprise. Without spontaneity, the movement became scripted, predictable, and in the end, controllable: steps that killed one of the important aspects of its message and appeal.

And the weight of church real estate threatens to take away our future. As I said, buildings have been draining congregational resources as they age. The once pristine temples of piety are crumbling through age, pollution, and neglect. That's a tax on our hope as well. Our spirit of expectancy is declining along with our finances. Not only do many lively and well-meaning congregations twist themselves inside out to meet impossible utilities costs, they tell themselves that they are failures, unfaithful to the gift that generations have bequeathed, because they can't make the budget. A double curse: crumbling buildings and rising hopelessness.[10]

Then we add one final problem: the pandemic. While it may well be over, in the sense of being an immediate threat, the first waves of COVID-19 seriously destabilized the health of many Christian communities. Unable to meet, and therefore, unable to benefit from weekly donations, many churches began to have very serious financial problems. Costs remained static, while revenues were in free fall. And while Zoom services helped to keep some people connected, there were many communities of faith which imploded under the pressure of stay-at-home orders. The nerve of volunteerism, which was the foundation of church work, was cut. People got out of the habit of supporting their church, attending to its needs and activities. And an already aging leadership used the pandemic as a way to gracefully retire. Of course, church communities were already precarious, given the increasingly older age demographic. The pandemic just speeded up the inevitable. As a friend, Stan Dotson, put it: the pandemic was like pneumonia[11] in a senior's residence. It accelerated the inevitable death of many churches that were on the road to dying, but which hadn't reached a critical condition, yet. March 2020 marked the end for many congregations.

Was the pandemic a blessing? It is perhaps too soon to tell. At this point, it is reasonable to suggest that, for the congregations that remain, we are feeling adrift. The psychic energy to build back communities that have been forced to remain home is in short supply. Minsters report not knowing how or when to expect new life. The rising costs of our buildings, coupled with this sense of lostness, have pushed church communities into amalgamations, architectural redevelopment, or even closure—none of which has had very satisfactory results, largely because the obstacles of real estate are simply a symptom of deeper problems. The current community of faith has marched itself into a theological dead end. We have nowhere to go.

10. Many of our sanctuaries perpetuate in believers a miserable, spiritual inadequacy. Twenty years ago, I was serving in a building that could seat 1100: the largest auditorium in town. Its Methodist founders built for growth. On a regular Sunday morning, we would have 120 faithful souls attending worship . . . close to 85% participation of the entire active church membership; a praise-worthy standard. But the architecture was shouting a different message: that we were losers, a dying community. Every empty seat was testament to our failure.

11. Didn't we call pneumonia the "old person's friend," meaning it shortened the lives of those who would otherwise have suffered through a lingering, drawn out, and undignified process of dying?

THE UNREALITY OF THE CHURCH: MISORIENTED MISSION

What's our mission, when the road is blocked, the building is lost, and the community is disintegrating? What do Christians do to act out their faith, when their church building is gone?

Years ago, now, the babysitter of my son, Griffin, came to the house sporting her new bracelet. She was very proud of it and made a point of showing it to me, since I was a minister. It was a simple braid of beads, with four letters featured in the middle: WWJD. I looked at that for a moment, puzzling over the significance of this acronym, and then I recalled a news broadcast on this movement among young people. What Would Jesus Do. It worked well for those inexperienced in life. Any doubts about what decision to make and you asked yourself, what would Jesus do?

But using Jesus as a model for our lives can pose some serious problems: 1) he was reputed to be one with God, whereas we are mere mortals; 2) he was perfect in judgment (apparently free some sin), while we are all too frail; 3) what did he actually do? We may not be able to know what Jesus would do, since the gospel records are not always consistent; and 4) even if we were able to discern his actions, our follow through may be less than adequate—given contextual differences between his time and ours. Modern situations are unimaginable to the Jesus of the gospels. We are left to guess his responses.

Nevertheless, the ethical contextual shortcomings notwithstanding, imitating Jesus does offer us some measure of assurance on what constitutes faithful discipleship. So, what did Jesus do?

The next chapter examines all three synoptic gospels and weighs the number of verses that describe Jesus' behavior. From this broad quantitative analysis, we can get a glimpse of what took up his time. For the purposes of this chapter, let us dispel some of the misconceptions about Jesus. Using what theologians call the negative path, the *via negativa*, we ask what did he *not* do? The gospel of Mark is a good measuring stick for this exercise.[12] Jesus did not spend most of his time in worship or prayer. It is true he went to isolated places to pray or reflect. Mark mentions this practice on

---

12. At this point, let us accept that the historical accuracy of the gospels is in serious doubt. For a number of reasons to be outlined briefly in the next chapter, they cannot be relied upon as an accurate picture of Jesus' life. However, as a voice of the local "Jesus" community, the gospels can tell us what people remember or believed Jesus said and did. And with this proviso, they can be helpful in outlining some general aspects of the community's memory of Jesus.

a number of occasions.[13] These are the times that it is mentioned explicitly. But one can surmise that there were more occasions, when Jesus traveled out into isolated locations around the lake just to get away and find some peace. His ministry was so busy that Mark reports twice how the disciples didn't even have time to eat. However, Mark also points out regularly that the crowds would not allow Jesus to isolate himself. They followed him in the wilderness, chasing around the shoreline to reach home, crowding out his home in Capernaum. Early on in his ministry, Jesus even stays away from towns, because he knew he couldn't have peace if he entered a village in Galilee; such was his appeal (Mark 1:45). So, while he may have wanted peace and freedom from the crowd, Mark's portrait of Jesus is of a frenetic pace that gives little time for personal devotions.

Likewise, Jesus never exhorts his disciples, his followers, or those whom he heals, to worship more often. He does mention once that certain kinds of evil spirits cannot be dispelled except through prayer (Mark 9: 29) and does tell a healed leper to go to a priest in order to make the proper offerings in thanksgiving (Mark 1:43–44). But these few instances are overshadowed by the number of times when Jesus simply asks for faith and trust—not prayer or piety.

Jesus does go to the synagogue . . . often. According to Mark, he seems to have used it as the primary locus of his teaching, at least initially. He was regarded as one who taught with a new authority, even by the home-town crowd of Nazareth (Mark 6:1). But Jesus could never simply teach in the synagogue. Mark points out, in his first stories of Jesus' presence in the synagogue, that he got himself in trouble for healing on the sabbath. The religious authorities began watching him, wanting to catch him in a contradiction. And one has the impression, from the flow of the story, that he was less and less welcome in the circle of the righteous, and consequently, went less and less to that gathering, and continued his teaching and healing in the countryside, by the lakeshore, and wherever people gathered.

A note on synagogue life. While Mark mentions often that Jesus went to the synagogue, these were probably not buildings so much as places where the townsfolk gathered. Think of the town square, a specific courtyard of the local spiritual authority or synagogue official. There are no priests in the synagogue. It is a teaching/devotional center, not a site for sacrificial rites presided over by designated "authority." In the local synagogue, there would have been patterns of readings and regular prayers, but to the modern eye, it would appear more like a spiritual, open-air classroom than a church sanctuary.

---

13. See Mark 1:35, 6:31, 6:46,14:32.as instances when Jesus is portrayed as prayerful.

According to the witnesses of the first community that shaped the gospels, Jesus did go to the temple for one Passover season, at least. And apart from some specific moments during the teaching parables on the temple mount, his presence at that great place of worship was, to be polite, troublesome. Like many of the prophets before him, he caused a disturbance. By overturning the tables of money changers and scattering the stalls of animal sellers (both of which were necessary aspects of the sacrificial cult on which the temple and Judean piety were based), Jesus acted out his assertion that the temple had become a hiding place for cheats and thieves, rather than a house of prayer. That is to say, the corrupt and colluding religious authorities had used the temple as a store house for their ill-gotten gains.[14] The money changing was not a problem—they were not the thieves. They were conveniently available, public agents of temple authority. Jesus disrupted their functioning as a way to dismantle, symbolically, a corrupted temple. It was more than likely this "attack" on the temple resulted in his execution. I can imagine temple authorities having agreements with Roman officials that any one disturbing the peace during a high festival would be immediately punished.[15]

So, the first gospel writer recalls that Jesus does not devote much time to prayer, even though he might have wanted to do more. He attends synagogue but appears to have gotten into trouble by his activities there, and when he does "go to church," i.e., the temple, he starts a ball of animosity rolling, which eventually gets him crucified. When he does prescribe behavior for those he heals, it is most often to live as if the reign of God has arrived. Leave behind old ways and live the good news (Mark 1:15). And the good news appears to be that the lame are healed, the lost are found, and the hungry are fed. When confronted directly about what a devout person should do in response to God's reign, Jesus responds with the famous phrase: "Sell all you have and give it to the poor and come follow me" (Mark 10:21).

My point at this junction is quite simple. In the early image of Jesus given to us by that first gospel community, he does not do worship/

14. It should be noted that the temple precincts were the location for financial archives. All the loan documents and legal paper work that recorded the loss of family holdings, the decline of the small farm and the rise of commercial estates, were held in the temple. When the Zealots took charge of the city of Jerusalem in 68 CE, their first act was to burn these real estate documents.

15. In chapter 14 of Mark's gospel, the opening verse speaks of how the religious authorities had a slogan: "Not during the festival, otherwise the people will riot." That sounds very much like a stated policy, one that the Romans would agree with and enforce, since any public disturbances had the unwelcome outcome of inspiring resistance and revolt.

devotion, at least not as a central or guiding principle of his mission. Nor does he exhort his followers to matters of piety apart from trust in God. They are instructed in casting out demons and healing the sick. And there is the explanation of prayer, in both Matthew and Luke, which is concluded with the Lord's Prayer.[16]

So how does it happen that, in the modern church that bears his name, we focus almost exclusively on weekly worship? That sacred hour on Sunday morning is the gold standard of discipleship and the measure of our success as a community of faith. With respect, I believe we have our priorities reversed, telling ourselves that our Sunday worship is the key, central activity that fortifies us to be just and righteous believers the rest of the week. Worship leads to justice. For Jesus it is reversed. Justice is worship. Following from the tradition of the prophets, Jesus lives justice and forgiveness and in so doing gives honor to God.

A few years ago, I was unemployed. Thus freed from regular Sunday duties, I took to reading ministry classified ads. They give one a peculiar and very specific portrait of church life. In particular, I was taken by the lists of priorities churches set for themselves in looking for a new leader. Apart from wanting a replica of Jesus Christ (entirely understandable and unrealistic), churches place preaching and worship leadership at the top of their pastor's work requirements. It is not uncommon for this single event, Sunday worship, to take up 40% of the minister's time. That is a significant allocation of talent and resources.

A quick look around any church building will verify that worship is the primary concern of Christian communities. We focus our best energies on worship. We have lifted it up above all else as the standard of discipleship, as if this is what Jesus asked most of his followers. Clearly, that is not the case.

At best, we could draw from Jesus' own life that regular community life in prayer and teachings is important, even essential. But to focus on worship/prayer to the exclusion of all else, or to place it way above all other activities of discipleship, is a gross distortion of the Kingdom of God movement Jesus calls his followers to join.

A word from the prophet Micah might be helpful at this point to remind us that Jesus is speaking in continuity with the Hebraic tradition of justice. The prophet asks what God wants: sacrifices in the temple, gifts of oil? And then answers his own question: "God has shown you, o mortal, what is good; and what does God require of you but to do justice, love mercy, and walk humbly with your God?" (Micah 6:8) How would our church

16. See Matthew 6:5–15, and Luke 11:1–13.

activities change, if we took the prophet's word and the life of Jesus as models for our community of faith?

THE UNREALITY OF THE CHURCH:
A POVERTY OF SPIRIT

If we accept that we have a humble path of justice-making and mercy-loving set before us, and if the Christian church is only destined to die when it fails to take that path, what's the problem? Why don't we do it? Herein lies perhaps the chief and most troublesome obstacle to our life as a community of faith. We don't believe the prophet or Jesus. Not really. Perhaps we lack real faith.

Of course, every Sunday, we gather and proclaim unwavering trust in our Creator. We sing about our courage, matched with an inspiring mission. We listen to the "old, old story," and hearing of unseen things above, we proclaim that we will be faithful disciples. But while we voice the words, they rarely reach the level of action, and when they do, our action is all too often furtive and insecure.

Here's a small example. As a ministry educator, in my own denomination, I can plot the pathway of our unbelieving. When we ceased having "summer missions" for ministry candidates and we called them "internships," we moved away from the mission motivation of church life and adopted survival as our goal. It was the 1980s, and our church was mirroring the world around us that was likewise getting more particular and concise about its vocations. To be sure, the vocabulary is a small matter, but it portrays a move away from belief-based, action-oriented movement, to professional, conduct-focused, self-serving organization. And that shift signals a dramatic alteration in our theology. In changing a few words, we have transitioned from faith to compliance, from trust in an unknown future to tabulating "attainable" learning outcomes. This shift took place for the best of intentions and with very much goodwill, and it was one example of how an institution chooses security and accommodation over vision and sacrifice.

And what happened in the shift of vocabulary, with respect to ministry training, was replicated throughout the institution. We said to ourselves that we were making ourselves relevant, keeping up with modern expectations of professionalism. In the move to accommodate ourselves to social norms, we lost the ability and the will to burn with the passion of faith. Put bluntly, in the name of security, we chose to moderate our believing. It's a small example, and one that spans a relatively short period of the church's life. But in the last few decades, I sense my denomination has domesticated its mission in procedures and protocols. The role of faith and the "call" to mission have been lost.

Let me be very careful at this point. I am not arguing that current believers are without faith and trust. How many examples come to mind of incredible faithfulness among God's people in the U.S. and Canada? I have personally witnessed quite noble, sacrificial generosity and many costly acts of compassion. They take your breath away. Indeed, I continue to work in the community of faith, because it is in God's household that I encounter people, who have startled me with the depth of their devotion.

Nevertheless, there is something we are missing. It is as if there is tremendous goodwill, but this doesn't result in transformation. Perhaps, if we turn to the famous story of a rich man seeking eternal life (quoted partially above), we can discover the kernel of our problem. Found in all the synoptics, Mark's version is certainly the source of the encounter. While Matthew calls this man "young" and both Luke and Matthew drop the beautiful statement that Jesus loved him at first sight, the story remains essentially the same in all three gospels. Here is Mark's version (Mark 10:17–23):

> 17 As Jesus started on his way, a man ran up to him and fell on his knees before him. "Good teacher," he asked, "what must I do to inherit eternal life?" 18 "Why do you call me good?" Jesus answered. "No one is good—except God alone. 19 You know the commandments: 'You shall not murder, you shall not commit adultery, you shall not steal, you shall not give false testimony, you shall not defraud, honor your father and mother.'" 20 "Teacher," he declared, "all these I have kept since I was a boy." 21 Jesus looked at him and loved him. "One thing you lack," he said. "Go, sell everything you have and give to the poor, and you will have treasure in heaven. Then come, follow me." 22 At this the man's face fell. He went away sad, because he had great wealth. 23 Jesus looked around and said to his disciples, "How hard it is for the rich to enter the kingdom of God!

Americans and Canadians have often heard this story as the hopeless quest of a rich man to secure riches, not just here on earth, but also in heaven. Makes sense. Someone who possesses everything needful in life will naturally seek to do the same in the time after death.

I prefer to think of this story within the context of first-century sensitivities that had no real concept of "heaven" as an endlessness of days in a place of perfect peace and harmony. The wealthy individual asks about obtaining eternal life, but we might translate that concept into a request like "how do I touch or experience the eternal?" Think of eternity not as a chronological objective but a question of quality and depth of time. The rich man is seeking "a closer walk with thee," so to speak.

In response, Jesus runs through the predictable questions. If you would be close to God, you need to follow the commandments, which the man has apparently done since his youth. "What do I lack?" asks the young man.

In most modern translations, the response of Jesus begins with a list of suggestions, the most severe of which is to relinquish his wealth for the sake of the poor. It sounds insurmountable, and our minds start to balk at the suggestions. So, we often miss the first thing Jesus tells us to do, translated most often as a simple command: "Go!" I like the translation of the Scholar's Version,[17] which amplifies the meaning of the Greek words into: "Make your move." Put politely, we might render it in modern parlance as: "It's time to get off our back sides." "This is our moment." "The time is now." "Don't wait any longer."

What is missing in our churches right now is Jesus' command: "Go!" To be precise, we do not give ourselves permission to act differently. There are plenty of examples of how a church community might transform itself: intentional communities of spiritual reform, social justice circles focused on the street, international development missions, local house communities of faith. The possibilities are before us, and we'll explore some in chapter 7. And it's not as if we are without the resources and the courage to act differently. I have witnessed enormous sacrifice on the part of believers, hoping to keep their church community alive. And how much of this effort goes into preserving the buildings? The fact remains that, when asked, everyone will admit that the building is of no consequence, when compared with the community of support that has been housed in their local church. Given a choice, even the staunchest conservatives would abandon the building (reluctantly of course), if it meant their community of compassion and support could continue in a healthy manner.

The young man asks Jesus, "What am I missing (Matt. 19:20)?"

It may be that we, like this young man, lack imagination. We just can't picture how a new community of faith might look, if it reoriented its focus away from worship to a ministry of hospitality and healing. That's part of our problem, certainly, and I am writing this book precisely to spark our imagining. Can we give theological justification for a shift in perspective and provide a few practical examples of how a new theological orientation and church mission might be lived out?

What else is missing?

17. The Scholars Version is a translation from the original Greek published by the members of Jesus Seminar and found in Miller, *Complete*.

Do we lack the courage or permission to think outside the box? Are we afraid to live into our dreams? There is some truth in this assertion. Who doesn't sense a niggling reticence to act in new way? Recently, I had a circle of people for dinner, and they were facing a crossroads. Not able to go back to their former church and having no alternative communities at hand, they were stymied. I suggested they start a new congregation, and I might as well have argued we fly to the moon. "Can you do that?" "What will the church say?" It was such a hard thought: to begin anew and to act on our dreams. We're expecting someone to stop us; looking for permission from an authority. But there is no need to wait, hiding behind the impulse to seek permission. It is not permission we lack! It's courage. We have been unable to find the strength of heart to live out our mission.

Is anything else missing?

In the final analysis, I believe we lack the Spirit to start. Perhaps we don't believe we can really change anything, especially ourselves. We speak the words in worship, how God's Spirit transforms the earth, invites us to participate in the recreation of the world. But, so far, these are just words. They don't hit the core.

In the end, we may be suffering from the same curse of the man in Mark's story. We have too many treasures. We don't need the world in order to change very much. We can command all we need through economic power and political influence. There is no necessity to work at changing anything.

A NEW REALITY: APRON THEOLOGY

Up this point, I have been quite critical of my community of faith. Let me conclude with some hope. Perhaps the most beneficial aspect of facing our unreality[18] as a church is the possibility that a new reality might arise from the ashes of our old model of being. If Christendom dies, who knows what might come next?

If it is the case that northern Christians are of goodwill, that they are prepared to use their resources in a sacrificial way for building a strong community of faith, and if all they need is courage to act on their imaginations, then what remains is the strategy to get over the obstacle of wealth.

Perhaps our resources as church should be put into alternate models of being—one that is characterized by relinquishment.

18. I have been influenced in my thinking about the church and its unreality by my good friend and mentor Douglas John Hall, who wrote a book early in his career, *Reality of the Gospel*.

Using the vocabulary of relinquishment, I am aware that there are segments of our society that have lived with a regime of "forced" letting go for centuries: women, people of difference races or sexual orientation. My point is that the once-privileged institution of Christianity must now learn what those "others" have known first-hand. Relinquishment is not pretty. It is now our turn to suffer the indignities and humiliations associated with it.

And while letting go is tough work, I believe we can learn to walk in this unfettered way, one step at a time. I am writing this text to explore how what I call "apron theology" can help us. It's a form of thinking our faith into action that begins with serving and, in a very real sense, serving bread.

If, as I mentioned in the introduction, we have lost our pathway with respect to the "Lord's Supper," perhaps we can develop ways to invite the God of the poor and disenfranchised back to a common table. In this way, we might move us into an incremental participation in the "pain" (Kitamori) of God in the world.

So, my central question: Can we get back to the kitchen table? Would it be possible to let go of the high altar? Can we reverse the historical trend of the Jesus meal and move back from the stylized ritual to a real shared, common meal? If we find a way for people to use their resources for the poor, to share bread freely and without condition, to live out their justice, bit by bit, around a kitchen table, then we can build bridges of trust between peoples, so that doing justice comes naturally. Loving mercy is second nature.

Apron theology begins with a rethinking of our story. What is it all about? What was the original intention of Jesus of Nazareth and his meal fellowship? Can we get back to the time before our community began to model itself on empire? If we return to scripture with the heart and mind open to pre-imperial standards and values, then perhaps we can reorient our understanding as the mission and meal of Jesus. Let's begin by exploring how a meal happened in first-century Palestine and how Jesus used it to explain the Kingdom of God. It is to that project that we turn in the next chapter.

AL AND'S Celebration Bread

This recipe was written for Allan Donovan to celebrate his birthday and to tell him how important he is. We could call this bread "ALLAN's Bread," but only he and a few others would know how the voice software of my wife, Ellen, spells his name. Rather than "ALLAN" it peppers her messages to him with "AL AND." Hence, the funny name.

This is an egg bread fashioned after what is known as "Rosh Hashanah Challah"—because of the braided shape and the inclusion of extra sugar and raisins. It is best served with coffee or as a breakfast treat—it is made with hope and joy baked right in, since it's a bread that celebrates the possibilities of a new year . . . with all the miracles and marvels yet to come. Given's Allan's humble, understated goodwill, it is a perfect reflection of apron theology.

MIX:

8 cups flour
½ cup white sugar
1 Tablespoon salt
½ cup oil
3 Tablespoons active dry yeast
4 eggs
1 ¾ cups warm water
1 cup dry raisins

PREPARATION:

1. Water may vary depending on how fulsome your flour scoops are and how humid your environment. What you are looking for is a spongy light dough—not too sticky. It should come clean off your fingers as you mix it and the gluten starts to work.

2. Work the dough into a ball and knead it for 8–10 minutes (play "Bohemian Rhapsody" once through, while you work the dough). I use the heel of my palms to spread, flip, and roll the dough. Flip, fold, and roll the dough, over and over.

3. Let stand in a covered, greased bowl for 2 hours.

4. Shape into 12 balls . . . let stand for 10 minutes. Roll each ball into a 12 inch long, cylinder-shaped strand. Lay 2 strands horizontally together, place 2 more strands at right angles on top. Next, weave one horizontal *under and over* the two vertical strands and the second horizontal strand goes *over and under* the vertical strands. And then, working clockwise, braid the loose ends around the entire circle. Once complete, braid the loose ends counterclockwise around the entire circle. Tuck in the small loose ends, place on a parchment-covered cookie sheet. (Repeat twice—using 4 balls each time; you may want to google "Rosh Hashanah bread" to get some idea of how the final result is supposed to look.). Paint all the rounds with an egg wash (1 egg whipped), sprinkle generously with white sugar, and let rise for 2 hours.

BAKING:

Pre-heat oven to 350 degrees F. and bake for 30–40 minutes (a bit longer if you don't have a convection oven), until top and bottom are firm and brown.

SERVE:

I would have a good, whipped cream cheese or crème fraiche ready to serve with this bread. Honey or jam would be another possibility. Add a double shot espresso, and you've got the perfect breakfast.

2

Having the Real Jesus for Dinner

In addition to determining which of the stories about Jesus are based on historical reminiscences and which not, we will want to develop a criticism of the myth and plot of the foundational stories. And we will need to continue our work in evaluating the sayings tradition, sorting out authentic from secondary elements. This agenda takes us back to the beginnings of Christianity, to a time well before it assumed its classical form at Nicaea. Just as the first believers did, we will have to start all over again with a clean theological slate, with only the parables, aphorisms, parabolic acts and deeds of Jesus as the basis on which to formulate a new version of the faith.[1]

INTRODUCTION

Who is your Jesus? Isn't that the question every believer asks themselves? And what does your Jesus say and do? Doctrine and dogma are important, but they are clearly derivative. The "who" of faith comes before the "what." Why else would we name a unique bread after an individual, as in the recipe preceding this chapter. It's because the "who" is what makes everything make sense.

---

1. Funk, *Honest to Jesus*, 301.

Hence, before touching on the uniqueness of the Jesus meal and the reasons some religious authorities and detractors were offended by it, it is important that we bring our Jesus into focus.

While admitting that we have shaped our Jesus according to current social trends and our own personal preferences, it is nonetheless important to ask: "Who is your Jesus?"

Is he a white Caucasian, with smiling blues eyes, flowing blond hair? The kind of St. Francis-like messiah who walks hand in hand with little children, calmly stills the storms of life with an outstretched arm, and has chirping birds nestled on his shoulders. He is most often knocking on the doors of his city, welcoming himself in to have tea in the kitchen. Everyone seems to know him. You will see that Jesus in Sunday school rooms across the country. Like a Victorian gentleman, he reclines calmly on a rock in the desert, discussing thorny problems with his disciples. He has the perfect balance of intelligence and compassion. There is assurance in his circle. This Jesus takes your hand gently, and you know God is in heaven and all is right down here on earth. Is that your Savior?

How about a dark-skinned, wild-tempered radical? This Jesus' face is plastered on T-shirts in every university dorm in the land. Looking a lot like Che Guevara, this Jesus is a relentless prophet, who points a condemning finger at social injustice and chains himself to the fences that restrict the free flow of truth. He's at the head of the protest march and the first to lift up those who stumble. If he's not comforting lost souls in the drunk tank while he awaits trial for civil disobedience, you can find him eating at the soup kitchen with the homeless and lost. Sit beside him, and your first impression is of fire. His spirit is an intoxicating mixture of hot passion and down-home common sense. He should make you uncomfortable; but with him you feel no fear. There's no evil power he has not faced squarely. The dark side holds no power over him! Before you know it, this Jesus has linked arms with you, and you're out on the street shouting peace slogans. Is that your Lord?

Then again, your Jesus might be in the Cathedral—his back is bent, his eyes are downcast. You can always find him walking the spiritual pathways of the devout. And while he seems to be praying constantly, he always has time to talk. There is neither ruffle nor ruse in his demeanor. He has that unique inviting and gentle manner, which welcomes all questions. Having the wisdom of the ages in his eyes, you know there is nothing you can confess that would shock or frighten him. And you don't have to say anything, if you don't feel like it. He accepts you as you are, even if all you need to do is enjoy the peace of his company, matching his pace as you circle the sanctuary. Is that Jesus for you?

How about this picture? Is your Jesus standing by the side of the road with a placard that points toward heaven. Never mincing his words, this Jesus' message is stark and direct. "Your time is up. Prepare to meet your God. Are you ready?" Not a subtle approach, he brings you up short. You meet him most often when the biopsy report comes back positive or your parents admit they can't take much more pain. Perhaps it is when the road ahead is blocked or you are lost in the mists of depression; he is always open to prayers and petitions. This Jesus is ageless. Looking at him, you can't tell if he is an ancient or an adolescent. He has seen death so often, it does not touch him. Oh, don't try to chat him up. He has no small talk. No polite placebos. His world is filled with ultimate concerns: Where is truth? What is worthy? What makes a real difference? Where am I headed, and where am I going? There is no question too silly to ask. But hold onto your hearts; this Jesus speaks with disarming directness. He looks into your soul and knows you. There is little doubt that he was there when you were born. He has stood beside you as you made the noble and naughty decisions of your life. He never abandoned you . . . even in your darkest hour and he won't abandon you in death. So, while it is terribly disconcerting to be known so well, there is also a tremendous sense of peace in his embrace. You do not have to pretend any longer. Is this your Jesus?

One last image. Is your Jesus washing floors in local shelter? He's always there, an apron around his waist and smile on his face. He's never short of good humor and seems to have an inexhaustible storehouse of goodwill. Late at night, he's massaging a bag lady's feet, or washing a pair of pants for the druggie, who had an accident because the McDonald's staff would no longer allow him to use the washroom. This Jesus has a scruffy beard, unkempt clothing, and could be mistaken for an indigent himself. He might be better dressed, except that he keeps giving away his new clothes to those who have nothing. It's a wonder he has anything at all; he seems so ready to share what he has with others. Once you saw him give a beggar everything he had in his wallet—a week's pay. And yet he never seems to display anything close to envy or regret. There's a whistle in his step, a joke to share with anyone who will listen, and a willing hand to help all those who have fallen. His laughter is rich and deep, the most contagious thing around the shelter: when he starts one of his long stories, the TV is turned down, men shuffle over to sit closer, and women crowd in-between to catch the punch line. And not just with the poor people; this Jesus has a way with the rich patrons who pay sporadic visits to their favorite charity. He takes them by the arm, and before they know what they are doing, they've taken off their stiff suit jackets and are ladling out soup to the homeless, calling them by name, as if they've been lifelong friends. Is that your Jesus?

Who is he . . . your Jesus?

That is the question that Christians have asked since the first generation of eye witnesses passed on. Once we had lost their historical connection,
Jesus became the product of contextual exigencies and personal dreams. We
created the portrait we needed, in order to face the demands of our today.

This development and redevelopment of images of Jesus may seem
dishonest to the modern mind, but it is a natural process, and we can see
it happening in the gospels themselves. For instance, the Jesus of Mark is
driven, always on an urgent mission to inspire his disciples and others to live
according to God's reign on earth. One has the feeling that the Jesus in Mark
is always running to get ahead of his own fame and direct his fortunes towards God's coming realm. He's started the ball rolling and seems to have no
regrets; but the twists and turns of his journey sometimes take him by surprise—so that he changes his mind (Mark 7:29). He's not in absolute control
of events and in the end is overtaken by the opposition to his mission, even
feeling abandoned (Mark 15: 34) by God. If we imagine that this first gospel
was written during the first-century uprising against Rome (68–70 CE), it
makes sense that Jesus is surrounded by storms and stresses. In contrast to
the other gospels, he calms the storm twice in this first gospel . . . a fitting
symbol of his role in the lives of those who first heard Mark's gospel.

In contrast, the Jesus of John's gospel is in charge of everything. From
his seven signs[2] which point to his glory and power, to his theologically
thick prayers, this Jesus knows all and sees all. The joke among scholars
goes like this: How do you crucify Jesus in John's gospel? The answer: "Very
carefully," because this Jesus is God incarnate, and he knows it! There is no
cry of abandonment from the cross! In John, Jesus dies with a command-
ing resolve, arranging for the care of his mother, just before he dies (John
19:26–27), like a faithful son. There is no hint of dismay. He's not confused,
but in charge right to the very end. In the fourth gospel, the guiding mission
of Jesus shifts away from declaring the Kingdom of God to demonstrating
that he is God's son and that salvation is found only through him (John 3:16,
John 6:47). John's Jesus no longer invites his disciples to share bread. John's
Jesus proclaims himself to *be* the bread of life (John 6:48).

Another example of the shift in the gospels' picture of Jesus, and one
that is close to the heart of this text, is what happens to the feeding of the

2. John structures his gospel around seven "signs" which point to his authenticity
as the long-awaited messiah. They are: (1) Changing water into wine at Cana in John
2:1–11; (2) Healing the royal official's son found at John 4:46; (3) Healing the paralytic
at the pool in John 5:1–18; (4) Feeding the 5000 with fish and loaves in John 6:1–14; (5)
Walking on water found at John 6:1–14; (6) Healing the man born blind found at John
9:1–14; and (7) the raising of Lazarus in John 11:1–46.

multitude. Found in two places in Mark, for reasons to be discussed below, the story begins as the dilemma of a hungry crowd. How do we feed so many people out there in the wilderness? Jesus is distressed and uncertain. He has to ask about how much food any of disciples can find! And then, when he gets the five loaves and a couple fish, he feeds them. The story focuses on the abundance of food.

The same tale is repeated by John, but only once (John 6:1–15). And in the fourth gospel, it fits into a pattern of "signs," which point to the power of Jesus. And making a significant shift, John portrays Jesus as omniscient. He knows in advance how much food will be available and what he will do with it (John 6:6).[3] So, the tale proceeds according to Jesus' plan. The multitude are fed, but it is not their hunger alone that is satisfied. They are looking for a king, and Jesus appears to be a lively candidate. The story ends with Jesus leaving, so they cannot crown him by force, and one is left with the impression that the feeding was a pretext for displaying Jesus' power over creation (John 6:14) and the people's growing awareness of his role as their true God-like messiah.

In the space of four gospels, we have traveled quite a theological distance: from the uncertain, wild-eyed radical, unsure of how it will all end, to the in-control messiah who stage manages everything up to and beyond the final curtain.

Just as Mark's Jesus is a reflection of the war-torn tempest within which and for which Mark was written, the portrait of Jesus found in the fourth gospel corresponds to the demands of a second-century audience. They were clearly separating themselves from Pharisaic Judaism and were wanting to establish their distinctiveness as a religious tradition. In addition, they had to accommodate themselves to the increasing pressure from gentile Christians, who wanted a more imperial spiritual leader—at least one whose values and ambitions did not blatantly contradict those of the empire.

The challenge for the modern Christian is to accept that there is no clear consensus, even in scriptures, with respect to the question of Jesus' self-understanding and identity. All too often, we read the controlled and self-aware Jesus of John's gospel back into the synoptic gospels, imputing to the Jesus in Mark an assurance that he does not possess.

Of course, we like the superhero Jesus in John. He knows he's the messiah. There's no crisis of identity, and we are spared the anxiety of trying to figure it out. We naturally assign John's unwavering Jesus to Mark's unsure, unsung hero. And while that may be an innocent mistake, the transference

---

3. In the fourth gospel, Jesus never asks a question to which he does not already have the answer.

of John's omniscient image to Mark actually blurs and blunts that first gospel story.[4] The stated mission of Jesus in Mark, which was to announce the Kingdom of God, is turned into a spiritual quest. If Jesus came from God, as John implies (John 1:2), and if his final mission is to return to be with God, then what happens in the here and now is of less importance. After all, Jesus has conquered sin and death. There's nothing more to do. Our role as believers is to watch and worship. Jesus does the rest. That turns the earth into a staging ground for the glory which is to come; our eyes, quite naturally, are turned heavenward.

To put this dilemma into a Christological framework, the current North American Jesus is clearly John's God/man, an unashamed Savior, who is bent on dying for human sin. John's portrait of Jesus accentuates his divinity, and it is a portrait that dominates our religious thinking and action. His actions are unswerving and unilateral. Any attempt from our side to assist him in his mission is viewed as regrettable hubris. "Salvation through the cross" means we stand back and watch, as Jesus saves us through his atoning power.

Do you feel left out yet? The problem of John's Jesus is that his divinity is not just powerful, its overpowering. There's nothing from my side that I can or should do! I have no way to bridge the gap between Jesus' perfect world and the life I live here, below.

If we have a challenge as northern Christians, it is to revalidate the humanity of Jesus. In general terms, we might say that our work is to restore the picture of Jesus found in the synoptic gospels as distinct from John. It is not only a question of making Christian ideas more accessible and relevant to a post-modern world, our revitalization of Jesus' humanity is an essential piece of moving the tradition beyond its current malaise. Can we allow Jesus to have that "prophetic imagination,"[5] which fired his vision for a world restored according to God's plans? Such a Jesus does not have all the bases covered. Rather than being a one-sided act of salvation, the cross becomes an invitation to collaboration. Discipleship is not worshipping the all-mighty Savior Jesus, but working with the toiling servant Jesus.

Let's leave that Christological challenge to one side for the moment.

I think I have made my point. The image of Jesus shifts from gospel to gospel. We see the difference between Mark and John. The Jesus in the other gospels is equally distinctive. In Matthew, Jesus is a thinly veiled new Moses, proclaiming a re-written, radical law. He is calling the Jewish nation back to its roots of justice and righteousness, lifting up a higher standard

---

4. Recall that I have argued, as the majority of scholars do, that Mark was the earliest and what I would call "first" gospel to be written and included in the Christian canon.

5. This is the title of a seminal work on the biblical prophets written by Brueggemann, *Prophetic Imagination*.

of personal piety than the religious establishment. There's an imperative in Matthew's Jesus. I can hear him say, "Let's get it right, right now!" Contrast this basically conservative Jesus with the political revolutionary, in Luke, who is overturning all the social norms of his day. In Luke, Jesus hosts meals, tells jokes, changes lives, and builds a new world order from the kitchen table up. He's starting small, but this Jesus is aiming high. His mission is what appears, on face value, to be a ridiculously extravagant grand vision: the conversion of the entire world to God's reign. A visionary for the long haul, Luke's Jesus is born in a backwater little town, and his rule will finally extend to the center of the universe: Rome.[6]

So, who's your Jesus?

For more than two hundred years, scripture scholars have asked that question. Called "The Quest for the Historical Jesus," their hunt for a reliable image of Jesus was frustrated by the inconsistencies I have outlined above and confounded by the simple fact that the gospels do not embody nor claim historical accuracy, not in a way that the modern world would accept. And having very little supplementary documentation by which to evaluate the gospel's account, we are doubly hamstrung. On this level, the Quest was summarized, and in some sense, concluded by Albert Schweitzer, who wrote of the unknowability of our question of Jesus identity:

> He comes to us as One, unknown, without a name, as of old, by the lakeside, He came to those men who knew him not. He speaks to us the same word, "Follow thou me." . . . He commands. And to those who obey Him, whether they be wise or simple, He will reveal Himself in the toils, the conflicts, the sufferings which they shall pass through in His fellowship, and, as an ineffable mystery, they shall learn in their own experience Who He is.[7]

Much like Luke, Schweitzer invites us out of the sanctuary and into the world where we will be met by the One who is our Savior. No point in trying to make careful distinctions yet. Jesus is only known on the road.

And this on-the-job identity is the reason we will all shape our picture of Jesus according to our personal "conflicts and sufferings." That's why we call it "good news." It's "good" because Jesus saves us, and it's "news" because it is updated (Crossan).[8] However, as we set about shaping a Jesus to speak

---

6. For a more detailed vision of how Luke makes his case for this vision through his two books: "The gospel of Luke" and "Acts of the Apostles," I would refer you to the book by Crossan, *Render unto Caesar*.

7. Schweitzer, *Quest for the Historical Jesus*, 401.

8. A common adage of John Dominic Crossan, first heard in lectures at St. Stephen's

to our time, are we not called upon to balance our personal estimations with the gospel story? You may ask: Can we not preface our vision of the bread-based Jesus movement outlined in the following chapters with some guidance from the gospel record? If we are seeking something that is beyond cultural distortion or religious exaggeration, where do we begin?

Let's start with two broad assertions that are beyond modern distortions or coloring. First, Jesus, the peasant from a small hamlet in southern Galilee, was executed by crucifixion. The cross is never in doubt as an historical fact.[9] And while that seems a very thin foundation upon which to base the edifice of Christianity, it says a great deal. Crucifixion was a form of execution reserved for runaway slaves and those who opposed the empire. It was Rome who crucified people, and they did it intentionally. Crucifixion is a public, legal, very intentional act. The cross was a sign post, a first-century social media message writ large, if you like: "You fuss with Rome, and this will Happen to You!"

Moreover, as anyone who has built log fences or post and beam houses will tell you, hefting large wood planks is not simple work. You need fulcrums, ropes, person power, and skill. Crucifixion is therefore an expensive undertaking, requiring both an administrative and financial commitment. It didn't happen on a whim or without some serious planning. So, Jesus was not the victim of uncontrolled mob violence. Death on the cross is evidence of an authorized execution that requires time and an experienced crew. In other words, Rome was offended enough by Jesus that it went to all the trouble of executing him.

So, my first assertion: Jesus was seen as a genuine threat to the imperial interests. Whether the emphasis should be on his "economic," or "social," or "spiritual" resistance to Rome, it was nonetheless overt and distinct enough to Roman authorities that it merited crucifixion.

A brief disclaimer. The Romans did not use the cross to make theological pronouncements. There's no evidence that a messiah type figure claiming to have special healing powers would be executed by crucifixion, because he declared himself to be the "Son of God" (Matt. 26:63) or a God-like figure. In contrast to the gospel of Matthew's account, it is unlikely that Pilate would have been swayed by arguments that Jesus was upsetting the religious equilibrium in Second Temple Judaism. If Jesus was a spiritual threat, as one scholar put it, I can imagine Pilate whispering to the high priests, "that's

College in the 1997 lecture series.

9. There are two references to Jesus outside Christian sources, each one states that Jesus was crucified: Tacitus, *Annals*, 15:44, and Josephus, *Antiquities of the Jews*, Book 18, chapter 3:64. 130.

what we have dark alleys for. Take him out and make him disappear."[10] The cross was a political statement and only to the extent to which Jesus and his Kingdom movement posed a real or presumed threat to the occupying Roman forces would he have been crucified.

A second assertion: Jesus was seen to be a "non-violent" threat. His followers were not rounded up and executed with him.[11] There was no need to capture the others, since they posed no immediate threat. The logic is simple. Cut off the head and the rest of the body withers—which is just what Herod Antipas did with John the Baptizer and his repentance movement. Once John was gone, the crowds at the Jordan dwindled away. The way to handle non-violent resistance is to execute the leader. From this simple fact that Jesus was crucified without his followers or even some of his disciples, we can deduce that his resistance to Rome was not violent.

Whatever else we might want to say about Jesus, our descriptions and devotions must somehow reflect these two facts: his resistance to Empire and his non-violence.

And from these two assertions arises the question that directs this text. What did Jesus do to deserve this kind of execution by the occupying Roman forces? Surely, if we knew what Jesus did, we would have some direction for our modern expressions of following him.

As one approach to answering that question, let's do a quick summary of what the gospel writers say about Jesus and what he did. How often do they describe him doing the same thing? According to the biblical record, what priorities does Jesus give to his own time? Quite separate from where we might want to place our emphasis, where does Jesus' actual energy get placed? It doesn't answer all our questions, but it gives us a broad impression of what Jesus did and therefore some measure of who he was and how, if possible, he was seen by others, especially those who might oppose him.

10. Crossan mentioned this at several conference events in Matanzas, Cuba, March 2009, and in Toronto, April 2011.

11. Violent zealots are arrested as a group along with their leader. In Mark, we are told about an insurgent, "Barabbas," who was imprisoned for murder in an insurrection, and the gospel writer adds his own footnote that Barabbas was there with his fellow insurgents (Mark 15:7).

My method: leaving John aside,[12] I examined all three synoptic gospels and recorded each gospel's verses according to 16 pre-determined topics:[13] From these broad topics I chose to focus on the top three activities Jesus is described as doing/speaking more than any other. What takes up most of his time?[14] If we were able to analyze his planner, so to speak, what would we find are his top priorities?

Here's a quick summary: There is a common pattern in all three synoptic gospels. Jesus heals people. It's his number one activity. Second comes his warning/teaching about the times and how everyone must be ready to live in God's new reign, right now! Finally, Jesus eats with outcasts and feeds the hungry.

Let's examine each of those ideas in turn.

JESUS, THE GREAT HEALER

Post-enlightenment thinking has always stumbled over the healing stories of Jesus. They are the dominant tone of Mark's gospel, a tone that is still pronounced in the gospel of Luke and more muted, but essential, nevertheless, in Matthew. All the biblical evidence notwithstanding, our modern minds balk at accepting healing stories at face value. They can't be historically accurate! We are pestered by the seeming impossibility of the actual events.

For instance, how can Jesus cure what appear to be long-entrenched psychiatric disorders? The bible calls the people who live with such conditions as having "evil spirits," and it may be the case that the actual diseases Jesus cured were a combination of psychological and physiological states—variants of epilepsy, schizophrenia, or bipolar disorder. No matter the actual ailment, it seems highly unlikely to current thinking that an individual could cure these diseases by speaking sternly to the person in question, as

12. I intentionally avoid using John as a basis for forming a portrait of what Jesus might have done or said. I am in agreement with John Shelby Spong in his assertion that much of the gospel of John is ahistorical and not a very reliable record of what actually happened. In his book, *Fourth Gospel*, 10, Spong asserts that ". . . none of the sayings attributed to Jesus in this gospel [John] was in all probability ever spoken by the Jesus of history . . . none of the miracles, called "signs" in this book, and attributed to Jesus, ever actually happened . . . most of the characters who populate the pages of this gospel are literary or fictionalized creations of the author and were never real people who ever lived."

13. These topics were: historical narrative, control of creation, family, discipleship, the law, messiahship, sacraments and ritual, parables, warnings, proclamations, instruction, prayer, healing, complaints, and feeding/food.

14. I would invite the reader to test out my hypothesis by doing the same thing: read all the gospels and discover what takes up most of Jesus' time.

seen in Mark 1:25, for example. So, we doubt these psychological and emotional healing miracles.

Likewise, the physical cures stretch credulity. Whether the people following Jesus are lame, or blind, or plagued with leprosy, how does Jesus restore them to wholeness? With a simple touch, Jesus cures leprosy (Mark 1:40). Using a singular command, he straightens crippled hands (Mark 3:5), mends immobile limbs (Mark 2:11), and gives sight to the blind (Mark 10:5). He cures a stricken young girl from a distance (Mark 5:36) and is even able to restore health without conscious effort. So great is his power that, when a sick woman merely touches his robe, she is cured of her chronic hemorrhaging (Mark 5:27).

Impossible!

Is it possible to make two distinctions that will help us get beyond our incredulity? The first may appear to be a matter of semantics, but I find it useful. There is a difference between "truth" and "fact." At issue in the healing stories is the problem of fact. We can't see them as anything close to being historically factual. We know that instantaneous cures can happen: a deadly tumor disappears, or a paraplegic learns to walk again against all odds. But these instances are rare. You can, but shouldn't, place your hope in them. The science is against miraculous cures. It's for good reason that we, who are schooled in the scientific method, have trouble with the fact of instant curing, especially as an event that can be called up on command. Of course, inexplicable changes in health do take place. I have spoken with patients whose cancer unaccountably disappeared. But these instances are exceptional and by no means predictable.

The *fact* of the healing is questionable; however the *truth* is, people knew they were healed in Jesus' presence. There is no way to understand it otherwise. He is *the* great healer. While we may not be able to explain the facts, there is no refuting the truth that above all else his authority as a teacher, his credentials as potential messiah, his popularity among the people of Galilee are all based on the truth: Jesus heals! Those who came to Jesus bent and broken walked away from the encounter knowing they were made whole. That's our good news. So rather than dredging up arguments about psychosomatic abilities to cure crippled limbs (John 5:1–15) or investigating the restorative power of spit and mud with regard to blindness (John 9:6), perhaps our energy is better spent agreeing that we don't understand the facts. The truth, however, is evident. People are restored in Jesus' presence, often.

My second distinction is the difference between "healing" and "cure." A careful reading of the paragraphs above will reveal that I use those words very carefully. Let us agree that any physical or psychological disorder has two aspects: the "illness" and the "disease."

The "disease" is the actual physiological or psychological ailment, be it a viral or bacterial infection, a chronic condition, or a cancerous growth, a chemical imbalance, or cerebral malfunction. It is something concrete that needs to be "cured." And sometimes modern medicine is able to do just that, and in other instances we are helpless to effect any change.

In contrast, the "illness" is how a patient is treated or sees themselves, because of the disease they are facing. Every disease has an illness. The best is example is AIDS. When it was first diagnosed, AIDS was a death sentence. But it was also a terror: contagious and transmittable. As a society, we met it with a full slate of prejudices. Touching the gay community first, we assumed it was evidence of the evils of homosexuality. "They" were to blame for their pernicious behavior. So those patients who were living with the disease of AIDS also had to deal with the illness of shame, isolation, and fear. We turned them into modern untouchables, hated and reviled. The disease was bad enough, but the illness was far worse. In less strident ways, we try to diminish the frightful aspects of the disease of lung cancer, by resorting to our condemnation of smoking—blaming the disease on bad behavior. The disease of lung cancer is tough. The concomitant illness of guilt and recrimination is tougher still.

COVID-19 is a most recent illustration of the distinction I am making. The disease is caused by the SARS-CoV-2 virus, that attacks the respiratory system of its victims. As we all know too well, it can affect a person's breathing, sense of taste or smell, and ability to function without serious fatigue. Alas, the disease can be fatal. The illness of COVID-19 is a combination of fear, latent guilt, and shame. It's exacerbated by an almost absolute isolation from loved ones and is further complicated by the disbelief and latent anger voiced by certain segments of our society—arguing that the disease is not real.[15]

It goes without saying that the illness is as real as the disease and, in many cases, is the most difficult aspect to confront, since it is often that which isolates or belittles the patient. How often have I heard something like this: "I can live with the pain, but the loneliness is killing me."

It has been my experience as a pastor that it is often possible to heal the illness, even though the disease is terminal. A quick story[16] I have

15. Who hasn't heard the pandemic being reviled as an invention of "deep state" operatives. It's not real! It's called a "Plandemic."

16. I make this distinction and tell this story as the central thesis in my recent book, Levan, *Healing Death*, 59.

told before:[17] When I had my appendix out at age 40, I was placed in a room with four other patients. One, the man in the bed beside me, was afflicted with a disease that was incredibly hard to bear. Not only was he dying, but whenever his dressings were changed, the room filled with such a stench that everyone and everything that could left the room. Visitors, staff, cleaning personnel . . . they all made a beeline to the door. I am sure the wallpaper would have detached itself from the wall, if it could have done so. It was awful.

I was stuck in bed, so I watched as my roommate suffered the indignity of his illness. I could see the pain of his illness. Whatever his disease might have been, it was his illness that was crushing him. As the smell rose and the room emptied, he knew he was repugnant and untouchable. No longer worthy to be good company, his illness of isolation made him less than human.

A few days into my stay, I witnessed a healing. A young nurse came in with basin of warm water and a towel, pulled the curtain around him, and gave this man a back rub and bath! When he was settled back in his place and I could see him again, the change was miraculous. It was so clear. He was smiling. His isolation had been broken. He was worthy of being touched and a real human being once more. No longer just a smell, he was a real man. He was healed of his illness! A miracle. That same day, he died.

In light of this story, you can see how the distinction I have made between curing the disease and healing the illness is not inconsequential.

If we turn to the bible, we will see a similar pattern in the healing stories of Jesus. I have chosen to focus on an incident that took place during the initial stages of Jesus' ministry. It's one of the first healing stories of Mark's gospel, taken from the first chapter. It is like a template for later stories and has a basic fourfold structure: (1) the approach; (2) the healing act: (3) the retort/admonition; and (4) the resultant dismay and adoration. Most healing stories contain these elements, though not always in that order.

Now here's what I suggest you do. Read quickly through the following text, without too much reflection, and make a mental note of what sticks out for you, what is surprising or new. Ask yourself, "What have I never heard before?" Then read the passage again carefully, taking note of the placement of those items on your list that were called to your attention:

> Mark 1:41–45 40 A man with leprosy came to him and begged
> him on his knees, "If you are willing, you can make me clean."
> 41 Jesus was indignant. He reached out his hand and touched
> the man. "I am willing," he said. "Be clean!" 42 Immediately the

17. There is a more fulsome explanation of the healing ministry of Jesus along with this story found in my book on the Lord's Supper: Levan, *Prayer*.

leprosy left him and he was cleansed. 43 Jesus sent him away at once with a strong warning: 44 "See that you don't tell this to anyone. But go, show yourself to the priest and offer the sacrifices that Moses commanded for your cleansing, as a testimony to them." 45 Instead he went out and began to talk freely, spreading the news. As a result, Jesus could no longer enter a town openly but stayed outside in lonely places. Yet the people still came to him from everywhere.

Here's my list of the strange or novel things I noticed when reading this passage again as if for the first time:[18] 1) Jesus is short tempered; 2) The touch and the words perform the action of healing; 3) Jesus wants to keep his healing power hidden, along with his identity; and 4) The healed man tells the story so often, Jesus loses all privacy. Perhaps those items were on your list, too.

This initial healing story sets a pattern. There is no question that the Jesus in Mark's gospel is in a hurry, harried, and lacking any time alone. And he seems strangely ill at ease. The leper approaches almost humbly and, on bended knee, asks for wholeness, relief from his condition. And as if he has lost his patience, Mark's Jesus speaks harshly. In verse 41, we have a peculiar problem of manuscript translation. In most bibles, you will read that Jesus "had compassion" for the man. This is taken from several trustworthy manuscripts. However, one of the most reliable manuscripts in Greek (Codex Bezae) contains this reading: Jesus is upset, indignant, bothered, or feeling pestered.[19] This sense of indignation is reinforced in the next phrase when Jesus snaps at him (literally "snorts"). I know we would prefer to have an eloquent, reverent, and peaceful Jesus. But either Mark's capacity with Greek is not subtle enough to rub off the rough edges of the Jesus tradition he has inherited, or he is repeating what has been passed down to him as historical. That being as it may, we'll have to wait for Matthew and Luke to

18. It was Marcus Borg who coined the phrase *Meeting Jesus Again for the First Time* in his book by that title. He captured the idea that the old, old story has two dimensions at least—the things we remember dearly about Jesus, and the way every encounter mediated by the gospels is fresh and startling new.

19. Many manuscripts have the Greek verb: σπλαγχνισθείς translated: "'he was moved with compassion," but the Codex Bezae has the verb: οργισθείς meaning "he was angry." When we are dealing with such a discrepancy between manuscripts, the scholars ask which is more likely—that a copyist would replace an "angry" Jesus with a compassionate one, or would anyone be tempted to remove the Jesus who is moved out of pity and replace him with one who is caught in a fit of rage? Of course, it is all conjecture, but it seems more likely that the change would favor a better portrait of Jesus and therefore the verb "he was angry" seems the more likely original and therefore closer to the original intent of the gospel writer.

"edit" Mark, so that Jesus appears more compassionate. My point? In Mark, Jesus is allowed to be human, to the point of being a little frustrated, even angry.

Next, I am struck by the sense in which action and word work in concert in this story. Jesus has but to speak and reality changes. In a single motion the cure happens instantly before our eyes. The man's disease of leprosy is gone—but so, too, is the illness. Do you catch overtones of the disease/illness distinction we made above? Certainly, Jesus is not only curing a physiological disease—his touch signals a very important shift for the leper. He is no longer outside the circle, unworthy, and untouchable. The mere touch of a spiritual leader signals a healing. This man, who was consigned to the outer realm of the dead, is now welcomed back into the land of the living. The touch broke down a very important wall dividing the leper from the righteous world where God dwells. In passing, it is interesting to note that Jesus does counsel this man to follow the prescribed program for verifying his cure. Seeking out a priest and making offerings in thanksgiving are akin to a modern visit to the doctor to get a clean bill of health—a negative COVID test perhaps.

In this passage, we also have an example of Jesus' resistance to being known either as a healer or a candidate for messiahship. His many attempts to conceal his identity[20] are part of what scholars call the messianic "secret" of Mark. On one level, the secretive side of Jesus is just part of his human nature. He's both modest and wanting freedom from the prying and pestering demands of those who want to take from him what they can get. His secretiveness is a natural response. On quite another level, Mark uses the "secret" as a rhetorical devise to entice his audience to keep asking themselves about Jesus. Making his readers work at their own answer to the question of who Jesus might be is a clever way to help them get over the obstacles mentioned in the introduction with regard to a crucified messiah. If they follow the logic of their own answers to the secret of Jesus, they may be more persuaded to believe in him.

At its deepest level, this secret identity of Jesus speaks to the issue of knowing God. It is not that simple. God is not always found where you would expect to find the Almighty. This will certainly be Mark's final conclusion. God will eventually become known in the cross, an instrument of death. Put succinctly, the messianic secret is another way of saying that God is hidden in God's opposite (Luther). We come to know God, when we are faced with what is definitely not God: suffering and abandonment.

---

20. See also Mark 1:25–28, 34, 3:12, 5:43, 7:36, 8:26.

My final observation in this first curing/healing story has been mentioned already. The fame of Jesus spreads so rapidly, he starts avoiding towns and villages for fear of being mobbed. Jesus discovers what any Hollywood star knows. Fame is a highly overrated thing. Not only is your privacy gone. People seem to have a proprietorial claim on your time. They think they can own you. This requires Jesus to take evasive action, and while it's an understandable response, the fact that Jesus faces this kind of problem makes the story all the more credible and accessible. He is facing what we know happens to many famous people, and it further enhances the human side of Mark's Jesus.

Whether he is willing, or reluctant, or both, Jesus was clearly an exceptional man, who could cure any number of human diseases. Likewise, he was a miraculous healer of illnesses. His curing of diseases and the healing of illness go hand in hand. Jesus does not appear to want either his curing or healing to become a trademark or example of his personal power. While he is a phenomenal curer/healer, not surprisingly, he doesn't seek to profit from it. In contrast to John's version, the Jesus of the synoptic gospels does not use the appeal of his miraculous healing as a means to achieve an ulterior motive, to underline his proximity to God, for instance. It is certainly not a mechanism to show off his personal power or parade his messianic credentials. Healing is for the restoration of life and not a tool to persuading people to believe in the Almighty or even to join in the Kingdom of God movement. In short, it is entirely accurate and true to state that Jesus' healing is given without condition. It is the embodiment of God's free gift of life.

THE APOCALYPTIC JESUS: STAY ALERT

Apocalyptic warnings take the second place in terms of time spent in the gospels recording Jesus' activity. Within this broad category are all the times when Jesus warns his disciples about false expectations surrounding the coming reign of God (Mark 10:39), misguided understandings of his parables (Mark 8:14–21), the distractions and misconceptions of religious leaders, which Jesus called at one point the "leaven of the Pharisees" (Mark 8:15), his predictions of the destruction of the temple (Mark 13:1–2), and his warnings against false religious practice (Matthew 23:13–39).

It is sometimes difficult to separate out his apocalyptic warnings from his teaching. But apocalypticism differentiates itself by its urgency and expectation. The language is often drastic and dark. Calamitous events are described as just around the corner! Earthquakes, world changing battles. There is no time to dither or doubt. Like John the Baptizer's call in the wilderness, the Jesus who is described in Mark (and subsequently replayed by Matthew and Luke) is pressed by the immediacy of the coming judgment of God. History is coming very soon to its consummation.

The expectancy of apocalyptic language has changed over time. Currently, we hear the end of history described as a great tribulation, punctuated by a "rapture" of those who are to be saved (1 The. 4:16–17). In this modern variant of apocalypticism, hope arises from the destruction of an evil world. And for modern believers, their fondest wish is not to be "left behind"[21] when the fire falls. It is difficult to discern if this is also an expectation of the Jesus speaking in Mark's gospel. In Matthew 25:1–13, there is certainly a vague sense that only the righteous will survive . . . those who are "alert" to the true signs of the times and also to any false premonitions. According to the Jesus in Mark, the end of time will be associated with false prophecy, imposters trying to claim messiahship. The great tribulation of suffering, through which the chosen ones will pass, will result in a new earth and new heaven. Jerusalem will fall; fire and famine will devour the community. Pray that you will be spared.

We have a taste of this dark premonition taken from what scholars call the "small apocalypse:"

> Mark 13:3–8 3 As Jesus was sitting on the Mount of Olives opposite the temple, Peter, James, John and Andrew asked him privately, 4 "Tell us, when will these things happen? And what will be the sign that they are all about to be fulfilled?"
>
> 5 Jesus said to them: "Watch out that no one deceives you. 6 Many will come in my name, claiming, 'I am he,' and will deceive many. 7 When you hear of wars and rumors of wars, do not be alarmed. Such things must happen, but the end is still to come. 8 Nation will rise against nation, and kingdom against kingdom. There will be earthquakes in various places, and famines. These are the beginning of birth pains."
>
> Mark 13:32–37 32 "But about that day or hour no one knows, not even the angels in heaven, nor the Son, but only the Father. 33 Be on guard! Be alert! You do not know when that time will come. 34 It's like a man going away: He leaves his house and puts his servants in charge, each with their assigned task, and tells the one at the door to keep watch.35 Therefore keep watch because you do not know when the owner of the house will come back— whether in the evening, or at midnight, or when the rooster

21. *Left Behind* is the first book, in a 17-volume series of novels written by Tim LaHaye and Jerry Jenkins, which describes the coming "tribulation and the rapture" made famous by Lindsey, *Late Great Planet Earth*.

crows, or at dawn. 36 If he comes suddenly, do not let him find
you sleeping. 37 What I say to you, I say to everyone: 'Watch!'

Notice how often the people are asked to "watch." In modern parlance
we might say "stay alert." Is this not the voice of the community of the gospel
writer speaking? Through Jesus, Mark is saying to himself and his audience
that no one should get too comfortable. Don't take things for granted. The
obvious reason Mark feels constrained to say this is that there was a strong
impulse to let up on the throttle of evangelism and discipleship. No doubt,
his audience had many examples of Jesus circles that had become self-satis-
fied or misguided by false pronouncements of presumptuous leaders. Perhaps in the frenetic pace of war, which was clearly when Mark was writing,[22]
there are bound to be many rumors of destruction and disaster and it would
be incumbent on everyone to stay "alert" and discern the times. One must
separate falsehood and fear from reality and truth.

And quite clearly, the immanent and urgent apocalypticism of Mark,
transferred in different measures to Matthew and Luke, is the result of the
revolt/civil war that erupted while it was being written. It may be that some,
if not all, of the calamities described in Mark 13 had already taken place.
Jerusalem was laid siege, and subsequently its stones tumbled down, one
by one (Mark 13:2), from the ferocity of the legions. Families were split by
violence, and it appeared that the entire world order was imploding.

For liberal Christians, the picture of Jesus as the wild-eyed prophet,
calling for the end of the world, is disconcerting. We don't want our Jesus
to be standing by the side of the road holding a placard, "The End is Nigh."
We'd rather see him working the sidewalks and gutters of a crumbling
world, trying to build up what was being lost. However, an unbiased ap-
praisal of scripture is difficult to discount. No matter the historical facts, the
community of Mark saw Jesus, in part or in whole, as a messenger of doom
and judgment. And far from being turned off, both his followers and his
detractors are exercised and excited by knowing the signs and the timing of
the consummation of history.

If we peel back the historical layers from the time when Mark was
written (during and after the First Jewish War) and move backward to the
Jesus of 30 CE, two issues seem to be important. First, the radical expectation of a new world was part and parcel of his message. Jesus came into his
ministry in this world with the full expectation of transforming it into the
reign of God. Taking the vision and spirit of John the Baptizer and adapting

22. Most scholars place Mark as being written around the time of the fall of the
temple, in Jerusalem, which was 70 CE and at the conclusion of what is called "the First
Jewish War."

it to his life around the sea of Galilee, Jesus preaches a "new world coming": the Kingdom of God.

And history bears out his claim. It may not have been what he or others expected, but his ideas and actions changed the planet. It would therefore be natural that the followers of Jesus would expect to see him as a prophet preaching repentance and change in his own time, a repentance and a change that would take centuries to be actualized but which were entirely reasonable to predict.

Second, apocalyptic thinking was a natural and growing phenomenon of the fledgling Jesus movement. The initial generations of Christ followers were under tremendous pressures: responding to the "call" to spread Jesus' message, building new communities, resisting the animosity of neighbors, the preservation of the original creative and open spirit of Jesus' itinerant ministry. All this activity was taking place within a growing distrust of their fellowship on the part of principalities and powers. Who wouldn't be thinking about a climatic turn of events? According to one early historian, by the time Paul arrives in Rome (56–60 CE), Christians already had the reputation of being like a contagious pestilence.[23] There is little doubt that by the time the oral traditions about Jesus were finding their way into written forms, they could feel the walls closing in. It's a natural hope that the implicit promises of a transformed social order, found within the teaching of the Kingdom of God, would take place in their lifetime. Paul was obviously familiar with these expectations and hopes. He was often obliged to speak of how his proclamation of the resurrection of Jesus could be squared with the fact that true believers were dying before they witnessed the "glory" of God's reign.

As mentioned above, Matthew and Luke each take Mark's apocalyptic picture of Jesus and shift the focus in slightly different ways. Matthew mutes the wild-eyed, urgent Jesus, of Mark 13, and turns him into a wise pharisaic-like, wisdom teacher and spiritual authority. There is still an end

23. The first, non-Christian mention of Jesus is found in a work by the Roman historian, Senator Tacitus, (mentioned in footnote 9 above), who in his work, *Annals* (15:44), describes Christians as being the culprits in the great fire in Rome. Speaking of the origins of that fire, he states: "But all human efforts, all the lavish gifts of the emperor, and the propitiations of the gods, did not banish the sinister belief that the conflagration was the result of an order. Consequently, to get rid of the report, Nero fastened the guilt and inflicted the most exquisite tortures on a class hated for their abominations, called Christians by the populace. Christus, from whom the name had its origin, suffered the extreme penalty during the reign of Tiberius at the hands of one of our procurators, Pontius Pilatus, and a most mischievous superstition, thus checked for the moment, again broke out not only in Judæa, the first source of the evil, but even in Rome, where all things hideous and shameful from every part of the world find their center and become popular."

of the world coming, but in Matthew, Jesus aims his concerns against the competition down the street, i.e., the Pharisees. Matthew is less concerned to show Jesus as a world reformer and more intent upon proving he is the natural and authentic inheritor of the religious heritage of Israel. And concomitantly, his Jesus points out more dramatically the faults and failings of the religious establishment. In Matthew, the apocalyptic Jesus is a new Moses, calling the people back to a more conservative, exacting fulfillment of his reinterpreted law.

Luke retains even less of the apocalyptic Jesus. His gospel is not aiming its appeals for repentance and dramatic change at the chosen people. His gospel opens to the world and focuses on the plight of the marginalized. His text is written for a church that knows the dramatic end of history is still quite a distance off. If Matthew is a church manual to preserve virtue in the relatively short interim between today and the end times, Luke's book is a travel guide for the journey: how to make it in the wider, wilder world as faithful travelers on the long, long road ahead. He instructs the church how to thrive and grow in the interim time. His answer: eat together and break bread with the strangers you meet on the way. It is to examine that final and major priority in the mission and ministry of Jesus that we now turn.

"THEY ALL HAD ENOUGH TO EAT"

What I am about to describe happens in many churches, but as I write this chapter, mine is located in a poor neighborhood in La Habana, Cuba. There's bread dough downstairs waiting to be made into pizzas. It's Friday afternoon, and the church bible study is about to begin. It wouldn't be the same without fresh bread. Sure, I imagine some of the same crowd would attend, even if there was no food, but with a heavier heart for sure. I love to see the spark in people's eyes, when, after having invited them to come and discuss the gospel message, I add that we are going to have fresh, homemade pizza. "Count me in!" To be fair, it's not just a marketing tool, though it works pretty well as an enticement to learn. It is also the embodiment of the gospel message—food for the soul begins with food for the body.

I learned this lesson first from my mother. When I was a youngster, she would host her annual Yuletide open house. In small town Ontario, it was a big event. The local newspaper covered it with a full-page spread. Over the course of two sittings, one in the afternoon and the other in the evening, hundreds of members from the church would come to share a sandwich and exchange stories. The afternoon session was held for those who could not drive at night—usually the older church goers—the tea cups and white gloves crowd. The evening party was more riotous and free-wheeling. Do I just imagine cigar smoke and wild jokes? My mom was very proud of those parties. They were her contribution to the ministry of the church, and I now see that they did more for the spirit of the congregation than a month of sermons. It was then that I learned how Christians eat and why.

Taking a cue from the mission of Jesus, my mom used food to nourish and create the contentment and sense of security that are essential to the company of faith.

There is little doubt that the same sense of security and contentment were features of the early movements surrounding Jesus. He is featured in providing food for his disciples (Mark 6:42, 8:6), inviting them into secluded places where they can be free from the crowd, so as to catch a meal (Mark 6:31). And when the disciples want to determine the resurrected Christ is actually their leader, they have a meal together (Luke 21:42).

There can be no more central picture of the Jesus who feeds his followers than the story taken from Mark's gospel and repeated by all the other gospel writers—a central tale. We call it the feeding of the multitudes:

> Mark 6:35–44 35 By this time it was late in the day, so his disciples came to him. "This is a remote place," they said, "and it's already very late. 36 Send the people away so that they can go to the surrounding countryside and villages and buy themselves something to eat." 37 But he answered, "You give them something to eat."
> They said to him, "That would take more than half a year's wages! Are we to go and spend that much on bread and give it to them to eat?" 38 "How many loaves do you have?" he asked. "Go and see." When they found out, they said, "Five—and two fish." 39 Then Jesus directed them to have all the people sit down in groups on the green grass. 40 So they sat down in groups of hundreds and fifties. 41 Taking the five loaves and the two fish and looking up to heaven, he gave thanks and broke the loaves. Then he gave them to his disciples to distribute to the people. He also divided the two fish among them all. 42 They all ate and were satisfied, 43 and the disciples picked up twelve basketfuls of broken pieces of bread and fish. 44 The number of the men who had eaten was five thousand.

Could this be the early church speaking of itself? In Mark's gospel, the focus is on the large number of people, who are without food and hungry, and the miracle of abundance. It looks impossible that all the people will be fed.

In this story, we have the clash of mindsets. The apostles are thinking of themselves as the ones who are in charge. Given their paternalism, they imagine that they have to find a solution to the crowd's needs. From their perspective, there is no way the little band of disciples could come up with the money or means to feed such a mob of hungry people. Jesus turns the tables, inviting the disciples to trust the people who have come. They have bread. Go ask them! And, sure enough, there is a little bread, which, when shared, stretches to feed everyone. Rather than trying to figure out how five small loaves feed five thousand people, can we accept the story as the testimony of the first generations of the Kingdom movement? When we get together in the name of Jesus, food is never a problem. We are well satisfied and content.

And in case we didn't get the message from this first feeding story, Mark repeats it a few chapters later, almost exactly the same event. I used to believe that this doubling was a result of poor editing. But Mark goes out of his way to have Jesus explain the feeding of the two crowds as object lessons in God's abundance and care.[24]

This is a single example of how Jesus was seen as the one who feeds the hungry—quite literally. Given the context of scarcity and the general lack of food security in first-century Palestine, it is not hard to understand how food played a common and powerful role in the building of the community of the Kingdom of God. In fact, as I will argue in the next chapter, shared bread was one of the central tools for embodying the miracles of this reign of God.

To summarize, if we look behind the first three gospels—particularly Mark—what is the image of the Jesus that appears? Allowing the verses themselves to speak, we get a human, real Jesus. He is an open, free healer, whose goodwill is sometimes overtaken by a sense of desperation for a new world. He touches all who come to him, warns against assigning any glory to himself. There is always a mounting urgency in his voice, as he feels the powers of darkness rising, and he can't stay quiet about the pain and suffering he sees about him. In the midst of the desperation and the clamor for his leadership, Jesus does what he can. He heals and preaches about a rising reign of God. And he embodies these proclamations by feeding people, openly and without distinction. He turns his meal fellowship into a means for incarnating and furthering his vision of a new realm built in contradistinction to the empire.

So, when we join his circle, what happens? How do we eat with Jesus in his Kingdom of God, and how does that differ from what happens when we have a meal in Caesar's world? To answer those questions, let's turn to the next chapter, which explores what actually will take place when we have Jesus for dinner.

24. See Mark 8:17–21.

Baguettes—My Last Meal on Earth

Baguettes are like Pinot Noir—a delicate simple taste that comes to the table in a humble fashion. No fanfare, just understated excellence. Some might say that baguettes are the quintessential bread (I would!). And behind this modest loaf is some of the best baking you can ever experience. A good baguette is tricky to make, time consuming, and always worth the effort. I often tell my family and friends that my last meal on earth will be a baguette, with wine and cheese, on the banks of the Seine opposite Notre Dame Cathedral—such is its place in my heart.

This recipe takes about 17 ½ hours, so plan to be around the kitchen for a few days, if you want to make a really good baguette. It makes about 18 twelve-inch baguettes. There's a lot of explaining to do . . . so I ask your patience. It will certainly be worth the effort.

Lesson one: the longer the yeast works a dough, the more flavor you have. Time is on your side.

Lesson two: Helping the yeast by adding Dry Diastatic Malt Powder (get it online)—it enhances yeast performance and adds good flavor.

Lesson three: steaming or spritzing baking dough with water gives you the essential chewy crust.

Lesson four: You'll need a few items not found in most kitchens: 3 *couche*—special cloths that the shaped baguettes sit in before baking; a baker's lame—a special knife for slashing each baguette; a transfer peel (a 30-inch flat board used to transfer dough from the *couche* to the baguette pan); a plastic spritz bottle—you can buy them at the local hardware store (don't reuse a spritz bottle from something else—we want clean water on our baguettes); finally, I would use baguette baking sheets that come with room for two or four baguettes each. Failing baguette baking sheets, you can use ordinary ones with parchment.

FIRST MIX (12 HOURS)

3 cups of white flour
3 cups of warm water
2 Tablespoons of active yeast
1 teaspoon Dry Diastatic Malt powder
Stir in a large bowl until all are dissolved and you have a slurry type mixture—not like dough; a bit thicker than soup. Cover bowl by stretching plastic wrap across the brim of the bowl and letting it sit in a warm place for 12 hours.

SECOND MIX

To the first mixture add:
9 cups of flour
4 Tablespoons of salt
4 Tablespoons active yeast
1 Tablespoon Dry Diastatic Malt powder
3–4 cups of warm water
You may need to add more or less water . . . start mixing in the flour with your hands and add water gradually. You are looking to create a spongy, slightly sticky, dough. This is where experience will improve your results. If the dough is too dry, it will not have that airy, chewy texture. Once you have the right consistency, knead the dough on a floured surface for seven minutes (sing "O Canada" four times—"Star Spangled Banner" three times). Place in a well-oiled, large bowl and cover with a damp cloth.

THREE RISINGS (3 HOURS)

Baguette dough needs to rise three times. That means you allow 1 hour for the each rising. You will punch it down twice. On the third time, you will then punch it down and cut it as described below.

SHAPING

Roll the dough out on a floured surface and divide it into 18 balls (each should weigh about 230 grams).

Let balls sit for 10 minutes, and then roll them into baguette shaped cylinders— about 13 to 14 inches long. I use a rolling pin—grease the wood surface with a light smear of olive oil. You can also use your hands, if you like. This is the second area where experience will guide you. The more baguettes you make, the more even and symmetrical will be your final product. (You can go online and see some examples of shaping baguettes.) I take the ball of dough, and with the rolling pin, I stretch it out into a long tube-like shape (4 inches wide by 18 inches long) and then roll up one edged so that it becomes a solid tube shape 16–18 inches long.

Lay out the *couches* and flour them well.

Place your first baguette dough on the end of a *couche* and then pull up the *couche*, to make a ridge as high as the dough, and place your second dough on the other side of that ridge—repeat for all the baguettes. Flour slightly. What you should have is about 4 baguettes per *couche*—each separated from one another so they are allowed to rise.

Take the lame and slice each baguette diagonally three times along its length.

Place a plastic sheet (a clean garbage bag will do—food grade plastic is best) over all the baguettes and let rise for at least 1 hour.

BAKING

Preheat oven to 475 degrees F.

Flour your transfer peel and place it parallel to the first baguette on the *couche*; roll the baguette onto the peel gently and transfer it to a baguette baking sheet or a cookie sheet covered with parchment. If you now pull gently and evenly where this baguette dough was lying, the other baguettes on the *couche* will separate out easily, and you can use the peel to transfer them. (You'll see what I mean, when you try it. Makes life easier. I promise!)

Once the baguettes are all on sheets, put them in the oven.

Every 2 minutes, spritz the inside of the oven with lots of water. (I use ½ quart per baking.) You can spray directly on the baguettes, as well as on the sides of the oven. I have taken to putting a cast iron frying pan in the bottom of the oven, and once the desired temperature is reached, I dump ice cubes into this frying pan. Instant steam. Then I put the baguettes into the oven to enjoy that steam.

It should take between 15 and 18 minutes to bake.

TASTING

Roll them out onto a cooling rack and wait about an hour before tasting them. Have butter, cheese, and wine at the ready. (If you can arrange for the trip to the Seine while you arrange your picnic, all the better.)

No better meal on earth.

3

The Real Meal Deal

Tell me, said the anthropologist, how you eat and I will tell you how you live; show me your table and I will know your society, How do you dine with your God? Are the seating arrangements and food distributions open or regulated, egalitarian or hierarchical . . . How do you eat with Augustus and/or Herod and/or Antipas in the Kingdom of Rome? And how, above all, do you eat and drink with Jesus of Nazareth in the Kingdom of God?[1]

INTRODUCTION: "CAN WE KEEP THE DONKEY"

Years ago, when distance learning meant writing and reading at home and sending assignments by mail to a distant, faceless college, the seminary where I worked instituted a province-wide bible study—by phone. A novel idea that now pales in the light of the ubiquitous nature of internet Zoom meetings. Back then, we gathered our community once a week by conference call. It worked quite well. We discussed topics ranging from the historical Jesus to modern church dilemmas. The genius of the project was its simplicity. Small congregational groups needed nothing more than a hands-free phone. With that, we would bring the best scholarship in the country to their doorstep.

Given the size of Alberta, it was quite remarkable that we would be able to link up such small groups in vastly distant towns. Our format was

1. Reed and Crossan, *Excavating Jesus,* 129.

pretty standard. Of the two hours spent together, half would be used listening to presentations of well-known academics. That was then followed up by an hour of questions and answers. During our second season, we spent the weeks in Advent exploring the historical nature of the birth of Jesus. For that session, there were participants from as far away as Yellowknife, in the Northwest Territories, and Milk River, down by the Montana border, and everywhere in-between. To help us, we invited a New Testament scholar from Ontario to speak with us: Robert Bater. At the time, Bob was recognized as a church leader, a courageous community advocate, and a member of the Jesus seminar—a collective of academics dedicated to making the historical Jesus both understandable and relevant for modern audiences.

Bob was also well-known for speaking plainly and without fear. No beating around the bush. I introduced him and explained to our audience that our topic was the historicity of the birth of Jesus. What is realistically verifiable behind the elaborate nativity celebrations we all knew and loved. What was historically probable in the nativity narratives found in Matthew and Luke? Bob began almost immediately with a list of nonevents in the Christmas story. Citing the most recent scholarship, he listed what to him were irrefutable facts: There was no "star in the east." There were no wise men, no gold, frankincense, and myrrh, and no slaughter of the innocents. There was no star-lit journey from Nazareth to Bethlehem, no holy couple— Joseph leading, while Mary was sitting on a donkey. There was no crowded inn in Bethlehem. Forget the manger, the cow stall, and little lambs. No angels sang "Gloria" on high, and no shepherds were struck speechless down below. There was no hasty visit to Bethlehem by wild-eyed shepherds, and there was definitely no drummer boy. Utter silence greeted his opening remarks. What to say? And then came a small voice out of Milk River: "Can we keep the donkey?"

Much as we don't want to admit it, we need the reassurance that some of our myths have a foundation in history. We grew up with them, held them close in our imaginations. Like a security blanket, we wrapped them around our shoulders, when the winds of change blew and the storm clouds of dissent appeared. These "stories of Jesus" shielded us from doubt and held down our fears. Can't we keep some of them? And even as we grow into adulthood, we cherish those early memories. They act like a nostalgic anchor in the sea of contingency that characterizes modern life. And sometimes we retreat back into them, when we are shaken.

Nevertheless, our constant task as believers is to live into the fact that many of our cherished pictures of Jesus are just that: pictures. These imaginings point us to the truth of his saving love, but they have no correspondence with the lived reality of his ministry. A tough pill to swallow for some. We want to "keep the donkey."

What is true of the nativity narrative also holds with respect to first-century eating etiquette. Despite our misgivings, when it comes to the table and meal fellowship of Jesus, we are on the same pathway of letting go of our preconceived notions. Leonardo Da Vinci's iconic mural of the Last Supper notwithstanding, there are a vast number of objects we have to remove from our portrait of a first-century meal gathering.

Let's suppose, for the sake of this chapter, that you are going to invite Jesus for dinner. What will happen? Let's pretend that he was passing through your little lakeside village of Magdala, and in a moment of fearlessness, you strode forward to welcome him as he reached the first few compounds of your town. Bowing, you asked him if he would do you the honor of sharing a meal. Of course, he and you know that the meal was just one aspect of hospitality. A place to sleep, a secure, safe, and sheltered space, some soothing ointments or purity baths were also included in such an invitation.

Now that you stuck you head out and asked him to visit, what can you expect? What will you see and taste? How will the meal be served, and who else should be invited? How is this meal going to unfold?

Before we can explore what will actually happen when you eat together with Jesus, let's first ask what is not going to happen—dispel our misconceptions at the outset.

WHAT EATING ISN'T

And we begin with the obvious. There's no table. As I mentioned in the Introduction, having Jesus for dinner means taking away any notion of a flat raised surface on which food is laid and around which people sit. The ultrarich might have a raised dais covered in silks or blankets, but even that was not a table in the modern sense. No sitting up to a board or flat surface with your legs underneath. If there was such a dais for eating, we would see it more as a low platform, a convenience to get food platters further way from the floor. But such an extravagance is not in evidence in your poor peasant's compound in Magdala. Of course, tables existed at the time of Jesus, but they were not used for shared meals or serving food. Rich people had small tables set by each reclining couch, but even they wouldn't sit at them to eat. Why would they?

Imagine today: You can certainly set a meal on the hood of a Chevy, but what's the point? It's inconvenient for guests and hardly polite or respectful.

It's not what you do when you invite someone for dinner and certainly not for someone as well-known and respected as Jesus.

In your poor, peasant town, most formal meals were eaten on the ground, served on a carpet, blanket, or well-swept floor. Perhaps there's an outdoor courtyard, built and set aside specifically for eating purposes. In that ancient world, a "sit-down" dinner begins with a "lying-down" circle of people reclining on the floor around a central space where food would be placed. It goes without saying that in less formal times, the family might squat around a fire where a common pot was warming, but no one would imagine sharing a meal in such a fashion, when important company was coming. (Can you picture inviting a member of Congress to your home and serving frozen pizza on TV trays in front of the television? You get the picture—it's not on!) "Company coming" means you recline to eat. Remember you invited Jesus and his followers to a meal, and as the host, your honor is on the line, and that means proper attention to etiquette and common practice. He's a spiritual somebody, and given the cultural sensitivities of your time, hospitality meant rolling out the carpet, quite literally.

As mentioned above, in wealthier homes, low platforms might be used to keep food off the unsanitary floor. In this case, they would be one-sided tables . . . people would be arranged around the outside in a semi-circle or u-shape which allowed food to be served easily to guests.

But that's rich people. In your humble home, you have a well-swept dirt floor and the multi-colored banquet shawl passed down from your grandmother's household. Its vibrancy has faded with use, and it has a few carefully sewn patches, but it holds such rich memories that you wouldn't dare use anything else.

Next, in our minds, we should take away the chairs. Again, they existed in the time of Jesus, but why would you use them to eat? In our modern world, ask yourself if you would ever serve guests their dinner in the shower? It's doable, but very unconventional, not to mention awkward. So, if you're having Jesus for dinner, chairs are equally unwelcome. Banish the thought.

At your meal with Jesus, guests will recline on their left arm around the common carpet or blanket. In well-to-do homes, there would be a pillow or rolled up cloak to give to each guest, something firm to put under their elbow for comfort. In your case, the house has a selection of very worn pillows, which do double duty as bed rests. Your wife will gather them up, give them a good beating to shake out the dust and any hidden bugs, and lay them carefully around your grandmother's banquet shawl.

Now we can picture a circle of reclining guests. Their feet (they are the lowest and most impure part of the body—we don't even mention them in polite company) are furthest from the food.[2] There's a space somewhere in the circle which allows servers (a woman, or a servant, or a child) to place common platters in the middle of the circle. Good!

And as will become evident when we speak of the positive aspect of having Jesus for dinner, this reclining configuration keeps people close and in place. It is not so easy to leave the circle around the common food space. It is certainly more disruptive to crawl away from the meal, when everyone is reclining and close enough together to reach the common platter, than it is when we have separate, well-spaced chairs.[3]

Next on our "not" list: utensils. You can forget about having a place setting. Your fingers are your fork, knife, and spoon. To be sure, such instruments played a part in cooking, and depending on the wealth of a family, there may have been multiples of each. But utensils were for the cooking, not the dining.[4] Your fingers do the work. With the aid of a crust of bread or a slice of vegetable, they dip into the food to take out a single mouthful portion at a time. And, you are going to use your right hand only. That's the clean one. The left hand stays under your body, tucked away, since it is the dirty hand that we use for other, less sanitary, necessities.

There's no way around this. To the modern mind, this is where it gets ugly. Picture a circle of reclining individuals, all reaching for a common platter. You can't avoid it. Your neighbor's fingers are going to be rooting around in your stew—often. The opposite of social distancing, first-century meals are all very up close and very personal. And you knew this when you invited Jesus and his followers to join you for a meal. You were welcoming them into an intimacy that our world would find quite disconcerting. He's going to get close, so close, in fact, that we will easily smell him and touch him. He will do the same with us.

That being the case, first we're going to be quite conscious of our own hygiene. Check our fingernails; look at our palms. Are they clean? You may not know about germs, but you can certainly see what looks presentable and what does not. Next, you are going to look very carefully at your neighbor,

2. From this arrangement you can understand how the unwanted sinner woman, as she is described in Luke's story of Simon the Pharisee (Luke 7:36–50), can easily anoint Jesus' feet, since they are accessible on the outside of the circle.

3. If you are reading this book as part of a study group, now would be a good time to set a turkey platter on a tea towel on the floor and have participants recline around it, as I have outlined above. Notice how close you have to get to each other for everyone to be able to reach the common plate.

4. It is interesting to note that the fork as a personal instrument for eating was not "invented" until somewhere in the fifth century. Of course, people may have used sharp sticks to spear food items while they were cooking, but a multipronged tool was not common.

at Jesus himself, indeed, did at everyone in the circle. What do they have that you might catch? Are they keeping clean? Have they followed the basic etiquette of cleanliness[5]?

Prior to 2020, when I described these questions of purity that circled around a first-century meal, we thought it was outrageous. How could people be so narrow-minded? Can people be excluded from eating just because they are not clean enough? We saw such mealtime sensitivities as prejudicial, if not downright paranoid. Look how superstitious and elitist they were!

However, in the middle of the pandemic, everyone was hypersensitive to their surroundings—especially at mealtime. We restricted our contacts with outsiders, didn't invite strangers to join us for a meal, and kept to the people within our bubble. This was not the result of prejudice or animosity; we were just being careful. Even when it wasn't an issue of actually eating together, we became quite picky about others. Is the woman ahead of us in the coffee shop line coughing too much? Does that man by the produce counter have a stuffy nose, and a cold, or the virus? We asked these questions as part of staying safe.

The same dynamics and logic are at play in the circle of people having dinner with Jesus. It was common sense. You're wondering about the other guests in the circle and where they might have been, what contaminants or contagions they may be harboring—wittingly or unwittingly. You can feel yourself doing a quick scan of the circle joining you for the meal. Is anyone showing signs of sickness: lesions on the skin or discharges of any kind?

And there's no need to think first-century diners are inhospitable or paranoid about the people they join for dinner. To set the correct moral/ hygienic framework, let's live back into COVID times, when we naturally asked our host about the other guests invited to that person's dinner party. They're sitting across from us, after all. Are they vaccinated? Are they careful, following the medical guidelines and state-sanctioned restrictions? Likewise, we ask of ourselves: Am I safe? Am I doing the right thing? Proximity breeds apprehension, and to those who are sincere, it heightens attention to important details like proper washing and sanitation.

Can you feel the walls rising around the dinner table? We want to keep out the "unclean" people. No one will come, if the anti-vaxxers are in attendance. Keep that restrictive mentality in mind as we continue with our list of what is not in evidence when Jesus comes from dinner.

---

5. One of the complaints leveled at Jesus is that his disciples failed to wash their hands before eating (Mark 7:1–5). To modern ears that might sound picky, but if those hands are going to be dipping into a common bowl, it is a reasonable complaint.

There are no plates. Did I mention that already? Surprise! When I hosted a "Jesus-feast" meal during my time as an academic, the gathered community would be relaxed—though a bit nonplused when they came into the "dining" room to find cushions and blankets instead of chairs and tables. They even accepted eating with their hands—after all isn't that how we all started? And for travelers, they know full well some Southeast and South Asian cultures like Malaysia, Indonesia, Sri Lanka, and India still favor eating with fingers. So, it's a little awkward, but doable. But, when it became clear there were no plates—everyone tenses up. It's a simple thing to remove plates from our meal practice, but it's much harder to wipe them from our imaginations.

Having no plates raises significant implications. It means that a meal with Jesus was something to be shared—literally. It's a joint exercise. You can't have a portion reserved for yourself. Eating is reduced to what you can hold in your fingers. Having no plates means that the people around the circle have no expectation of serving or receiving a discrete portion for themselves. As I write this, I am in a cafeteria, and it is striking how everything implies and depends on discrete, personal portions. The fixed tables and chairs, the placement of food counters, the lighting and exits, the trays and cutlery . . . they are all based on individual eating practicing. Food is not a team sport.

At the modern table, even when you are part of pack, you are a lone wolf, consuming what you select and sequester for yourself. Having your own plate not only offers a modicum of privacy, it also connotes control over your food, the pace of consumption, and within the context of each meal course, the selection of food combinations. Do you eat your veggies first, allow the meat sauce to flavor the potatoes, or combine sweet flavors with tart ones? All this freedom of choice comes with a plate.

No plate: no choice.

The lack of plates also restricts portion size. As you recline to eat with Jesus, you will be presented with a common bowl or platter—that's your dinner. Indeed, that's everyone's dinner. In the very wealthy homes, this shared serving dish might be brought to each person in turn. Either way, the meal is based on a common platter from which you and all your guests will select only a finger portion to eat. To separate out a serving of the food and reserve it for yourself only would be seen as rude, selfish, and snobbish. You eat only a mouthful at a time. If there was bread, you might use it as a scoop and have a little more on it than you could put in your mouth at one time, but you didn't finger out a meal's worth of dinner and plop it on your bread. How uncouth!

Can you picture yourself reclining to eat with Jesus, and while everyone one else is using fingers for a single helping, you set down a mound of food at your place for only you to eat? Only a glutton or social boor would imagine such a thing! In our day, it would be equivalent to someone taking the Thanksgiving turkey, placing it in front of their own place, and proceeding to eat it with a knife and fork.

So, in your case, you are cleaning the three clay serving platters that hold an honored place in your household. They will have to do double duty, since you have more than three dishes in mind as you plan out the menu. One is chipped and another is cracked—they will work for the drier dishes. The best platter was a gift from the local synagogue leader to your father, and it will hold the prize dish, a special recipe from your wife's mother.

In summary: no table, no chairs, no utensils, or plates. That's the short list of meal mechanics and what you can expect not to have while having Jesus for dinner. The actual food selection and what may or may not be on offer to eat will be explored below. There is one last point about the "what," or in this case, the "who" is not at the meal. Before Jesus comes to your home, you will no doubt have heard that he brings along some questionable companions. You have been a righteous Jew your whole life, and that meant keeping opposites in balance. Men eat together first; women eat later with the children and servants, if there are any. Anyone with bodily secretions (blood, pus, or undefined seepage) would be excluded from food preparation and/or serving. And they would eat at a distance from everyone else. No shame—just good, healthy practice. Those, who displayed evidence of God's s disfavor and therefore who are sinful, would likewise be discouraged from attending if not be outright excluded altogether from eating with the family. Hence, the blind, the lame, the crippled, or consumptive would not be welcome. And, of course, there were those people who by their very nature or occupation were unclean: prostitutes, tax collectors, morticians, grave diggers—strike them from the guest list. They are not welcome in a respectable house, and they know it.

For years, I would explain this exclusivist approach to eating as evidence of first-century best practice. My classes would be sorely tempted to heap scorn on such an "elitist" approach to eating. But let us not jump on our high horse too quickly. First-century meal practice in the Jewish world was shaped by a combination of medical intuition, social common sense, and spiritual conviction. And to be clear, the Jewish propensity to build high walls of exclusion around food resulted in saving lives.

As I mentioned above, at the height of the COVID pandemic, exclusion became mainstream. Anyone who tested positive would not be welcome for supper! Sure, we might make then a care package to be delivered to their door, but we would not have them in our company. And we would expect guests to abide by all the health directives: to wear face coverings and observe social distance! Now is not the time for independent nonconformity. We all follow the COVID guidelines, because it keeps everyone safe. Is the first-century preoccupation with the "who" of eating any different?

So, when we invite Jesus for dinner, we would naturally expect the common sense rules around the circle to apply: men eat first, women later, sinners and risky types are left outside and might be fed at a distance with scraps.

And the fact that Jesus is reported not to abide by these simple rules is putting everyone in your household on edge. As the hour approaches, you ask yourself whatever possessed you to invite him. What if he has women in his circle, who recline to eat without being invited? And what if some of the town's rejects show up at his side? And "they" will expect to be served along with "us," and that will spell chaos, not just for the immediate predicament of the meal, but for the contamination it causes in the kitchen and the long-term repercussions surrounding your household's honor and righteousness. Your gossipy neighbor told you just now that Jesus is trouble. He eats with lepers and prostitutes! Didn't you hear that? Now . . . how do you explain to your household that everyone with Jesus will be treated with respect—no matter who they are? This will take some doing.

I hope you are feeling uncomfortable. If we are not on edge, we have not understood the chasm that separates us from Jesus. Moving our meal back to the first century will require us to strip away many of the guidelines and practices which give us a sense of power and control. We're arriving in a strange place. Food is food. It doesn't change much from century to century. But how we serve and consume it makes all the difference. Show me a culture's eating practices, and I will be able to explain a great deal about their values and principles, hopes, and dreams.[6]

But before we get to the actual eating, can we turn toward the place where food is prepared? How does the kitchen operate, when we are having Jesus for dinner?

WHAT'S IN THE KITCHEN?

Are you like me, a kitchen hog? When I visit a new house, I make a beeline for the kitchen to see the set up. How wide are the counters? What about the stove and cooking utensils? Is there a decent set of knives? How about

---

6. Reed and Crossan, *Excavating Jesus*, 129: "*Tell me, said the anthropologist, how you eat and I will tell you how you live; show me your table and I will know your society, . . .* "

layout? Is the fridge in the right relationship to the range? And what is the coffee set up? All essential questions to those of us who love to cook.

Having invited Jesus for dinner, you'd better come to grips with the fact that there is precious little you can use to actually prepare the food. Of course, first-century homemakers would take for granted the small selection of cooking utensils, spices, and produce. They'd know how to make it work; but to our eyes it would be precious little.

There would be a household fire pit with a tripod or a bar to hold pots. Failing that, we can imagine a selection of rocks or an iron spit for holding pans above the fire. You might have some brass pots now black with soot having been passed down through generations. For sure, there is a selection of clay bowls and platters, a wooden ladle or two. You will have a frying surface or pan. There might be a communal bake oven in your house compound and perhaps a deep well or cave for keeping food cool. Near the "kitchen" you would have a preparation surface for grinding grain, rolling out bread dough, cutting vegetables, and mixing ingredients. And while it may be a small area or one that has precious few conveniences, I imagine first-century cooks were as adept as modern ones in streamlining and organizing food preparation.

The biggest difference would be the lack of stores. For the most part, each meal begins from scratch, since there is very little that can be preserved from meal to meal with any assurance it will be fit to eat. Dry spices, grains and ground legumes, root vegetables and berries . . . they might be available. But dairy products spoil in the Mediterranean heat. Milk turns sour or, if worked carefully, becomes yogurt. Meat, if it isn't cooked, salted, or dried, will spoil. Greens and oils are fine. Likewise, grain-based foods, like porridge or bread, have a longer shelf life. You might not have to grind barley or wheat[7] to make flour for every meal, but it's a regular chore for someone. As there is no fridge, you can forget about leftovers or partially prepared meals; no freezers with emergency appetizers waiting to be reheated. So, if you invited Jesus for dinner in the morning, you are going to spend most of the day gathering and preparing the ingredients for the meal.

There is your fire pit—with accompanying utensils. Somewhere, you would have a cutting surface and grinding utensils. Good luck. If it's a baking day, you can count on bread and perhaps some roasted protein. But all heat sources require the gathering of fuel: wood or dried animal waste—so someone, usually a child, will have their morning cut out for them just finding wood.

---

7. Depending on the size of the household mill and the skill of the homemaker, grain for the day's bread might take upwards of three hours to grind from seed to flour.

That's not to say you are helpless. From tradition and family experience, you are very skilled at frying and boiling your courses, using a small selection of flavoring agents to produce a wide variety of dishes.

But . . . nothing is going to be quick. Fast food is a modern anomaly. For the vast number of human beings in the past and for many even still today, meal preparation is the dominant preoccupation of the women in our households.

WHAT ISN'T FOR DINNER?

That's the physical set up, more or less.

I know when I am considering what to provide for a dinner invitation, I am often inspired by the food I have on hand, the people who might come—shaping dietary preferences to the season of the year and the staples I have to hand. As we travel back to have dinner with Jesus, our constant struggle will be to lower our expectations and assumptions. Only a very small percentage of the population enjoyed anything close to what we would consider to be basic standards of food selection and dietary variety.

And before we ask what's for dinner, let's recognize what isn't on the menu. For the most part meat-based protein is problematic. Whether it is goat, lamb, beef, or chicken, any consumption of flesh requires the elimination of a farming resource. Chickens provide eggs. Goats and cows offer milk and, by extension, yogurt. Sheep give wool, and once processed, it turns into clothing garments, household linens. protection against the elements, and material to be sold or bartered. Steers are work animals as are horses and donkeys—and their value puts them well out of reach for most Palestinian farms.

You don't eat your assets,[8] and so the daily intake of protein would not normally involve using one of these farm animals. Wild meat (when available) might prove to be possible. Fish is certainly an option—free for those who have the proximity to the sea and ability to catch and process seafood. But for the most part, protein will come from dairy products and legumes.[9]

8. In the story of the two sons, found in Luke 15:11–32, mention is made of the party preparations to celebrate the lost son's return. ". . . kill the fatted calf, let us eat and be merry" says the father, "for this my son was dead and is alive; he was lost and is found." (vs.23–24). In light of preserving farm animals as a way to ensure food security, this sacrifice of the "the fatted calf" was quite an extravagant gesture. In our age, imagine a father remortgaging the family home to host a wedding banquet for a son returning from foreign wars.

9. Eggs could provide protein, and they are not forbidden by Jewish law. So, we can imagine that they might be part of Jesus' diet. He mentions them only once: Luke 11:12

THE HOLY TRINITY

There is a "holy trinity" of food staples available to you, as you prepare to cook dinner for Jesus: olives/oil, wheat/barley, and grapes/wine. They are made sacred by virtue of their foundational nature—we build our meal from these three places and add to them as diet and availability shift. Each one has its own method of processing, and we may use them at various stages of their preparedness as our menu and diet require. Likewise, we may vary their use, subject to seasonal and economic pressures, local traditions, and technology.

THE LOWLY, EXALTED OLIVE

It is difficult to exaggerate the centrality and importance of the olive as a staple for the Palestinian diet. It's everywhere—a multi-purpose source of food, a symbol for life's meaning, and a signpost for eternity.

As a source of food, the olive is both reliable in times of food insecurity and a source of essential nutrients and proteins. It works well as an on-the-run snack and a lingering-over-dinner treat.

Beyond its nutritional value, the olive had important social and cultural significance. Olive trees, given their longevity and ubiquity, were seen as a symbol of prosperity, stability, and beauty, not to mention national pride. Given their seemingly eternal staying power, the olive, in general, and the olive branch, in particular, became synonymous with lasting covenants. They speak of permanence and security. And for millennia, the olive branch has embodied the hope for eternal or, at least, long-lasting well-being. Among other things, it was featured on first-century Roman coins. It was described by Tertullian (a second-century church leader and theologian) as the twig carried by the dove back to Noah's ark to signal redemption.[10] Even today, we talk about "offering an olive branch" as a euphemism for making overtures for restoration and peace.[11]

---

in a teaching about prayer. But it seems eggs were considered more of a rich person's food and not commonly eaten in peasants' homes.

10. Speaking about baptism, Tertullian claimed that the olive branch: "announced to the world the assuagement of divine wrath, when she had been sent out of the ark and returned with the olive branch." 2009d.

11. In 1974, Palestinian leader Yasser Arafat took an olive branch to the UN General Assembly and said, "Today I have come bearing an olive branch and a freedom-fighter's gun. Do not let the olive branch fall from my hand." "*Mahmoud Abbas: haunted by ghost of Yasser Arafat.*" The Daily Telegraph. London. 23 September 2011.

It is not a surprise that you can find the olive's presence and peace-filled connotations in important places. For example, there are two stylized olive branches surrounding a map of the world on the flag of the United Nations. They are clearly meant to denote world peace. A bunch of olive branches, symbolizing goodwill and harmony, held by the eagle in the seal of the United States of America, is the balance to the clutch of the war-like arrows held by its other claw. And the olive branch is still today featured on some Mediterranean national flags.[12]

As a food stuff, olives offered a number of very important advantages.

First, it was versatile, being both a firm fruit that could be chewed and, when processed, used as a side dish to proteins. When turned into a liquid, it could complement other dried goods. We have evidence that, during the time of Jesus, olive oil was used as a healing agent, a condiment, a topping for bread, a grease to use in frying other foods, and a natural oil to preserve leftovers for later use.

Second, olives are eternal. Olive trees seemingly lasted forever. They're ancient and ubiquitous in lower Galilee, and so, as we prepare to make dinner for Jesus, we may be relying on our family's orchard, one that has sustained our household for generations. The longevity of olive trees gave rise to the comparison between olives and prosperity. They quite literally held the promise of survival in tough times—embodying peace but also security.

Third, given their seeming impermeability, it follows that olive trees and their produce were seen as valuable assets. At certain times, olive oil was used as a currency of exchange. Stored in deep wells, it could be traded for other agricultural products, used to secure and pay off debts, while, at the same time, being used as the foundation for the country's daily diet.

So, a multipurpose fruit.

Anyone who has picked a ripe olive from the tree and popped it into their mouth will tell you that a fresh olive is nothing like the olive that comes on your plate. Indeed, the fresh olive is often too bitter to be eaten, being filled with oleuropein, a compound that must be removed prior to eating. Olive harvesting is naturally followed by a two-step process of curing and brining. Essentially, we are going to pickle the olive before we eat it. This adds to the complexity of its flavors and gives the olive a much longer shelf life. We cure the olives by immersing them in water. Olives can be dried and cured with lye, if abundant water is not available. Once cured for a few weeks, they are placed in a salt solution. That's the step of brining. Like all pickled items, they are required to sit in this brine for a length of time, before they are consumed. No doubt, every household had its own traditions

12. See the flag of Cyprus and Eritrea.

and secrets, when it came to the curing and brining of their olives. In addition, every variety of olive provides a different flavor, and when mixed with garlic or other herbs, the complexity of tastes is endless. Even though it's a simple food and we are a poor peasant family, one should not assume our olives are bland or uninspiring. On the contrary, as we prepare to serve Jesus, perhaps we get out that special jar of olives—the ones all our neighbors rave about—so that he can taste how a humble olive can be a regal delicacy.

If raw olives take time and care to be turned into the delicious meal we all know, the same could be said of olive oil. It requires considerable energy and skill to produce. Olive oil is made when ripe olives are washed and crushed. In Jesus' time they would have been ground by a millstone, if one was available, or, in more traditional ways—foot stomped using wooden shoes. Either way, the point is to turn the olives into a paste that allows for natural enzymes to form. Once crushed, the olive mash would be pressed to extract the oil. While there is evidence of some more sophisticated mechanisms in use in Palestine, in the bible belt region around the sea of Galilee, the old pressing methods would have been more common. In that case, you place the mash in a vat or chamber with holes to allow oil to escape and then lower a weight on top of the mash to push it down. A long lever, with stone weights at the far end opposite the vat, would be used to add weight and pressure to the pressing process. Eventually, oil would be gathered and stored. Olive oil, apart from its many uses, had the added advantage of being a stable product, even in Mediterranean heat.

So, as we approach the kitchen/cooking area, knowing we have to serve Jesus and his followers a good meal, we begin with olives—the ultimate finger food. Perhaps we will use them as a first course, served in their own oil, with added salt to give some punch. It goes without saying that we would add them to a vegetable dish or use them as a topping for fried bread. Lots of options. Given the importance of this meal, I can imagine we will go with trusted old family recipes. Why not grandmother's tangy olive bread, a lovely tart delight that, when coupled with her honey-soaked figs, is a perfect balance of sweet and sour?

Besides being a first platter and a complement to other dishes—adding its unique multilayered, acidic flavor to second and third courses —we'll use olive oil to grease the pan when frying, as the foundation for soups and as one dimension to a sauce to cover other ingredients. If Jesus is coming to us in the cold season, we'll use olive oil to give depth and texture to a hot sauce. And if it's summer, we'll cool things down with olive oil mixed with citrus juice—as a light drizzle over vegetables is all we need.

Having settled on a selection of courses, we move to the next part of the trinity: barley or wheat-based produce.

FIVE SMALL BARLEY LOAVES

Borrowing the story of the feeding of the multitudes from the other gospels, the author of John adds a few very concrete dimensions to the original story. Told first in Mark (Mark 6:30–44), Jesus originally asks about bread to feed the crowd, and the disciples reply they have five loaves and two fish: a pretty sparse plot with few details. In John, however, bread and fish are the offering of an unnamed boy, signaling the generosity of innocence. And instead of generic "loaves," we are told he has "barley" loaves (John 6:9). Whatever John's purpose might be in giving a descriptive adjective to this bread,[13] it does point to a peasant reality. Most meals were accompanied by the cheaper, more resilient and ubiquitous barley. Wheat production is not easy, especially in a climate where intermittent drought or excessive heat could ruin a crop. Barley is tough, drought-resistant, and it was also harvested first, a month or so before wheat. It stores and dries well. Whole barley does add substance to stews and soups, and there's no question that it has the advantage of being cheap and easy to grind.

Barley bread would not be my first choice for a starch; as porridge mush, it might be digestible, but as bread, if it is not mixed with other lighter flours, it makes a loaf that is closer to cardboard than bread. However, in John's version of the feeding of the multitude, it signals that the people gathering to hear Jesus are impoverished peasants, share croppers, and itinerant workers. They don't have the luxury of fine, wheat bread. Barley bread is like no-name Wonder Bread in our day. It's cheap, plentiful, never tasty, always available. A poor person's staple.

Along with olives, bread—barley or wheat—is a necessity. So, when it comes to feeding Jesus, we will need to prepare some form of bread. That's not an option.

Let's just remember two simple facts about bread making in first-century Palestine: time and time. It takes time to produce flour. Perhaps someone has already begun the grinding of grain for other reasons, or perhaps we have some left over from a previous day's work. Nonetheless, making bread requires the time to grind the wheat or barley into flour.[14] We can't just go to the cupboard and haul out 8 cups of flour for our recipe. Likewise, it takes

13. I can't help but feel John is trying to add historical credence to his version of the story. It sounds much more convincing to describe the detail, of an object or subject, when telling a tale. Who will believe you, if you state that Jesus took some bread? It sounds much more convincing if he held "barley" bread.

14. The length of time needed to grind our grain would depend on whether we have a small mill stone (operated by hand) or if we use the more traditional method of using what we could call a rolling pin, slowly grinding the grains into flour on a stone slab.

time for the bread dough to rise. There was no source of leavening agent during the time of Jesus, apart from some form of sourdough or whatever natural air-born yeasts might be present. That being the case, bread making is a long day's journey. Of course, the longer the dough takes to rise, the better and more multilayered the flavors, but it's still not simple. Hopefully, before you asked Jesus to dine at your home, you remembered that last night's sourdough was ready to bake today. So, we're covered.

If it's a baking day, the communal oven will offer plenty of possibilities. Taking the dough that was rising during the evening, we'll shape our bread according to the heat of the oven. My first stop would be pita bread. The round, hollow buns that allow for any number of uses: a small piece can be used as a scoop for stews and soups. The hollow shape of pita works well as a tiny plate for holding vegetables and a pastry-like container for sweet fruits and sauces. At high temperatures, pita bakes quickly (seven minutes) and stays fresh for the day. It works separately as a treat, when dipped in olive oil and smeared with yogurt. It can carry a lunch to laborers, in the field, or be the snack that keeps hungry hands away from the main course, while it boiling over the fire. Pita: a very versatile bread.

Apart from pita, we could also shape our dough into small loaves—perhaps stuffed with other ingredients, like olives or dried fruits. We'd save these to bake for when the oven is cooler. It goes without saying that loaves are more substantial, adding more bulk to a meal. With them, we can fill in the gaps in our menu, if we have fewer ingredients for further courses.[15]

If, however, the invitation to have Jesus for dinner was an on-the-spur-of-the-moment deal, we may not have the time to bake. The oven requires us to light a fire inside, allow it burn to ashes, and then thoroughly rake out the cinders from the baking flour before we start. That's a time consuming process, and we haven't even counted in the hours it takes to gather fuel. So, with little notice, we might end up frying a flat bread to be used as a scoop for food. Like a cracker or tortilla, this bread could be leavened or unleavened. As it cools, it could be rolled up with ingredients inside or left flat. It could be used like a platter itself, on which other treats are heaped. And flat bread doesn't have to be tasteless. Before baking, if we roll out the dough on a surface with salt or herbs, cracked wheat or course flour, our flat bread will have some texture and taste. Painting it with olive oil adds depth. How about a sprinkling of olive bits and chopped greens? Lots of possibilities.

---

15. In Latin America, today, peasants add chili to meatless dishes to stretch their meal and add flavor to mask the simplicity of ingredients. People will say of such families that they are "puro chili" —unadulterated chili. It's a sign of poverty. In a similar manner, we can imagine a meal served to Jesus would be bulked up with starch, if other proteins and staples were unavailable. Fresh bread dipped in olive oil can be very tasty.

Much like olives, bread is not just bread. It conveys meaning on many levels. It is first a sign of goodness, a reflection of God's gift of creation. As we eat bread, we are easily reminded of the wonders surrounding this staple of our diet: the transformation of seeds into flour, the magical rising of the dough to make bread. By extension, bread is a vehicle of recognizing and giving thanks for the miracle of God's bounty.

In Jesus' time, there is a priestly ritual made possible through bread. On the altar in the holy of holies in the temple in Jerusalem, there is a weekly tradition of displaying and then consuming "show bread." This bread was a sign and reminder of God's covenant in the wilderness to send bread from heaven, daily. It was the embodiment of salvation. Only the priests could consume it.

Given its importance in the day-to-day diet of peasants, it is not by accident that bread is featured so centrally in household spirituality. In the Seder meal for instance, unleavened bread is always on the table. It is used like a sandwich—shown to be a symbol of delight, and even gets employed a toy. As we eat bread during the Seder, we are able to look back with thanksgiving over what God has given us—bread for the journey. And we can look forward with hope to the bread served in the banquet "next year in Jerusalem." While the current pattern of the Seder was not created until well after the time of Jesus, the Passover "meal" Jesus knew and organized (Mark14:12) for his circle no doubt was a similar, well-developed family feast which featured bread (matzah) as one of the key ingredients for remembering and hoping.

On a more fundamental level, shared bread is an enactment of vulnerability and trust among strangers. The host breaks bread and passes it to his guests to show they are welcome. As we eat together, we open ourselves to seeing each other's humanity. As creatures, we are not immortal, but must feed our bodies. Doing this feeding in the company of others makes us vulnerable. A meal is a time when your natural defenses are down and taking the crust of bread from a neighbor connotes communion and acceptance. So, on a spiritual level, we are eating our way into a covenant—it could be merely a temporary truce or a long-lasting peace, but shared bread is the vehicle for saying what cannot or perhaps would not be said: "I trust you."

Among friends and family, a shared bread is a re-enactment of our common bond. For instance, in some cultures, couples having just been married share a first slice of cake together before serving others. In my household, the bowl of buns make the round of the table before anything else. And when friends come to visit, there is coffee—but how much richer and homier it is to also offer a cookie or sticky buns to go with it.

Bread is also the reminder in our family circles that we are not abandoned. When a child cries and a father wants to bring comfort, how often does he hand over a slice of bread or sugary biscuit? In my mother's kitchen, there were always tins of cookies for hungry hands. My brother would walk off with a stack of five or six in both fists. And while we drained those cookie tins relentlessly, I know it pleased my mother tremendously that her kids were being fed. She was often working, but the cookies were a sign that we had not been forgotten.

All of these memories and connotations surrounding bread were as present in first-century Palestine as they are today. So, when Jesus takes bread, blesses, breaks, and shares it, there is no question his followers felt more than satisfied physically . . . though that happened of course. They knew they were trusted, loved, and accepted.

So, when Jesus comes for dinner, there will be bread. I am going to suggest we have a cracked wheat flat bread, spiced with a touch of salt and a generous wash of olive oil.

We'll get to other side dishes in a moment, but first we have to account for the third element of the trinity: wine.

FRUIT OF THE VINE

Given the recent tendency for Protestant churches to resist or denigrate alcohol, it has not been fashionable to associate Jesus with wine.[16] Apart from the one story of the marriage feast in Cana, found only in John's gospel (John 2:1–12), we see Jesus drinking wine only during the last supper, and perhaps we say to ourselves, that since at that point he was enacting a ritual rather than eating a meal, he didn't really taste the wine that much. Because of our sensitivity to issues surrounding addictions and given the influence of the temperance movement still alive in many religious denominations, most reformed churches in the U.S and Canada have substituted grape juice for wine in their eucharist celebrations. For these reasons, we don't speak of wine and Jesus in the same sentence, at least not when referring to his daily life. But there is no doubt that wine was a regular necessity, a source of life-saving liquid, and a staple of his diet.

Let's back up. Wine has been in evidence for millennia in Palestine. Moses was convinced that the promised land was indeed plentiful, when two scouts (spies?), who had been across the Jordan, brought back to him

---

16. In my early career as a minister in rural Quebec, it was common for people to apologetically tell me that Jesus didn't really change the water into real wine. It was actually non-alcoholic wine.

a vine clustered with bunches of grapes. King David is said to have had two wine stewards: one for his vines and the other for his cellars. Plenty of archeological evidence illustrates that there was a high level of refinement in viniculture well before Jesus was born. From ancient times, it has been a source of revenue, and during the first part of the first century, wine was the major export from Palestine.

Like apple orchards in colder climates, grape vines were a standard part of any healthy family farm.[17] Tended according to ancient traditions and harvested with care, grape vines provided much needed resources: fruit to dry for nourishment, grape juice to ferment for daily consumption, and wine to sell or barter for other necessities.

At harvest time, grapes would be gathered by hand and taken to the wine press (called a "gat" in Hebrew), which was often found very close to the vineyard. to save on wastage and time. A wine press was a shallow "well"-like structure—perhaps cut in rock or shaped by hardened earth and clay, lined with stone, covered by a canopy or simple roof. This treading floor would be used to crush grapes. The tried-and-true traditional method was to stomp down the grapes by foot, a method that produced enough pressure to break the skins of the grapes, but not so much that it would break open the grape pips.[18] This was apparently men's work. To keep their balance on the slippery surface, there would be strategically placed ropes for holding one's balance. The canopy added shade from the sun. One can imagine inside jokes and old stories being shared among the men as they walked endlessly around the "gat."

As the grapes were crushed, the juice from the press would flow down a channel into a deeper pit or stone well called the "yekev" or "winery." A cross hatching of twigs or thorns was set across this channel to catch the larger bits of grape skin or other alien objects.

Once settled in the yekev, the yeast found naturally on the skins of grapes would begin the fermentation process, acting on the sugar from the fleshy part of the grape. The depth of the yekev would keep temperatures constant and this "tirosh" or "must" would work for four to five days. Fermentation is essentially the conversion of sugar into alcohol, with carbon dioxide being a byproduct of that process.

---

17. First-century Nazareth was a small village (not even rated among the top 1000 on a comprehensive lists of southern Galilean towns.) It was comprised of mud/clay buildings, and so when archeologists dig down to the "Jesus" layer, the only evidence they have of human habitation are the hewn-rock wine presses and storage systems. Life's necessities.

18. The pips, if cracked open, would add a bitter flavor to the wine.

Once the CO_2 was finished off-gassing, and before the wine began to oxidize, the liquid would be channeled to an even deeper pit, where it would be "bottled." In wealthy estates, it might be placed in Palestinian variants of Greek amphorae, and in peasant farms, wines were stored in large clay jars or wine skins.

This "wine" would then be consumed according to taste and need, recognizing that the longer it sat, the better it tasted.

We can imagine Jesus having wine regularly. It was safer than much of the water that might be available. In his circle, the wine would be diluted to extend its volume. Salt water, herbs, spices, like cinnamon, might be used to give wine a distinctive flavor. Date honey or dried fruits might be used to make it sweeter. Some wine was cooked and concentrated—used more like a liqueur.

Given wine's ability to withstand heat, it was a perfect liquid for the dry, hot climate of Galilee. Apart from drinking, wine found use as a healing agent, a dye, an aid to digestion, and, of course, a symbol of spiritual meaning used in religious rituals. Again, like bread, wine is a symbol of God's goodness, and so during the present-day Seder celebration, participants enjoy four glasses of wine, at least. When Jesus takes a cup after the dinner (described in Luke 22:20), it may well be that he is using one of those ritual cups (the last?) that was prescribed by his version of the Passover meal.

Wine mimics blood—the life-giving force of all beasts of the field and birds of the air (Genesis 1:30). To consume wine is to remember that connection between all animals and humanity.

Given its intoxicating qualities, we could say that wine was more than just wine. It was the gift of joy, the evidence of God's gracious benevolence. Relieving tensions and inspiring laughter, it also embodied the abundance and delight of creation. During the present-day Passover Seder, four times (immediately before drinking a cup of wine, the participants make this link between wine and Godliness by saying: *Baruch Atah Adonai, Eloheinu Melech ha-olam, borei p'ree hagafen.* "We praise God, Spirit of Everything, who creates the fruit of the vine").

And given its intoxicating capacity, wine is a magical agent that lifts us out of the daily grind and gives us a glimpse of paradise—a place and time when laughter comes easily and pain is banished. So wine is both a spiritual and physical foundational element of our diet.

Having Jesus for dinner will require us as hosts to choose the best wine that we can offer. There is still one half-filled jar of the vintage from three years back. Saved for important occasions, we last dipped into it at the feast for our grandfather's passing. That will do nicely. And we'll serve that good wine first and at its full strength—a rare indulgence. That's how you do hospitality in our time and place.[19]

And we will not stint on portions as we normally would—trying to stretch our supply as far as possible. Tonight, with this company coming, we'll have full wine goblets.[20] Abundance is our gift to Jesus.

And that brings up one final point about wine. It's more than a liquid. It's a symbol of peace and prosperity. Because it takes time to produce and requires an established manufacturing structure, wine production was synonymous with stable social conditions. For instance, Micah used the vine as a metaphor of God's reign in paradise: "But they shall sit every man under his vine and under his fig tree; and none shall make them afraid . . . " (Micah 4:4). When war is banished, wine will flourish—a sentiment not lost on our guests, as we serve the best wine to Jesus and his company.

Now that we have settled on the three foundational ingredients of our meal, we can progress to the items that are more optional—dependent on our farm's production and local circumstances.

THE MAIN COURSES

At a special meal, like the one we are preparing for Jesus, we can imagine a number of "courses" or platters being served. Not unlike modern palates, over the course of a meal, first-century tastes ran from rich, deep flavors to sweeter, lighter ones. We start with bread and oil perhaps, or bread with a light sauce, pass through protein, and end with dried fruits or honied vegetables.

It goes without saying that there will be yogurt as a condiment. As I mentioned above, milk does not last long in a Mediterranean climate, where cold storage is spotty, at best. We'll have made it into a yogurt-like dish that can be used to flavor almost anything. So, picture yogurt being "on the table," so to speak, in various states: as a dipping sauce, as a condiment, as the base for gravy. It's first-century ketchup.

19. In the story of the marriage feast in Cana, the host explains this practice of serving the best wine first (John 2:10), so that when people are in their cups, the poorer quality of the wine will not be noticed.

20. There is no better illustration of the importance of abundance as part of the host's responsibility than John's story of the marriage feast at Cana. When Jesus changes water into wine, the gospel writer outlines the volumes involved (John 2:6): six jars, each holding between twenty and thirty gallons. Do the math! By modern standards, Jesus has just made something between 750 and 800 bottles of wine. An astronomical amount. John loves to exaggerate, but his point is clear. In the company of Jesus, there is always untold abundance.

For sweeteners, we'll use honey. It comes sometimes as a pure liquid, to be used for dipping, and it can be included with bread, wine, meat, other protein, and/or vegetables to offer that special tang. Some dried fruits are stored in honey, and it comes with the specific coloring of that fruit: dates, figs, apricots, or raisins.

Likewise, these dried fruits would find their way into some of our main dishes. They can stand alone as a final course or be chopped to add accents to protein dishes.

For variety, we have a source of many added ingredients: mustard, capers, cumin, rue, saffron, coriander, mint, dill, rosemary, garlic, onions, and shallots. They would be combined with oils and sweeteners to make up our traditional platters.

In our daily diet, starch comes from bread, cooked or fried, as cracked wheat or barley. Potatoes are a new world vegetable, as are tomatoes. So, they are not present at the meal for Jesus and his circle. Likewise, while some bible translations in English may refer to corn,[21] it does not yet exist in Palestine, also being an import from North America in the sixteenth century. During the time of Jesus, rice had recently been introduced to his context, so we might use it. Cucumbers were popular.

For protein, we can imagine mixtures of cooked legumes and vegetables.[22] Sometimes, we would eat wild locusts—if they were available.[23]. As I mentioned in the introduction, meat from domestic animals would be rare, especially since we just made the invitation for Jesus to join us this morning. There's no time for fattening or slaughtering an animal. At high seasons of the year, we might have goat or lamb,[24] but not for a spur-of-the-moment meal. Pigeons are a possibility. Maybe a dove. Chickens are much rarer than we might imagine. And even though we don't eat a lot of eggs (that's a dish for rich people), we tend not to eat our livestock, unless it's really necessary. More than likely, we will have fish. It's versatile and available in many

21 See Samuel 2:19, 2 King 2:42, Nehemiah 5:2 for references to "corn."

22. Lettuce and wild grasses would be part of our diet when eating with Jesus, but also other common vegetables were radishes, onions, squash, leeks, garlic, kale, pine nuts, lentils, chickpeas, fava beans, and peas.

23. One source suggested there were 800 different forms of edible locusts: https://blog.adw.org/2014/07/yes-they-ate-locust-a-review-of-some-the-common-foods-at-the-time-of-jesus/

24. Family livestock was slaughtered for festival and planned parties. Given the problems of cold storage, any slaughtered animal needed to be consumed soon after it was roasted. That being the case, one would invite neighbors and friends to join in. The communal party became an imperative. And as hosts, we would serve our circle with our "fatted" calf, so to speak, in the knowledge that when their livestock need to be killed, we would be invited to their feast. Think of it as the dinner party social safety net.

forms: dried, salted, grilled, or baked. Perhaps, once the invitation to Jesus was made, we sent a son[25] out to try his luck on the seashore. Whatever he brings back will be a welcome addition to our feast. Fish combines well with many vegetables and spices and comes in a size that can be easily consumed at one sitting. And it's available to any who have patience. For that reason, no doubt, Jesus uses fish often as the basis for his meals with his followers.[26]

It may well be that the flash point for Judean rebellious feelings centered around the shifting nature of fish in the common person's diet—once they were free and available to any, who had the time and means to catch them. But as taxes and licenses increase in the time of Herod Antipas, it may well be that fish became a restricted commodity—caught only by those who had paid for the privilege. Everyone, from town aristocrat to village housewife would resent having to pay for something that was so central to daily eating and which had been, until recently, the cheapest and easiest source of protein. Is this why Jesus came down to the seashore for his ministry instead of staying in the mountains surrounding Nazareth? It was among the fishers that there was a real appetite for change. They had "ears to hear" Jesus' call to the join the Kingdom of God.

Of course, each of these added ingredients of vegetables, protein, greens, and fruits would be combined according to local customs and family traditions. In our case, let's follow up the bread dish with a tabbouleh-like salad of fresh greens and cracked barley and then progress to a simple grilled fish, nestled in a bed of sliced cucumbers. We'll finish off with figs dipped in sweet yogurt and end with a bowl of deep-fired, sweetened locusts.

That's the content of the menu; but there is much more to having Jesus for dinner than ingredients. What will happen? What are the rules? What is proper etiquette in first-century Palestine?

25. It's not just that a son would be available to do this work for the household; kids are able to pass under the radar of licensing officials who would otherwise penalize an adult for fishing "without a license," so to speak. See the next paragraph for the explanation of how fishing had become a taxable activity.

26. Apart from the centrality of fish featured in the feeding of the multitudes' stories found in all four gospels, cooked fish is also an important aspect of his post-Easter appearances. For instance, Jesus greets his disciples after the resurrection by the sea of Galilee with grilled fish (John 21:9). In the gospel of Luke, the disciples give Jesus some boiled fish, when he says he is hungry—a sign that he is "bodily" resurrected (Luke 24:42).

THE KEY INGREDIENTS: HONOR, VULNERABILITY, AND COMMUNITY

Let's begin with a common assumption made by the people who have invited Jesus and followers to dinner . . . one that is mostly invisible to modern eyes. The most valuable commodity of that ancient world is honor. And eating together is all about honor. There was material wealth, of course, and one needed a modicum of exchangeable items to survive or at least to trade for things that could not be produced on the family plot of land. Certainly, the rich enjoyed a much higher standard of living and life expectancy—so wealth was revered, if not coveted. But money was not the key source of valuation. The family's honor was.

Honor is a combination of perceived righteousness, good standing among neighbors, moral stature, and unswerving loyalty to commonly accepted social expectations.

Honor was conferred publicly through subtle gestures of deference and gratitude. It was part of a family's heritage, embodied in the head of the household and reinforced by the allegiance and constancy of family members. One's honor was recognized in public circles—through unspoken signals of esteem and the allocation of privileged positions.

To a highly mobile, modern audience, honor seems to be a fleetingly thin basis on which to pin one's self-esteem. I have trouble finding a comparison. In some eastern provinces of Canada, former British colonies, one might find a similar reverence for "United Empire Loyalists" —those who fled the independent United States during the war of 1776. And one could also associate the reverence for "fine, churchgoing" people evident in some small U.S. and Canadian towns, as a faint facsimile of first-century honor. But it's a stretch. Does one's standing on a social media platform make a good comparison? Honor is equal to plenty of "likes."

Honor is the job of the head of the household, and it is most at play during the meal. A host is required to show careful and extravagant care in the reception of guests. It's not just a social nicety, it's part of the structure of valuation—a commandment of the most high. Did not Lot invite two strangers (angels from God) into his house, treating them as family? (Genesis 19). Open hospitality was the responsibility of the householder. And one's honor rested on the care of these guests. It wasn't a show or empty play-acting. In a similar fashion, guests responded to this generosity with thanksgiving and propriety. There is no need to think of exaggerated flattery or extravagant selflessness on either side. While it is less important today, most hosts and guests abide by the same, unwritten rules of behavior: giving and receiving goodwill as part of the enjoyment of shared food.

And given the proximity of guests to each other and the host, the meal sets the scene for a defenseless time, when each one's physical need, and by extension their weakness, is made evident to all. Eating is a time of exposure, when we are least capable of defending ourselves. So, the offer to Jesus to join us for a meal is an invitation into shared vulnerability.

The antidote to the practiced helplessness of eating is community. Rather than feeling in danger at dinner, genuine community restores common strength and gives to the participants in a shared meal a real physical and spiritual sense of security and well-being. That's the goal of every good host: to make the solid connections, to bring restoration, satisfaction, and health to the guests, and to establish a community of mutual affection and respect.

Part of the structure in the community of a meal is the etiquette that surrounds it. First, there would be a mutually agreed upon level of hygiene. We would come to the shared platters with clean hands (perhaps our host would have provided water and wash towels), we would keep our feet as far away from the food as possible. Not only were feet unhygienic, having walked through germ-infested fields, as I mentioned above, they were considered to be the lowest part of the body—not mentioned in polite company.

As part of our upbringing in this culture, we would know that there is an order to dipping into the common dish. The host governs the process, granting to the most honored guest the right to eat first. One waited one's turn after that, a turn allocated according to one's position in the family or level of perceived privilege. It goes without saying that one did not grab food preemptively. Likewise, one waited to be served wine or to be invited to serve oneself.

HOW JESUS MAKES THE MEAL HOLY

When we invited Jesus to come for dinner, we were not foolish. We know his reputation: how he is derided by his detractors as a glutton and boor. We've been warned by our neighbors more than once—since we made that invitation—how he welcomes every sort of reprobate and backslider to share food at his table. There's a serious risk in this dinner.

And yet, as righteous and well-read Jews, we know that hospitality to those we do not know, who are strange to us, is part of our heritage. Faithful adherence to God's commandments requires it. Seeing an itinerant band on the road, we recall how we were once like that—sojourning in the wilderness. Seeing Jesus as a wanderer, we are reminded of the commandment: "You shall treat the stranger who sojourns with you as the native among you, and you shall love him as yourself, for you were strangers in the land of Egypt: I am the Lord your God" (Lev. 19:34). Devotion to hospitality is linked irrevocably to trust in God, who is the ultimate householder and host. So, we welcome the stranger. But what will he do?

From our modern perspective, we have no real evidence to suggest how exactly Jesus will act at our dinner. The gospels speak often of his meal fellowship but rarely of what he specifically says or does. Apart from the four stories (all related) that describe a woman anointing Jesus—a story we shall examine closely in the next chapter—we hear mostly of the final result of his shared dinners. People are transformed. The meal is miraculous. Crowds gather from everywhere to be in his company. It's healing and appealing.

If we backtrack from the way people have been changed by his dinner fellowship, we might assume two things. First, he is able during the meal to rearrange power relationships. The meek are lifted up (unnamed woman in Mark 14:9) and the powerful are made humble (Simon in Luke 7:36–50). Second, Jesus embraces the outsiders, the rejected ones that "good" people have scorned, and brings them into his circle (Levi in Luke 5:31, the unnamed woman in Luke 7:44). However, none of us was present at those meals, so much of what we say is conjecture. But I have two stories to relate in conclusion to this chapter which remind me that strangers can restore us to health—the first is a story from a drunk tank and the second, from a church hall.

First, the drunk tank. When Apartheid was still in force in South Africa, many people outside the country opposed it. As part of that movement, I joined a group of non-violent protesters, who tried to serve the South African High Commissioner to Canada with an arrest warrant for crimes against humanity. Needless to say, I got two steps onto the High Commission grounds before I was tackled by a police officer and sent to the local drunk tank to cool off. There must have been 100 of us stuck together—most were strangers, everyone was frightened. What would happen next? How long would we be held without access to washrooms, food, or water? Among the crowd was a South African agitator. Someone said he had just been released from jail as an ANC operative. No one really knew him, but he started us singing. It was a simple tune—the chorus was easy to mimic, and at every verse, there was a blank space. The activist invited everyone in turn to insert the name of their "hero" in that blank space, and we would then sing the verse and chorus in honor of that person. We heard Nelson Mandala mentioned, of course, and Mahatma Gandhi. Nellie McClung and Tommy Douglas were at the top of some Canadians' lists, the Beatles made an appearance, as did Bob Dylan. All our spiritual leaders visited us in that drunk tank. It took an hour or more to go right around the circle, and in those 60 minutes, fear was dispelled, and hope was renewed.

It sounds melodramatic now to recount, but those of us, who were present, were deeply moved. We came into that drunk tank humiliated and afraid. And when we left, we knew new boldness—the courage of our convictions. This was the work of that stranger. We didn't know him, but his spirit was infectious. From this personal experience, I can confirm that a single encounter with an exceptional individual can be transformative: the meek are lifted up.

The second story was repeated in my presence often in our church hall, so I know it wasn't just a one-time thing. In the community where I served in downtown Toronto, we would regularly have Sunday lunches. It was our custom to welcome everyone and anyone, who was able to eat, to join us for a meal. Some of the underhoused on our street corner would come in for the food. There was one fellow who liked our Sunday meals. Let's call him Victor. He was always in a rough way. Unable to get a regular shower, he suffered from some serious hygienic issues. Perhaps he was incontinent. Whatever the problem, Victor's body odor was pungent and legendary. It would proceed him into a room, and even his fellows would stand at a distance—they knew better. No one would sit near him.

No doubt, Victor's isolation and rejection was part of the considerable weight that crushed his spirit. He would mumble and apologize his way through the line at the banquet table. Taking his heaped plate, by habit, Victor would seek out a space away from the crowd—a corner where he could eat without disturbing others: self-isolation writ large.

In that church community we had two leaders, a married couple, immigrants from Germany. They had worked for decades to build and sustain that church. And they were the unofficial hosts of every congregational gathering. By the time I was a minister with them, the man, Horst, was well into his eighties. Nevertheless, he would come daily to the church to repair drywall and install washrooms and automatic doors. A quiet, understated man. Those who met him might think he was the epitome of the conservative, uptight Christian: an older male with stern looks, always sporting a bow tie. He might come across a little rough and tough.

But if you join us for lunch after church, you will see who Horst really is. Wherever Victor went to sit to be alone, Horst would join him. Not patronizing, Horst engaged Victor, as he would any member of the congregation. There were plenty of family groups, including his own, who would have welcomed Horst to sit with them, but he chose to be with Victor, the outsider. I can't say that Victor was cured of his physical condition, but having Horst share a lunch with him healed, in some small measure, his wounded spirit. He was no longer an outsider.

I am asked regularly why I put up with Christians, given our dark history and the intermittent, personal animosity I have experienced, and my reply is Horst. Here is someone who had every opportunity to ignore a ragged reject. But far from walking past, he joined him in shared bread. The lost are found.

Not everyone would agree with me. Believers can be offended by how and with whom we eat. Many at the time of Jesus complained about his meal fellowship. Whatever he did or said while dining with others disturbed them profoundly, and it's to learn from these naysayers that we turn to the next chapter.

Sourdough: where it all begins

MAKING THE STARTER

It takes seven days to make a sourdough starter. As I have said elsewhere, bread takes time, sourdough especially. Once made, it requires daily "feeding" and can be used once a week to make bread.[1]

The cheese bread recipe below is one of my favorites and a best seller on the Piper's Buns bake stand.

Let's begin by making the sourdough starter.

On Day #1, get a clean 1liter jar; fashion a lid/covering from cheese cloth that can be held over the top with an elastic. In this jar, mix (with a fork): ½ cup whole wheat flour and ¼ cup warm water. Set in a warm place for 24 hours.

On Day #2, you may see small bubbles appearing on the surface of the sourdough, and there may be a brown liquid (hooch).

On Day #3, pour off any hooch. Discard half the starter and, with a fork, mix in ½ cup flour and ¼ cup warm water. It should be the consistency of pancake batter—a bit stretchy. Add more water, if necessary, so that it is a smooth batter.

On Day #4 follow the same steps as Day #3.

On Days #5 and #6 follow the same steps as Day #3, except do not discard half the starter.

On Day #7, your starter should be double its original size, and it should have bubbles throughout. Mix it one last time with a fork. Give your starter a name (this is a must . . . mine is "Lázaro," Spanish for Lazarus—the friend who Jesus raised from the dead— John 11:38–44).

1. If you need it, you can use your sourdough daily. Just increase the quantities listed above. After the initial seven-day period to make sourdough, it will then be ready to use at whatever frequency you like. Don't forget to keep feeding it. If you are unable to use your sourdough for an extended time, you can slow it down considerably by putting the jar in the fridge. In that case, it can keep for up to a month and still be useable, once it is brought back to room temperature and fed for a few days.

A CHEESE SOURDOUGH

Grate 1 lb. of sharp cheddar cheese and set aside.

Break one egg and stir it into a smooth mixture and set aside.

Mix 1 cup sourdough starter with 4 cups flour and 1 ½ cups warm water, a Tablespoon of salt and 2/3 of the grated cheese.[2] When the dough is spongy, flip it onto a floured bread board and knead for 7–10 minutes. (Sing "Happy Birthday" 15 times.)

Place this dough in a greased bowl, cover with a wet cloth, and allow it to rise for three hours.

Turn out the dough and cut into four equal size pieces. (They should weigh approximately 150 gm each.) Shape into a tight round ball.

Grease four small 5" pie plates or line them with parchment, and place one ball in each.

Paint the top and sides of each ball thoroughly with the egg wash, and divide up the remaining cheese to sprinkle on top of each loaf.

Set the four loaves in a warm place and allow to rise for 4–8 hours. (This works well as an overnight bread. Place it on the counter before you go to sleep, and upon rising, it's ready to put in the oven.)

Bake at 350 degrees F. for 35–45 minutes; allow it to cool for 30 minutes before slicing.

NB

Once established, you can maintain your sourdough and use it at the frequency you desire by following the feeding steps listed under days #5 and #6 above. You should have enough sourdough starter to repeat the above seven-day process and make another recipe . . . so the sourdough has a life of its own. Some neighbors, on the island where I live, swear that their sourdough has lasted for years. Good luck!

---

2. One baker I know adds a small teaspoon of instant dry yeast to his sourdough . . . giving his bread the advantage of a quick rising while still keeping the tart flavor of sourdough. In that case, the second rising would be no more than 3 hours.

4

"He Eats with Them" . . .
Weighing the Complaints

It is easy enough to be friendly to one's friends. But to befriend the one who regards himself as your enemy is the quintessence of true religion. The other is mere business.[1] *—Mahatma Gandhi*

INTRODUCTION: THERE HE WASN'T

I couldn't believe my eyes. There Jesús wasn't. Not a trace of his cart, the waiting crowd, and most importantly, there wasn't a single one of his delicious ham sandwiches in sight.

It's 8 o'clock in the morning. I'm already sweating. It's Cuba, and I'm hungry. Jesús' food is my breakfast. They're called "Bocaditos" . . . "little mouthfuls," and they are the best in town.

"What! No bocaditos?" Was I too late? Had Jesús been abducted by sandwich thieves?

It had been an hour and thirty-five minutes of tough slogging, biking up and down the hills of Matanzas, the town in Cuba where the seminary is located at which I am teaching and writing. I was ready for my early morning treat. My trusted bike and I had been performing this daily, early morning exercise for three weeks now. Ninety minutes into the ride, I get my reward. After the hot, hungry work, I'd coast into Jesús' refreshment stand. He's the sandwich man, and we have become an item.

1. Gandhi and Merton, *Gandhi on Non-violence*, 62.

"Jesús" is a common Cuban name,[2] so there's no need to think of him as special or pretentious.

Here's my routine. Just after 8:00 a.m., I'd cycle up to his stand at the main intersection in town, wearing a red bike shirt, something that is rare in a world with nothing. And Jesús is decked out in an equally extravagant manner for a sandwich seller: a chef's uniform, white hat, apron, even white shoes. He's a real show—the only street vender I know who sports plastic sanitary gloves! I'm impressed!

When Jesús sees me coming, he starts preparing my favorite breakfast: fresh bread, slices of tomato, heaps of his newly carved ham, and a brown sauce to die for (I think it's oil, dry mustard, sugar and garlic, but I have never asked). He smiles broadly and has a word about baseball or the weather, whenever I stop. We joke about how it's easier to bike in the diesel fumes of passing trucks than snow storms of Canada. I began with only one bocadito. After 20 days, I am up to three.

There is something so comfortingly simple and charming in our camaraderie. It's about bread . . . a common language around the globe. So, when one morning, Jesús was not at his usual spot, I was left strangely empty. It wasn't just my hunger. More than nourishment, I was missing the connection. Sharing food forges links that are impossible any other way.

I tried another stall down the street, but it wasn't the same. Bread, served by a friend, tastes so much better than that which we get anonymously—[3] a fact not lost on the people of God as they passed from the wilderness, where they freely received daily bread from God's hand, and entered into the promised land, where the bread was sold by the king. Call it the first fact about bread: it is more than just flour, and water, and yeast. Bread is communion. The king's bread is never as flavorful as the loaves of homemade bread we received from our grandmother's labors, because the stuff we get at a box store or supermarket has no strings attached. There is no continuity between the work and dedication that inspire the one who makes the bread and the delight arising in the person who eats it. Without that connection between oven and table, the dead bread sold in most shops neither implies nor elicits an ongoing relationship. Certainly, you get what you pay for: a starch product designed as a delivery system for butter, cheese, or meat. But, as we all can testify, real bread can be so much more.

2. There are plenty of guys named "Jesús," and many go by the common pet name given to those with that name: "Chuchi." But my friend preferred his real name: "Jesús."

3. If you have been feeling strangely disconcerted when I tell a story in a pedestrian way about "Jesús" as an ordinary guy as opposed to the revered and holy "Jesus" of the bible, then you are working your way back into the gospel stories when Jesus was just one of the guys, a special man, but a man nonetheless.

Am I right?

Since communion is the first fact of bread, it goes without saying that it lies behind the appeal and success of Jesus' Kingdom movement. A shared loaf establishes connection and acceptance. It brings delight to the baker and the receiver. I have yet to be met with a sour face, when I show up at the door with fresh, warm bread. How can you argue with that?

So why did so many people oppose Jesus and his bread movement? Certainly, the religious authorities of his day did not appreciate his vision and then gossiped about his little community—called Jesus names, claiming he was not what he should or could be as a spiritual leader. What was at the heart of their complaints? How can anyone be opposed to the community of shared bread? Were they jealous—wanting the acclaim and trust of the people which Jesus seemed to enjoy? Was it fear? They sensed Jesus was taking the people down the road to unrest, which would not only undermine the authority of temple officials. His ideas of free bread could also disrupt the careful balance of accommodation to Roman occupation worked out on a village-by-village basis.

Maybe the complainers were just ordinary people, who resent change or who are so unhappy in themselves that they see other people's joy as an affront. If we are going to understand how Jesus' Kingdom movement shifted from one focused on a common shared meal to one based on a sacralised, exclusive ritual, then why not look closely at these complaints. Sometimes our detractors know more than we are willing to admit—to others of course, but especially to ourselves. Perhaps they can teach us some new lessons about Jesus and his fellowship.

Jesus asked his followers to love their enemies (Matthew 5:44), and Gandhi argued that the sign of a truly religious person is that they can befriend the ones who are enemies.[4] It may be impossible to have an emotional affection for the gossipers and detractors of Jesus, but we might accord them that form of friendship which takes their complaints seriously. Can we look into the gospels and see Jesus from their perspective and understand their misgivings? What can they teach us that we need to learn?

Again, let me be clear that I am not assuming the gospels are offering us a historically accurate picture of the disputes Jesus had with his disparagers. But we can imagine that the complaints found in the gospels themselves were examples of the confrontations met by the evangelists and their communities, as the Way of Jesus spread through the first century. In that sense, they reflect the frictions felt by several generations after Jesus lived. It follows that the way these criticisms are presented and resolved in the

---

4. See footnote 1 above.

scriptures will illustrate both how the followers of Jesus adapted their message to suit the demands of their time and how these complaints captured the misgivings of the wider culture. This is a rich resource for expanding our awareness of the development, appeal, and growth of Jesus' Kingdom of God undertaking.

ISN'T THIS THE CARPENTER?[5]

In a manner similar to the question of Jesus' identity (chapter 2), I followed a straightforward method of examining the Jesus detractors and what they said. Reading all the synoptic gospels carefully, I compiled and categorized the content of the complaints and the identity of the complainants. After some judicious organizing, it became clear that Jesus' actions and deeds were criticized from two major points of view: (1) how and with whom he ate, and (2) his authority to heal and preach as he did. There are also a number of miscellaneous complaints, some of which developed over time into serious disparaging reproaches. Let's start with these random denunciations and then progress through to the major issue: "he eats with tax collectors and sinners."[6]

First up: Jesus was nothing more than a peasant handyman living in a backwater village so small it doesn't even appear on the map. Not messiah material; he's nothing more than a fraud and a farce.

During the 2008 US presidential election and after, there was considerable energy devoted to the birthplace of Barak Obama. Eventually called "the birther conspiracy," conservatives and racists argued that Obama was not born in Hawaii as he claimed, but in Kenya . . . thus being ineligible to be President. Genealogy is important—even still today.

In first-century Palestine, it was also an issue. You got your authority, at least in a superficial way, from your family and their place within the hierarchical aristocratic structure of Judea. The Roman occupation notwithstanding, one's prospects for achieving honor and power were shaped by birth.

One of the initial, perhaps first, complaints about Jesus comes from his own hometown. They don't believe that one of their own could be revered as a spiritual leader. Familiarity breeds contempt. You can hear them so

---

5. Mark 6:3 states clearly that Jesus is a carpenter (*tekton*). In Matthew 13:55 he is named as the" son of a carpenter." A *tekton* was a first-century "handyman." Perhaps Matthew wants to avoid such a pedestrian association with his Jesus and makes him merely the son of a working-class guy.

6. For a comprehensive list of complaints see the Appendix of this text.

clearly. "Isn't this just the town carpenter? We know him. He's Mary's son, brother of James and Salome. They live right here beside us" (Mark 6:1–6). By implication, these detractors are saying, "Who does he think he is?" "He's no better than the rest of us." "He comes from nowhere." The complaint might just be the product of hometown gossip. There's a pernicious side to human nature, wanting to tear down those we think we know—especially if we think they are being pretentious. We remind them that they began as we did. We downplay their importance or virtue, so that we do not feel like we are left behind or less worthy. It's a form of jealousy or envy disguised as down-home loyalty and common sense.

What may have begun as petty backbiting grew to be one of the chief criticisms leveled at Jesus' followers, once their brand of Judaism grew to be a social movement of prominence. Jesus was a false messiah, not even a full-blooded Jew. Celsus,[7] a second century philosopher, gave voice to what he claimed as a common assertion that Jesus was an illegitimate son of a gentile. He had no royal affiliations or credentials, and his Jewishness was suspect. And while this complaint is not directly stated in the gospels, it obviously was prominent enough for both Matthew and Luke to create their own genealogies and birth stories, so that Jesus was given a proper Davidic heritage and birthright. In addition, Matthew calls Jesus "son of David" ten times, making it abundantly clear that he has the right royal lineage.

You may have noticed that Matthew's gospel particularly tries to root Jesus in the biblical heritage of the prophets and the law. It may well be that he is responding to the criticism that Jesus is not really a Jew. Or if he was Jewish, that he wasn't sufficiently mindful of the scriptures. Matthew is the proof against such false claims and slander. In the first gospel, you can hardly move from one chapter to the next, in Jesus' ministry, without it being accompanied by a scriptural reference. By one count, Matthew makes reference to or alludes to a biblical passage 96 times[8] in his gospel. And while Luke makes Jesus out to be a traveling preacher and healer, Matthew portrays him as a much more rooted spiritual leader. To the Jewish ear trained to hear allusions to past prophets and leaders, Matthew's Jesus appears to be speaking like a new Moses—especially in the Sermon on the Mount, when he claims he is bringing a "new" law to the people. How much more righteous can you get?

7. In Origen of Alexandria's *Contra Celsum* , he quoted criticism from this second century Greek philosopher, who ridiculed Jesus by stating that some Jewish leaders said Jesus was the illegitimate son of a Roman soldier, Panthera. 423.

8. For a complete list go to: https://catholic-resources.org/Bible/Matthew-OTQuotations.htm

What does this first complaint teach us? Certainly, his detractors are feeling threatened by his rise in popularity. The attack on his lineage and authority has racist, classist undertones. We're operating on a level of discontent that is visceral—not open to reason. Jesus and his popularity are touching on some very sensitive nerves—perhaps he's undermining our deeply held dreams, our hopes for a violent, punitive leader, who would give the Romans the thrashing they deserve. Whatever the source, Jesus was clearly not what some people expected from a messiah. No matter his deeds, he just doesn't fit the bill.

BE HEALED . . . NOT ON THE SABBATH

If Jesus spent much of his time healing the sick and was presumed to have an authority in word and deed that few others possessed (Mark 1:22), it is instructive to note that the gospels contain only one specific complaint against his healing ministry—repeated multiple times in various formats.[9] Let's examine the passage found in Luke's gospel, chapter 13. It is a variant of many other healing stories. At the synagogue gathering there is a woman, bent with infirmity, that has lasted eighteen years.[10] Interestingly, she does not ask for help, but Jesus calls to her, and lays his hands on her, and she is instantly healed.

The complaint by the local synagogue leader is that healing, which he construed as work, is inappropriate for the sabbath. Surely, Jesus, you can heal at some other time! On the surface, it's a pretty flimsy complaint— sounds much more like nit-picking born of sour grapes. In Mark's telling of this story (Mark 3:1–6), the one in need of healing is a man with a withered hand. The detractors in this case are Pharisees. They did not come with an open mind and were therefore not taken by surprise by Jesus' actions. Rather, they had arrived at the synagogue already hoping to find something objectionable in what Jesus was doing. They, too, latched onto sabbath rest requirements as a reason to object to Jesus. "He's working on God's holy day." But as Jesus points out, this is not a very sound argument. Is not the sabbath day a time for doing good? he suggested. In yet another variant of this story, Jesus argues in Luke (Luke 14:5) that any sane, righteous Jew would "work" on the sabbath day to save an ox or a child that had fallen into a well. How is healing any different? No argument is offered in rebuttal.

9. See Luke 13:14, Mark 3:6, Matthew 12:19, Luke 14:1–6, Luke 6:6–10,

10. It is interesting to note how this healing story gives a specific length of time that the infirmity lasted—no doubt to quell the skeptics who might suggest it was only a momentary illness.

Clearly outwitted, these detractors are either silent or they go away looking for some other means to entrap Jesus and even to "murder"[11] him.

Coming from a religious world myself, I am used to complaints, and these ones feel very much like issues of power and control. Jesus is usurping the religious leaders in the place where they would want and expect to have full jurisdiction. How dare he take over our show! Who gives him the right to mess with our rituals and traditions? We'll speak more of this issue of spiritual authority, below.

It could also be that the complaints about Jesus' healing on the sabbath were more of an evangelistic device than a historical fact. Is it possible the gospel writers include them to discredit synagogue leaders, in general, and the Pharisees, in particular, who were, in fact, the chief religious opposition to Jesus at the time the gospels were being written? After the fall of the temple in 70 CE, Pharisaic Judaism was the main competition down the street, so to speak. So, we paint them as conniving and mean-spirited—even denying people their access to healing. In this regard, it is noteworthy that these tales all end with the triumph of Jesus. His compassion wins the day, while his detractors appear to have small hearts and even smaller wits. In a perverse way, their complaints are a compliment to the healer Jesus.

That being said, it is of particular note that no one in the gospel record complains about the actual healing itself. Apart from the instance when the people of the region Gerasenes (Mark 5:17) ask Jesus to leave, because his healing has been so thorough, no one disparages or questions his ability to heal. Nor do they doubt the consequences of his healing actions. No one suggests he isn't a very good healer or that his cures only last a few days. There isn't a single suggestion that he is a charlatan. Below, we will examine how some suggest that his power over evil spirits comes from the fact that he himself is a devil. But even then, no one argues that his acts of healings are fake or unreal.

And it is important to remember that, during the time of Jesus, there were plenty of examples of other healers: the Greek God, Asclepius; Honi, the circle drawer; Apollonius of Tanya. Even the future emperor, Vespian, was credited with two miraculous healings. Presumably there were also many lesser-known traveling miracle workers and healers. But no one in the gospels makes comparisons between Jesus and these others. In the initial ministry described in Mark's gospel (Mark 1:22), Jesus is said to "speak" with

---

11. In Mark 3:6, the complainants leave and consult with Herodians on how they might "kill" Jesus. Unlike the Pharisees. Herodians are not well-known. Historical evidence is sparse, but from their name, one might presume that they were a conservative movement seeking to reassert or somehow reinstate a Herodian dynasty in Israel, free from Roman interference.

an authority that others do not possess. And we are left with the impression that his healing also had few precedents.

We can surmise, from the lack of complaints regarding his healing ministry, that the Jesus movement, as it grew, did not face opposition from critics who questioned Jesus' healing ability. He may have come from the wrong side of the tracks, but there seems to be little room or appetite for undermining the fledging Jesus followers by discrediting his miraculous power. And this is remarkable, since, as we determined above, his healing ministry was one of the three major activities that took up his time and perhaps the central reason for his initial success and popularity.

Could it be that, at the time of writing the gospels, the miracles of healing were a distant memory? Perhaps the Jesus movement, in its third and fourth generations, did not boast of Jesus' power to cure illnesses so much as his continued presence.

Is there anything these detractors can teach us? I could be flippant and repeat that old adage "no good deed goes unpunished."[12] And there is some truth to that. The depth of compassion shown by Jesus inspires a "naughty" reflex in those of us who are less than perfect. These complaints also point to an unfortunate fact about false religion. Wanting to preserve its own power rather than promote virtue, it inspires the kind of hypocrisy that rejects the very goodness we claim to admire. And as I see the religious leaders wagging a finger at Jesus when he oversteps a long-held boundary, I feel both the shame and guilt of having done the same thing.

Whatever the lessons to be learned, healing does not stir up much fuss in the gospels. And we can move on from these miscellaneous minor complaints to the two major objections posed by Jesus' detractors: (1) he doesn't have the proper authority to be a spiritual leader or messiah; (2) he undermines or belittles his righteousness by his eating habits and meal practice. Since these two issues have a logical connection, we'll turn to the question of authority and conclude this chapter with Jesus' dinner fellowship.

"ARE YOU THE MESSIAH?"

The question of Jesus' authority has roots in his landless, laborer background. All the language of "solidarity with the marginalized" and "preferential option for the poor" notwithstanding, in the context of Jesus, people without land were nothing. There was no nobility, either emotional

---

12. This inverted moralism is first attested to in Walter Maps 12th-century *De nugis curialium,* in which a perverse character "left no good deed unpunished, no bad one unrewarded." http://en.wikipedia.org/wiki/No_good_deed_goes_unpunished

or spiritual, attached to the role of being a peasant. "Salt of the earth," is a piece of nineteenth-century romanticism. Jesus was a *tekton (carpenter/ hand-man)* or the son of that sort of common laborer. That's not a very flattering occupation and certainly not one from which a messiah is born. He's probably illiterate,[13] has very few connections in the upper classes, and is viewed by people in power as less than nothing. He is certainly not one with any kind of social or religious authority. Hence the complaints and the jibes, when Jesus comes to the temple mount. He might have been viewed as a "somebody" in small town Capernaum, but in Jerusalem, he's one in a long line of pretenders. So, it is natural that he should be questioned and criticized about his presumed "right" to speak of holy things.

Of all the complaints about Jesus, the one centering on his "authority" makes the most sense to a religious audience, even in the twenty-first century. Legitimacy is key to orderly practice and a trustworthy community of faith. If we must have a leader, and most religious organizations would say that leadership is necessary, then there should be some means for testing and validating any who seek that role. In our modern world, leadership is vetted through spiritual structures, tested in practical internships, and accredited through a recognized educational institution.

While not using exactly the same names and procedures, leadership at the time of Jesus was tested in similar ways. Aspiring spiritual leaders were mentored by a teacher—perhaps for years. They would be schooled by other disciples of this teacher and, over time, given more and more responsibility. Depending on the teacher, this mentorship might include literacy training. It would certainly be supported by meditative or prayerful exercises, and as the years passed, one gained "stature" and was seen to have "authority." In this case, you don't get spiritual credentials just because you want them. They have to be earned and the detractors of Jesus are reasonably skeptical. Where did this guy come from? Who is his teacher? What testimonies or references does he have to prove he's genuine?

There is an advantage to reading the gospels carefully and in the sequence most scholars believe they were written. Obvious patterns begin to emerge. For instance, the empty tomb gets more crowded and more majestic as we move through time.[14] In a similar manner, as I mentioned above,

---

13. No doubt, you will quote the passages of scripture where Jesus stands up to read (Luke 4:16b), but it is more than likely that he was doing as many contemporaries did. He memorized the scriptures as a child and repeated them verbatim as an adult.

14. In Mark 16:1–8. The gospel written first tells us there were three named women who came to the tomb and they saw a single "young man dressed in a white robe (Mark 16:5)." In Matthew, there is a guard of Roman soldiers at the tomb, two named women approach; the young man has been turned into an angel (Matthew 28:3), and

Jesus becomes more self-aware and confident as he moves from one gospel to the next. With regard to complaints about Jesus' authority, the majority of detractors in Mark are chief priests and temple authorities, with the Pharisees putting in a relatively small appearance. But in Matthew, the Pharisees take the main stage and become the target of Jesus' blistering critique of temple Judaism, its diverse stipulations and commandments, and its many traditions.[15]

Let's look at the specific complaints of Jesus' authority . . . they come largely during his time when he was preaching on the temple mount. Beginning with Mark, let's do a simple comparison with Matthew's account. In Mark, chapter 12, we can list his critics as follows:[16]

1. Chief priests and scholars bent on arresting or killing Jesus are mentioned five times.

2. Only once do the Pharisees (along with Herodians) want to "trick" or catch Jesus in an error.

Turning to Matthew's gospel account of the same temple discourses, the range of detractors and conspirators shifts and increases substantially:

1. Chief priests and scholars are mentioned four times.

2. Pharisees are either questioning Jesus or the brunt of his criticisms fourteen times.[17]

---

his appearance is like lightning. In Luke, the women are not named and the one angel of Matthew has been replaced by two men whose clothes are like lightning (Like 24:3). In John's gospel (John 20:1) the "women" have been reduced to Mary of Magdala . . . who does not enter the tomb at all, and instead two male disciples run to the tomb and enter it. No angels or men in white; Jesus himself is walking in a resurrected form in the garden. There is a two-fold progression through the gospels: majesty is increased and glorified, while the presence and importance of women is diminished.

15 Some might suggest that Jesus' vindictive diatribe found in Matthew 23:33–35 is close to "hate speech," when it is seen through the lens of Christian anti-Judaism.

16. Mark 11:18 After the "cleansing of the temple" the chief priests and teachers of the law look for a way to kill Jesus.

Mark 11: 27 The chief priests and teachers of the law question Jesus' authority.

Mark 12:12 The chief priests and teachers of the law look for a way to arrest Jesus after the parable of the talents.

Mark 12:13 The Pharisees and Herodians ask about paying taxes.

Mark 12:18 The Sadducees ask about eternal life.

Mark 12:28 Teachers of the law ask about the greatest commandment.

Mark 12:38 Jesus warns against the teachers of the law.

17. Matthew 21:14 Chief priests and scholars are indignant when the crowds hail Jesus as "Son of David."

Matthew 21:23: Chief priests and elders of the people question Jesus' authority.

Clearly, from the first gospel written to the second, we have a dramatic increase in the number instances the Pharisees are portrayed as the chief enemy of Jesus and his ideas.

It could be argued that Matthew had access to a more fulsome report of those four days of preaching on the temple mount. Perhaps he knew an eyewitness with a better memory whom Mark could not or did not consult. Was Matthew privy to oral or written traditions that had not surfaced when Mark was writing his account?

At this stage, we are left with conjecture about the differences between the two gospel accounts. I take it as a given that human nature being what it is, the temptation when editing another's work is to elaborate and fill in gaps of accounts we feel are inadequate. One wants to clear up misunderstandings and make a better story. Given that Matthew does precisely that in other places,[18] I would suggest that Matthew's changes to the Markan account are his own imaginative additions to the original story.

Such a shift in adversaries is understandable, since by the time Matthew was written, the temple in Jerusalem had been destroyed by Vespasian's legions. With its demise went many of variant forms of Judaism, i.e., Zealots, Sadducees, Essenes. After Jerusalem was destroyed, Christian Judaism and Pharisaic Judaism were the two major "competitors" still standing, and each was vying to become the true expression of the Jewish heart and soul. For the gospel writers and the regular adherents to Jesus' path, what better way to discredit the opposition than to paint the Pharisees as hard-hearted and narrow-minded. They are the ones to blame for the corrupt priesthood, and it's their self-serving collaboration with the occupying Romans that resulted in Jesus' crucifixion. In a street fight, you call your opponent names, whether they deserve them or not.

But the issue of authority is also a high-level criticism. The powerful ask about it. They guard their own positions and status by limiting it. They

---

Matthew 21:28: The parable of the two sons is directed at the chief priests and scholars who did not embrace John, although prostitutes and tax collectors did.

Matthew 21:45 The chief priests and Pharisees plot to arrest Jesus.

Matthew 22:15: The Pharisees (alone . . . no Herodians mentioned) try to "trap" Jesus with the question of paying taxes.

Matthew 22:23: The Sadducees ask about resurrection.

Matthew 22:34: An expert Pharisee asks about the greatest commandment.

Matthew 22:41: Jesus directs his question of the Son of David to the Pharisees.

Matthew 23:1–36: Jesus warns against and blames the Pharisees and teachers of the law at least ten distinct times over their apparent duplicity and hypocrisy.

18 In Mark 1:27, the people of Capernaum are amazed at Jesus' preaching. "What is this?" They say, "A new teaching . . .?" But then the gospel writer does not outline what that teaching might be. Seeing this lacuna, Matthew adds the Sermon on the Mount (Matthew 5:1—7:28) to his gospel as an example of Jesus' "new teaching."

control the mob by imposing it, and they certainly aren't interested in shar-ing it—particularly with a no-name peasant from a pitiful hovel out in the sticks. So, we can assume that the question of Jesus' authority was a debate among elite religious leaders.

All their disdain notwithstanding, Jesus enjoyed the favor of the townspeople. He has his own power base, one that threatens the priestly, temple class. In Mark's gospel, we are told, several times,[19] that the spiritual rulers were intimidated by Jesus' popularity and the "authority" he enjoyed because of it.

Put bluntly: Jesus is competition. He's not presenting himself as a new "priest" or temple ruler. He doesn't want to take over, but his teachings have the effect of discrediting the temple and its practices and, by extension, the ones who do run that show. And whatever one might make of his inter-ference with the money changers and animal sellers on the Monday after his entry into Jerusalem,[20] there is no question that Jesus seems bent on disrupting, if not destroying, the proper functioning of what was, in his day, a world pilgrimage site. And those who depend on and profit from such an enterprise would quite naturally ask, "By what authority are you doing these things? . . . And who gave you authority to do this?" (Mark 11:28).

This is where I take a step back; perhaps I move to hide myself behind Jesus. As a Canadian, I was trained in good order, playing by the rules, and not jumping the queue. I don't presume to take leadership, unless I am asked and, even then, only gingerly. So, I can feel the tension in the air as the holy week progresses and Jesus gets tested time and again about his "right" to do and say what he does. Add to this emotional atmosphere the fact that Passover was a celebration of Israel's liberation and that pilgrims came to this holiest of sites to pray for that freedom to come again, and we have considerable political instability. Then, if we imagine that all this liberation

19. See Mark 11:18, Mark 12:12, Mark 14:1–2.

20. Tradition calls this act the "cleansing of the temple." In Mark's gospel, Jesus drives away the animal sellers and overturns the tables of those who would exchange gentile money for the money allowed as an offering in the temple itself. Apparently, he refuses to let people enter the temple precincts with an animal offering. One could argue that Jesus is "cleansing" this religious site of corrupt business practices. He's shutting down the commercialization of his religion. On a deeper level, it might be that Jesus is actu-ally "attacking" the temple as an illegitimate system in and of itself, since it has become a "den of thieves" (Mark 11:17). A thieves' "den" is where you hoard your treasure and hide from the police. So, the implication is that the temple authorities are storing their ill-gotten gains in the temple and escaping justice. By disrupting the proper functioning of the temple sacrificial system, Jesus is symbolically closing it down. And while that may seem to stretch credulity, for those readers who recall the peace movements of the 1960s, remember how some protesters poured blood on draft cards as a symbolic act of discrediting the entire war effort? Symbolic actions have significant power.

celebration was being watched by occupying soldiers from the palace walls overlooking the temple, we might agree with the chief priests and rulers that Passover was no time to arrest a popular, prophet-like preacher,[21] no matter where he comes from.

I can easily imagine how Jesus' presence in Jerusalem would lead to political intrigue. Temple rulers would be nervous on any account, but having a mob-supported, inspirational speaker preaching in the court of the gentiles was dangerous. It would not be a stretch to imagine the chief priest (whose nomination was approved by Rome) suggesting to his Roman counterpart that such a serious irritant was threatening the carefully constructed balance of power and control that kept "peace" within the holy city.[22]

"Let's get rid of him!"

To be clear, Jesus never claimed to have spiritual authority, nor did he pretend to have special power. Certainly, in Mark's gospel, Jesus seems to be doing the reverse. He tells those he heals not to spread the news about his gift. He wants to keep a low profile. Unlike those who know they are essentially without credibility, Jesus did not have to remind his audience about how smart he is[23] or how close he is to God. And he didn't come to Jerusalem to take over the temple or start a new religion. He brought his Kingdom of God movement to the capital city because, for better or for worse, he felt it was time to reform his religious landscape and reassert the values and principles of the God he encountered in the law and the prophets.

If Jesus had authority, it was not the result of his own boasting. It was a consequence of his teaching and healing. As mentioned above, at the very beginning of Mark's gospel, we are told that his fame spread like wild fire because he was perceived to have real "authority" (Mark 1:27). He taught like one who needs no promotion, no publicist, or propaganda machine. His deeds spoke for themselves. And Jesus' authenticity stems from the fact that he lived what he said. The Kingdom of God was not just a clever turn of phrase. It was made real every time he gathered his community for a meal.

---

21. Mark 14:1–2.

22. I would also imagine that Rome had their own reasons for wanting to eliminate Jesus. He made fun of them. What Christians call the triumphal entry into Jerusalem could also be called satirical street theater. While Pilate enters Jerusalem from the west with all the pomp and circumstance of occupying armies, Jesus enters the holy city from the east, playing the anti-king. Pilate was no neophyte when it came to the show of power, and I believe he knew quite well when he was being spoofed. Military power that is seeking to dominate an occupied territory does not have a sense of humor. And Jesus paid for his symbolic act with his life.

23. A recent President of the United States comes to mind in this regard.

Perhaps the Roman rulers could see that Jesus held "authority" because he lived out what he said, but the powerful are not usually that perceptive.[24] However, if any were to have looked closely, they would have recognized right away that he meant what he said. Jesus was appealing to his followers to live, as he did, in a world governed quite literally by God's rules. That being the case, Caesar's laws don't apply. They were irrelevant. That's treason, a crucifiable offence! Clearly some temple authorities could recognize a "true" prophet from a false one. They might have had first-hand knowledge of how his Kingdom gatherings worked or been told by informants. Either way, they could see that the words of Jesus were backed up by his deeds and that makes him especially dangerous.

If the question of "authority" brought Jesus to the attention of the Romans and their collaborators, the issue of how he lived out his preaching got him taken seriously enough that he had to be crucified.

HE WOULD KNOW WHO'S TOUCHING HIM[25]

A cursory reading of Mark reveals that Jesus' main project was the coming of the Kingdom of God. If John the Baptizer embodied his message of repentance through immersion in the cleansing water of the Jordan, Jesus made manifest the Kingdom of God in a common meal. We know this, not only from the number of times his bible stories revolve around a shared meal, but also from the number of times his detractors criticize Jesus' food practices. Of the total complaints about Jesus, the majority center on the "who" and the "how" of his eating fellowships. Captured early in the ministry of Jesus described by Mark, we get what sounds very much like a much-repeated slur: "Why does he eat with tax collectors and sinners?"[26] Something is happening at this Kingdom of God meal that annoys people, the local religious elites particularly. It may have begun as curiosity or gossip, but it soon became vindictive, and once we arrive in Jerusalem, these complaints become murderous.

What's really happening at Jesus' meal, and why is it a problem? At this point, let's do a quick summary of the three "miracles" described in

---

24. I am reminded from my days in the peace movement that the powerful had little real awareness of those they controlled—their daily lives, their passion, and fears. But those who were being controlled knew a great deal about the ones who claimed to have such authority over them.

25. Luke 7:39 When the Pharisee who had invited him saw this, he said to himself, "If this man were a prophet, he would know who is touching him and what kind of woman she is—that she is a sinner."

26. Mark 2:16b, also found at Luke 5:30 and Matthew 9:11b.

the Introduction. I believe by outlining these key characteristics of what is happening in the meal we share with Jesus, we'll be able to explore why such things are problematic. And as evidence, we'll conclude this chapter with the quintessential paradigm of Jesus and his eating etiquette *faux pas* found in the story of his dinner with Simon the Pharisee (Luke 7:36–50).

First, if Jesus made manifest the reality of the Kingdom of God through eating and feeding, it began with real food, and plenty of it. If the stories of the feeding of the multitudes are any indication, whether they are historically accurate or not, they express a truth. People came away from their encounter with Jesus having been fed real food. There is always plenty to eat. A simple and profound message: "in God's household everyone is fed." In this sense, Jesus is acting out a mission that is in keeping with the law[27] and the prophets.[28] Mealtime is not about exploitation, but on the contrary, it is a real and constant reenactment of God's will for distributive justice—everyone eats until they are satisfied. Abundance reigns.

Second, Jesus seems to invite everyone to eat with him, rich and poor, outcaste and insider. Women particularly join him at the table. And there is no distinction. All are welcomed and accepted. Quite the miracle, especially for those who have been excluded or cast out. And while there is only one complaint about Jesus eating too much,[29] there are many more that focus on this second miracle of acceptance. Indeed, in the one instance when Jesus is called a glutton, it is followed immediately by the seemingly concomitant accusation that he's eating with disreputable types.[30]

And third, while the disciples may argue about who is most important, by having an honored place in the meal circle, Jesus suggests that the best strategy is to be humble and not expect any special treatment.[31] In other words, the fellowship of Jesus is a true circle of equals and not a pyramid of power. His meals were a reflection and embodiment of that principle.

27. In Leviticus 25, the stipulations of God's jubilee year, in which distributive justice is the key factor, are outlined . . . none shall be exploited forever. Likewise, those who are poor are protected from paying exorbitantly for their food (Leviticus 25:37), since all should be able to eat and enjoy God's creation.

28. The prophet Isaiah echoes other prophets (Amos, Micah), who proclaim that God's rule over the earth will end food insecurity. Isaiah 55: 1–3 "Come, all you who are thirsty, come to the waters; and you who have no money, come, buy and eat! Come, buy wine and milk without money and without cost."

29. Matthew 11:19 and Luke 7:34 contain the exact same complaint, and it appears that they are sharing the same story.

30. Matthew 11:19: "The Son of Man came eating and drinking, and they say, 'Here is a glutton and a drunkard, a friend of tax collectors and sinners.'"

31. Luke 14:10.

So, what's the problem? Why would anyone complain about Jesus' eating practices. Is the abundance of food wrong? Can acceptance of outsiders as equals be misconstrued? Are women really not welcome at a banquet? Is there an issue with equal power and agency within a meal fellowship? To understand the complaints about Jesus' meal fellowship, we have to understand the values and presuppositions that governed his world.

Every culture has its own ethical inclinations that dictate public behavior. For instance, by in large, Canadians prefer order over individual rights. Lining up to buy coffee is not just logical, it is a moral necessity. Americans choose individuality over collective good. They'll put up with considerable social chaos, if it means they can continue to carry their own firearm, for instance. The French favor excellence and finesse, while the Quebecois accentuate a joy in living. Norwegians keep quietly to themselves, and Cubans laugh loudly through their day. And these predispositions quite naturally lead to commonly accepted social behavior. To use the last couplet as an example, Norwegians will routinely refrain from greeting strangers, even when they are in close contact in an elevator or on public transit. You're viewed as impolite or nosy, if you try to engage someone in small talk. In contrast, Cubans cannot meet except that they touch each other. No matter if you are a life-long friend or a complete stranger, one greets all women with a kiss on the right cheek. It is seen as standoffish or ignorant to keep to oneself.

In first-century Palestine, we might suggest that the Jewish soul also had its own preferences. It preferred an order of "same things." Mixing was suspect. Like things went with like things, and while the knowledge of which objects were the same and which were different might be subject to question by outsiders, people in the culture knew what went with what. For instance, you didn't mix materials used in clothing, crossbreed animals, or plant different grains in the same field (Leviticus 19:19). Out of a similar desire to keep distinct things separate, there is a long tradition of cooking and serving milk away from meat (Exodus 23:19, 34:26; Deuteronomy 14:21). Men ate separately from women. Women in their menstrual period were deemed unclean and were not allowed to mingle with those who were righteous.

Uncleanliness from bodily discharges barred one from mixing with others and certainly from the dinner table. Sinners—those who have forsaken the law — and those deemed to be unrighteous by virtue of their employment were likewise excluded. Some material things were unclean and unwelcome, as mentioned above—bodily fluids, blood, secretions, but deformity of any kind was also evidence of spiritual uncleanliness. And if one was in contact with any of these "unrighteous" people in any way, one was disqualified from a common meal.

Evidence of illness was generally assumed to be the result of sin. Those who had been favored by God are not afflicted by disease or disability—so the ancient theological argument goes. Conversely, anyone who suffered from a discernable ailment: blindness, withered hands or feet, serious skin disorders . . . they were deemed to have fallen out of favor with their Creator and were being punished—a very old formula. There is a similar dynamic operative in our modern world. You win the lottery and you call yourself "blessed," and if you lose a hockey game, you wonder "what have I done wrong?" It's not a hard and fast rule, but it's an unspoken inclination. It's the place where your heart goes, before your mind can intervene. Put simply: sickness is sin, health is righteousness. What that means in the context of first-century eating practices is that if you're crippled or deformed, you're not welcome to recline in the circle with others, because you are a sinner.

Then we must add to this theological argument that any incapacity equals sin, and the generally accepted assumption is that sin is contagious. You can catch impurity from someone else. A simple example will explain. If I live long enough with someone who had tuberculosis, the chances are that I will also contract it. Just as disease passes from one to another, so one can argue that sin is catching. That being the case, our common sense would tell us to keep sinful people away from righteous ones. Healthy individuals distance themselves from the sick. In a similar fashion, one guards one's purity by avoiding those we know are unclean—we don't want to catch their unholiness. These people would likely include anyone who collaborates or communes with gentiles and those who could have or would have touched unclean objects: money, grains and meats sacrificed to idols, blood, pigs, or unclean animals. Likewise, Samaritans and other heretics need to be shunned, given their sinfulness. From the first-century perspective, all these restrictions make good sense. Distance and isolation are our best defense against impurity and sin. And lest we become judgmental, this same lesson has been beaten into our world over the past three years of the pandemic, when we extol "self-isolation" and "social distancing" as our best defense against infection.

And if eating is a moment in the day when one is most vulnerable, the rules around keeping unlike things separate become more widely accepted and enforced at mealtime. In our day, no one would dream of putting a dirty, greasy hand into a bowl of chips laid out on a serving table for any and all to eat. So, in Jesus' day, there were many clear and well-meaning restrictions on keeping the impure from contaminating the pure when it came to a shared platter of food.

Using first-century logic, we can understand why some "unclean" people would not be welcome at our dinner table. On a simple level, women don't eat with men—we don't mix genders. Children are excluded from public functions for similar sensitivities. Anyone who works with bodily fluids: prostitutes, grave diggers, women having their period, hemophiliacs and people with a hemorrhaging disease, and anyone with a skin disorder . . . they don't recline with us to eat. Tax collectors are dirty—morally suspect, because they collaborate with Romans and extort others to make a living. By virtue of their work, they must mingle in the impurity of a gentile world—touching foreign coins for instance. Moreover, tax collectors were also the most visible form of the hated occupation. They collected the money, that sustained the Roman legions, and gathered taxes, that also paid for the worship of a foreign deity and idol (Caesar was crowned emperor and "god"). So, they are clearly not welcome to join us to eat. Gentiles and Samaritans would also be excluded. Hospitality laws dictate that we welcome strangers into our midst,[32] but common sense argues that we serve them separately. No one wants to catch their sinfulness, and who knows where their fingers have been? They can contaminate their own food over there.

Now, if we back away from the minutiae regarding eating and purity for a moment, we can simply say that mealtime brings about a number of stress points. It's the time in the predictable and basically pedestrian routine of your life, when one has to be watching their "p's" and "q's." Of course, some things would be second nature: waiting for the host to dip first, taking a place in the circle commensurate with one's status. But other things require conscious thought: who has been where? Is there anyone who is showing signs of "sin?" How about recent outbreaks of impurity? Are there any recognizable outcasts in our circle? Stressful.

Add to this low-level tension the fact of living in occupied territory, and now we can sense a greater than average sense of apprehension at the dinner table. Every choice has a double meaning. There's what's on the surface, and there's how any decision or gesture reflects on collaboration with or resistance to the Romans. We eat recognizable "Jewish" food, because it's what we like, but also because it reinforces our identity as Jews. We abide by our mealtime etiquette, because the religious authorities require it and our social spiritual inclinations agree with it. But in addition, what we do at the table—who is served and who is excluded, establishes our trustworthiness for any neighbors who might notice. Our dinner is a sign post: here lives a righteous Jew. We are not Romans; our table proves it.

32. See Leviticus 19:33–34. As with many such injunctions, the law about hospitality is linked to God's saving act in freeing the Israelites from slavery in Egypt. That is to say, it is a central ethical and theological precept. "The foreigner residing among you must be treated as your native-born. Love them as yourself, for you were foreigners in Egypt." (Vs. 34a).

Resistance to altering the seemingly ageless restrictions governing the common banquet makes even more sense, when one takes into account how some Judean elites were forsaking their roots and appropriating Roman practices and dress as a way to ingratiate themselves with the Empire. As we abide by our high moral standards regarding food, we scoff at these dubious rich Jews who have abandoned our ways, just as they have abandoned our God and the dream of a renewed Davidic reign over the land of Israel.

So, if Jesus disrupts these carefully established and spiritually accepted restrictions around eating by welcoming sinners, tax collectors, and the impure outcasts into our meal fellowship, we can imagine any number of reasons why he would get pushback. At this stage, let's examine four obvious irritants: (1) Jesus flaunts accepted, common sense, social, and spiritual principles; (2) he undermines Jewish identity; (3) he risks personal purity and security by his meal fellowship; and (4) his obvious popularity with the grassroots, who applaud his open meal practice, is the envy of religious sects, who wish they themselves enjoyed such popular support.

JESUS FLAUNTS THE RULES

First, Jesus didn't follow the rules around food and eating. In any circumstance, that is going to get you a second glance. In first-century Palestine, it gets you in trouble. Rules are in place for a reason. At that time, peasant life is structured to maximize our food security, while abiding by the law laid out by Moses. The grassroots communities have tried and tested their ways, so that they both adhere to the commandments of God and recognize local exigencies. When someone doesn't follow these ways, they flaunt their ignorance and make a virtue out of defiance. Everyone is on edge.

The religious authorities may have little power to alter Jesus' behavior, but they can certainly complain about it. He's being irresponsible and cavalier about his sinful behavior, breaking the barriers we have put in place for everyone's protection. And as a spiritual leader, he should know better.[33] There's no doubt about the people he entertains. They don't hide

---

33. One of the lessons from the pandemic is how simple matters of etiquette and good behavior can be deeply emotional. In the past year, we have witnessed how liberal, democratic societies get divided between those who follow COVID/vaccination protocols and those who defy them. Previously unseen, and now seemingly impassible, chasms appeared between the two sides. The level of animosity against the other position seems to have no relation to the question at hand. Simple requests to put on a mask were deemed to be a breach of fundamental individual rights. Those who defied the mask rules spat, quite literally, on the ones who insisted on mask wearing. With a similar level of visceral emotion, those who had been vaccinated derided those they

their unworthiness. He knows who is touching him, and, still, he lets it happen. Doesn't he know that he is spreading disease and sin with his cavalier actions?

In the gospel record, one can account for most of the complaints about Jesus on this basis. Jesus is one who knows the law, as a "rabbi," and yet he is willfully ignoring the best advice regarding spiritual purity. The actions are reprehensible for sure, but even worse is Jesus' willing disregard for what he must know is the right thing to do. In either case, Jesus' seeming disdain of meal traditions and eating etiquette is a key element in his detractors' complaints.

JESUS UNDERMINES JEWISH IDENTITY

Second, Jesus was disrupting the community's security by undermining their Jewish identity. Spiritual and social affiliation can be a protective blanket, so to speak, when your environment seems both dangerous and contingent—compromised by the fact of a foreign occupation. The hated Romans can take our money and our land, but they cannot rob us of what we think and how we pray, how we eat and what we believe. The intangibles, that constitute our identity as devout and righteous Jews, are our birthright and perhaps all we have left of our dignity. Hence, anyone, who might undermine that identity or confuse the elements that make it what it is, is not welcome in our town. Making friends with the unclean and eating with the outcast—may sound noble in the twenty-first century, but in Jesus' time, it could be seen as a callous contempt for the values that set us apart.

And being seen as a "genuine" Jew had it advantages. A succession of emperors had granted the Jewish community exemption from participating in civic religion, worshipping the divinity of emperor, and in some cases paying tributes to temples dedicated to Roman deities. Jews were also exempt from military service and enjoyed some freedoms from military requisitioning. Anyone who compromises that special status is going to be met with resistance from social and religious authorities.

So, a local boy, who doesn't act like the rest of us, needs to be brought into line and taught a lesson. Otherwise, our gentile neighbors, who already resent some of our "privileges," privileges they don't have even though they too suffer under the occupation, might argue that being Jewish is less definitive than we would like. I can hear the gossip in gentile towns like Sepphoris (4 kilometers from Nazareth): "Look at what Jesus does . . . one of your

---

called "anti-vaxxers."

Jewish Rabbis. If he can flaunt the rules and be Jewish, how about the rest of us? Maybe we could claim to be Jewish, too!"

Not only anonymous townsfolk, but community leaders would be threatened by a spiritual "guru," who enjoyed great fame and yet who also ignored the niceties of ethnic identity. Like all gatekeepers, it seems reasonable that synagogue rulers, Pharisees, and other religious types would naturally complain about Jesus' disregard for purity concerns. Naturally prone to resist change, those protecting orthodoxy see any deviance from accepted practice as an affront to common sense, almost a treasonous insult to the integrity and identity of the whole.

JESUS RISKS PERSONAL PURITY AND SECURITY

Third, one could suggest that those who complained about Jesus and how he ate with sinners and tax collectors, publicans, and prostitutes were troubled by issues of personal hygiene and health. While respecting Jesus as a spiritual and inspirational leader, they still might want to protect him from bad practice. Having dinner with a leper, for instance (Mark 14), can do temporary damage to one's righteousness and irreparable harm to one's physical health. Everyone knows that. Jesus is too astute not to know that he is risking his own well-being and that of his followers, by flaunting the rules that have kept everyone safe for hundreds of years. How dare he! Again, the comparison with the pandemic is too obvious not to mention. How often did we say to each other that those who don't wear masks are putting themselves and everyone else they meet in danger?[34] That's Jesus in the first century.

From this point of view, I find the Pharisees' complaints to be entirely understandable, and one might even say they were acting in everyone's best interests. And if people had become sick by participating in a Jesus meal, their concerns would also be justifiable.

OTHERS ARE JEALOUS OF HIS POPULARITY

Fourth and finally, if the concern for personal health puts the best light on the detractors' complaints about Jesus' eating practice, the issue of jealousy or envy may be the worst explanation for their criticisms.

---

34. During the pandemic, the level of anger and animosity between those who followed health guidelines and those who refused to get vaccinated is an illustration of how heated and acrimonious (even murderous) our divisions around proper hygiene can become. Is it any surprise that some of Jesus' detractors wanted to eliminate him?

Every religious movement seeks to garner public support and enjoy popular approval. Devotion to the temple and its concomitant demands was the overarching religious structure of daily life for Jesus' circle. But in small towns, any number of religious factions, camps, or sects vied for status and esteem. And just as we must not paint the Pharisees with a brush tainted by years of unflattering prejudice promoted by Christians, neither should we be naïve about how envy operates for all human beings. From the orthodox point of view, Jesus was getting away with murder, and the people loved him. His gift of healing was unmatched, and his preaching was spellbinding. You can't tell me that didn't inspire a serious amount of jealousy among the proponents of other variants of Jewish practice. Would the Zealots not want to enjoy Jesus' popularity? Did the followers of John not wish their leader had had such healing powers? And were the Pharisees, who were themselves an innovative movement, not be affronted by this new Rabbi's reclamation of the law? Pharisees proposed that keeping the law in your heart could be a reasonable substitute for a pilgrimage to the holy city. Wasn't Jesus proposing something similar, but using his own scheme called a Kingdom of God? Why does he get all the praise?

It feels petty and unacademic to suggest that one takes a contrary position simply out of envy. But having served on the faculty of a number of universities and theological colleges, this last explanation of the criticism of Jesus is, alas, all too credible.

"DO YOU SEE THIS WOMAN?"

The above explanations of the reasons behind the complaints about Jesus' meal practice may seem speculative or even fabricated, and so to base our suggestions on a concrete example, I propose we examine the meal Jesus has with Simon the Pharisee, found in Luke chapter 7. While this anointing story is told in all four gospels, it is only in Luke that it happens during a meal in a Pharisee's home. Using the New International Version as our biblical text, I will intersperse the verses with comments and commentary[35] to further our discussion.

---

35. If you are using this text as the basis for a bible study, this might be the point when you could read the text out loud, then go around the circle, examine it verse by verse, and discuss the comments I make along the way.

LUKE 7:36–50

Verse 36 When one of the Pharisees invited Jesus to have dinner
with him, he went to the Pharisee's house and reclined at the table.

It seems evident that Luke has borrowed this story from Mark's gospel (Mark 14:3–9), but he shifts the location and the personalities. In that process, he alters the focus of this tale. In Mark, we are eating at the home of Simon the leper—the bottom of the purity scale. He's a sinner and social outcast, and Mark's story revolves around an unnamed woman anointing Jesus, as if for burial and, by extension, for messiahship. In great contrast, Luke turns Simon into a Pharisee. Now the meal fellowship has jumped to the highest rung of purity, and the plot swings to center on table manners and hospitality. As any good story teller will admit, if you change the context surrounding your main characters, you're doing it for a good reason—to make the tale more engaging, to make clear what had otherwise been confusing, or to shift the meaning of the story altogether. This last option is what Luke is attempting. He uses the story, not to anticipate Jesus' death, but as a means to highlight his life and one of the key elements of his mission.

Verse 37 A woman in that town who lived a sinful life learned that
Jesus was eating at the Pharisee's house, so she came there with an
alabaster jar of perfume.

In Mark, the unnamed woman is just that—anonymous. Only the ointment hints at her occupation. In Luke, there is no doubt. This is a "sinner" or to put it bluntly: a sex worker. She brings with her the tool of her trade: a jar of ointment. Traditionally, prostitutes would hang a small jar of ointment around their necks to advertise their trade—its aroma and soothing properties being an enticement.

Verse 38 As she stood behind him at his feet weeping, she began
to wet his feet with her tears. Then she wiped them with her hair,
kissed them and poured perfume on them.

We've already mentioned that, since the guests at a meal are reclining with legs stretched out behind, there's no trouble for a woman to reach Jesus' feet. The fact that this woman is weeping signifies either uncontrollable joy or deep sorrow. Is there a hint of regret as well? The end of the story may indicate that her tears might be evidence of profound relief, even rejoicing. From the tears we go on to kissing, and this is the steamy part of the story. In the ancient world, "feet" were a lowly part of the body and not mentioned in polite company. So, it's a bit vulgar to mention her ministrations involving

Jesus' feet—something too intimate. On the surface, the washing of a guest's feet is common hospitality, but to weep over them, use your own hair as a towel, to kiss, and anoint them? Okay, now we've entered into a whole other realm of touching. Luke is clearly exaggerating, even sensationalizing, this woman's care for Jesus. Rubbing it in, so to speak, so that the audience is in no doubt about the close connection between Jesus and this sinner.

Let's think about the ointment for moment. If the jar is a symbol and tool of her trade, what does it mean that she poured it out on Jesus' feet. In Mark's story, she actually breaks the jar—a more dramatic gesture to be sure (Mark 14:3b). Does this mean she is spending some or all of her resources on one man? Is this an acknowledgement of his importance, or is it an act of relinquishment? At the end of the story, it will be clear that Jesus has already had some contact with this woman. So, is it possible that the previous encounter has resulted in her decision to spend it all and then be done? Could this be her letter of resignation written in ointment? She has no more need of it, because she's finished with the sex trade?

> Verse 39 When the Pharisee who had invited him saw this, he said to himself, "If this man were a prophet, he would know who is touching him and what kind of woman she is—that she is a sinner."

First things first, Jesus is willingly allowing an impure person to contaminate Simon's meal fellowship. That's a problem. She's a woman and a prostitute, two good reasons to keep her out. And Jesus as a spiritual leader knows that her sin is contagious, and he is therefore not only putting himself at risk, but also the health of the entire circle. Should he allow it? Of course not! It's a nonstarter, as far as table manners are concerned.

Here is also the evidence for the second justification for criticizing Jesus, mentioned above. He is willfully undermining the carefully constructed distinctions made by religious authorities. Righteous Jews do not consort with sinners, and especially not prostitutes. It is not only spiritually repugnant, it's morally reprehensible and politically dangerous. Jesus should know better. He does know better, and he doesn't care. That makes his actions as a "prophet" even more reprehensible. No good rabbi would allow a woman to be so familiar, so sensual in polite company. No matter how she feels, Jesus should have kept his distance, preserved his dignity, and illustrated to the guests at the meal that he was a trustworthy, respectable teacher of the law—one who pays special attention to the carefully established rules of etiquette. At best, he should have, could have, rebuked this woman and taught a good lesson in manners. At the least, he might have asked her to leave off such ministrations to a time and place more suited to such intimate acts of contrition. Either way, Jesus could have restored order, if he wanted to do so. Obviously, he chose not to abide by the well-established and well-meaning household rules. How dare he!

> *40 Jesus answered him, "Simon, I have something to tell you." "Tell me, teacher," he said.*

I always find this interchange to be very revealing. Jesus addresses his host by name, giving the impression that they are on a first-name basis, even friends. And Simon, while we have just been told he doesn't like what is happening, responds to Jesus with respect, even eagerness. (Given what he was thinking, Simon shows remarkable constraint!)

> *Verse 41: Two people owed money to a certain moneylender. One owed him five hundred denarii, and the other fifty. 42 Neither of them had the money to pay him back, so he forgave the debts of both. Now which of them will love him more?"*

Be careful how you answer this question. While the right response seems obvious, the implications are not. If we are to draw comparisons with the situation at this meal, as it is unfolding, which one of the guests is the bigger debtor[36] and which is the smaller? Given Luke's penchant for irony, it may well be in his mind that the one who owes much is Simon. And like many people who think they are virtuous, it is their very self-righteousness that both blinds them to their "debt" and masks its enormous size.

> *Verse 43 Simon replied, "I suppose the one who had the bigger debt forgiven." "You have judged correctly," Jesus said.*

So, Simon gives the obvious answer. Here, again, there seems to be a level of trust between these two. Simon doesn't try to qualify his answer or use his response to either boast of his own intelligence or put Jesus in his place. And Jesus commends Simon on his answer, also without qualification. There is a hint here of a possible rapprochement between Jesus and the Pharisees. They are both intelligent, highly skilled in debate, deeply concerned with the welfare of the people, struggling to maintain a healthy relationship with God and creation. They have much in common. There's no reason they wouldn't respect each other, even become friends. It puts an entirely different slant on the gospels, if we picture the Pharisees as distant, if perhaps doubting, allies of Jesus.

---

36. In first-century terms, the big debtor owes close to two months salary for an average peasant laborer, while the small debtor owes just over a month's salary.

> *Verse 44 Then he turned toward the woman and said to Simon, "Do you see this woman? I came into your house. You did not give me any water for my feet, but she wet my feet with her tears and wiped them with her hair.*

My friends will tell you that I am conflict-averse. I would rather run a marathon than address those whom I have wronged or with whom I have a problem. And when something critical happens and conflict seems inevitable, my first response is to try to ignore or downplay the situation. So, when I read this verse, I get very, very nervous. Rather than tactfully avoiding what he already knows is a contentious issue for Simon, Jesus rubs his nose in it. "Do you see this woman?" Of course, Simon does. That's the problem. She's not supposed to be there. And rather than easing the tension by inviting the woman to leave or suggesting she cease her ministrations, Jesus singles her out.

And my anxiety doubles when Jesus starts to question the hospitality of Simon. Even in modern days, no one would interrupt a dinner to tell the head of the household that his reception of his visitors has been "piss-poor." I use vulgar language advisedly, because Jesus does. In mentioning feet twice in the same sentence, he is debasing the conversation with reference to the lowest part of the body. And, as I said above, we do not mention "feet" in starched circles. I can feel Simon and the others cringing, from embarrassment and resentment. How dare Jesus publicly question Simon's hospitality? It's a direct attack on his honor. And if Jesus wasn't our esteemed leader, we would think he was acting like a social boor—which is what I think Luke wants his audience to feel. The gospel writer sets up two exaggerated options—like a choice. Either Jesus has come to change everything from the ground up, beginning with the power relations imbedded in table etiquette, or he's a loudmouthed malcontent that needs to be rejected out of hand. Which box do you tick? There's no third option.

> *Verse 45 You did not give me a kiss, but this woman, from the time I entered, has not stopped kissing my feet.*

Why doesn't Jesus just let it go? He's made his point, hasn't he? Why keep pounding Simon for his lack of hospitality? Now, Jesus is asking to be kissed, when he comes in for dinner and—wait for it—he mentions "feet" a third time. Now, there's no getting around it. Jesus is pushing us all to the edge.

> *Verse 46 You did not put oil on my head, but she has poured perfume on my feet.*

It's as if Jesus is standing in the circle, counting off Simon's faults . . . exposing his failures as an honored host for all to see. And yes . . . again, we get the "piss-poor" reference. I find myself looking away. I can't tolerate how insensitive and downright nasty Jesus has become. Of course, if I believe in Jesus and his Way, then what this exchange tells me is that he will not accommodate himself to table manners that exclude outsiders, women, and the unclean. No white lies and no polite indulgences for the sake of propriety. No matter if he appears crude or cruel; for Jesus it is a greater injustice to allow the distinctions of gender and purity to exclude anyone from the common meal. And Luke is asking his audience, "Where do you stand?" As I said, there's no middle ground. You're either with Simon and his form of purity or with Jesus with what some call a "higher"[37] righteousness.

> Verse 47 *Therefore, I tell you, her many sins have been forgiven— as her great love has shown. But whoever has been forgiven little loves little."*

Christian evangelists might be tempted to use this story as evidence of the pattern of repentance and forgiveness. When we turn to our savior with open, humble hearts, and show that we are wanting to change our ways, he will forgive us. There's a *quid pro quo* at play. A sense of forgiveness is the reward I get for admitting that I have been naughty. Good works are needed to achieve God's grace. But that is clearly not what is happening here. The woman has already been forgiven. Her show of devotion to Jesus is the result of that previous act. In theological terms, grace comes first, and then our natural response is faith.

This verse seems to indicate that the woman is the character in Jesus' parable who owed "much." As I said, there is always a sense of irony lurking behind Luke's Jesus and his pronouncements. Is it possible that we can hear it here? Is Jesus saying to Simon, of course, "those *who think* they have few sins, they will also show little love?" In ironic statements, there is a touch of humor and in humor there is the possibility of repentance. Can Simon laugh a bit at his presumptions? Did he really think he owed little?

> Verse 48 *Then Jesus said to her, "Your sins are forgiven."*

---

37. Brown, in his foundational text, *Birth of the Messiah*, uses the argument of "higher" justice, when explaining how the audience should understand the five particular women described in the genealogy of Jesus: Tamar, Rahab, Ruth, Bathsheba, and Mary his mother. These women, whose histories are checkered with scandal, chose a position that was just "higher" than the pedestrian morality and traditions of their day.

I hear this as a statement of a fact that has already existed and not a declaration of a new state. The woman is being told that her love is obvious, because her sins have been forgiven previously.

> *Verse 49 The other guests began to say among themselves, "Who is this who even forgives sins?"*

Luke adds the gossip of the crowd into the mix. Like a Greek chorus, they color the conclusion of this tale with a grey hint of foreboding. Their words echo the resentment that will be voiced more vociferously, the closer we get to Jerusalem. These affronted guests revert to another one of the complaints I mentioned above—questioning Jesus' authority. Who is he to forgive sins? Only God, or by extension, the temple priests, can forgive sins. One complaint leads to another. Jesus is clearly not trustworthy.

> *Verse 50 Jesus said to the woman, "Your faith has saved you; go in peace."*

The first-century audience would be saying to themselves at this point that Jesus restored this woman to health, He turned an outsider into an insider. And that is the key of his Kingdom of God.

It's the "who" of Jesus' meals that is troublesome. Jesus welcomes sinners. He is the agent of repentance and forgiveness.

And Luke makes sure we are not confused. The woman's faith was her salvation. A not-so-subtle way to remind his audience that each one of us can be restored, even if Jesus is not present. To quote Martin Luther and paraphrase the Beatles, "all we need is faith."

Now that we have some appreciation of the dynamics surrounding the meal practice of Jesus and have gained a little understanding with respect to what was troublesome to the religious authorities of his time, we can then ask the key question: How is it that the real meal, which accentuated abundance, acceptance, and equal access to all, became a ritualized celebration reserved only for those with elite status? How did we move from community to cannibalism? And more importantly, how did this shift change the Kingdom of God movement of Jesus? Those are the questions of the next chapter.

Croissants

BEFORE WE BEGIN

1. This recipe takes 18–24 hours, so be prepared with enough time to do it all as explained below.

2. You can increase or decrease the amounts proportionally, but this recipe will make between 35 and 45 croissants (depending on how you cut them).

3. Croissants are one of the fanciest breads to serve and work well with any meal or snack, but if you want "warm croissants for breakfast," it will mean getting up a couple of times in the night before (such is the life of a baker!).

4. You'll need a good rolling pin for this recipe, a good pizza cutter, patience, and a measure of upper body strength. (You were warned!)

THE DOUGH

Mix: 9 cups of all-purpose flour with:
    ½ cup sugar
    1 Tablespoon salt
    3 Tablespoons instant dry yeast
Melt: 2/3 cup butter

Beat together: butter, 3 eggs, 1/2 cup heavy cream and 1/2 cup warm water.

Combine egg mixture and flour mixture. You'll want to have a spongy dough (dry is bad), so add more warm water, if there is still flour at the bottom of your bowl as the dough begins to stick together. (It will take a few tries at this recipe to get the right balance of warm water to flour.) Once the dough is formed, knead for 10 minutes. (Sing the chorus of "Amazing Grace" 20 times.)

Set the dough to rise for two hours.

THE BUTTER (CROISSANTS ARE ACTUALLY A DELIVERY SYSTEM FOR BUTTER.)

On two sheets of parchment, mark out a rectangle 7 inches by 10 inches.

Cut the square of butter, creating 1/8-inch slices, and fill in the rectangle on both sheets of parchment with these butter slices. (It should take about 1 ½ pounds of butter.)

Cover the butter on the parchment with plastic wrap, and using a rolling pin, flatten the rectangles of butter so that the butter is one solid, even sheet.

Place the parchment/plastic wrap of butter in the fridge to get very hard. (It will take at least 3–4 hours.)

THE ROLLING

Line two half baking sheets (18 inches by 13 inches) with parchment.

Once the dough has risen, cut it into two equal parts.

Roll each part out so that it fits into the standard half baking sheet and cover them with plastic wrap. Place the two sheets in the fridge to cool (at least two hours).

Now we have to plan backwards from when you want to serve these fresh croissants. Baking time is 20 minutes, rising time is 2 ½ hours, rolling time is flexible, but there must be at least an hour between rollings, and we will need to do three rolling sessions. Here's a suggestion for fresh croissants to serve at an 8:30 am breakfast:

1. Do the dough, butter steps in the afternoon before you want to serve breakfasts croissants.

2. Do the first rolling at 9:00 pm and the second at midnight.

3. Set the alarm and wake at 4:30 am for the final rolling and cutting into croissants.

4. Bake the croissants at 7:30 am, so that they can cool for 20 minutes before eating. (Another option is to start the croissants the morning before, do the rollings through the afternoon and evening, place the shaped croissants in the fridge until 5 am and then take them out to rise and bake for breakfast. That eliminates one step in the middle of the night.)

FIRST ROLLING

1. Take out one half baking sheet of dough, unwrap it and place it on the counter. Place one of the butter sheets in the middle of the dough rectangle, so that the 10-inch side is across the vertical axis of the dough. Fold the ends of the rectangle over the butter to cover it completely.

2. Now flour your rolling surface; place the dough (which should now be the shape of a smaller rectangle: 13 inches x 9 inches) on the floured surface. Flour the top and roll the dough out to a rectangle 26 inches x 18 inches. This will take some muscle power!

3. Fold the dough in thirds and roll it out again to the 26 inches x 18 inches size.

4. Fold one last time in thirds and cover in plastic and place back in the fridge. (Repeat with the second dough in the fridge on the half baking sheet.)

5. As you can see, we are effectively making layers of butter between layers of dough. The more often we roll it, the flakier the dough gets. We put it into the fridge, so that the butter doesn't melt into the dough but stays hard and separate until baking time. So, allow the dough to get thoroughly cold again (1–2 hours).

SECOND ROLLING

Repeat steps 2–5 from the first rolling.

THIRD ROLLING AND SHAPING

1. Line four half baking sheets with parchment.

2. We will roll out each dough separately—leaving the second dough in the fridge, while you roll and shape the first dough. Roll the dough as thin as possible. (This is where the upper body strength comes in handy, because the dough will be pretty cold and unwilling to roll easily.) I would suggest a rectangle 24 inches x 36 inches.

3. To shape a croissant, we first cut this rectangle in half, horizontally. Then cut each of these narrower rectangles into smaller triangle wedges (4 inches at the wide end down to a point at the other). It may take a bit of practice, but you'll see that you can cut wedges of equal size

using the edge of one triangle to form the side of the next one beside it, only in a mirror image.

4. Take each triangle and stretch the pointed end out a bit . . . don't pull too hard . . . just a slow stretching. Take the straight, wide end of the triangle and stretch that ever so lightly. Cut a 1-inch slit in the middle of this wide end of the triangle and begin rolling the dough on itself, taking the wide end of the triangle and rolling toward the pointy end, until you have a croissant shape. Bend the two ends of each croissant so that the dough makes a crescent shape and set it on the parchment. Repeat until all the triangles are shaped into croissants.

5. Repeat step 2–4 with the second dough.

6. All things being equal, you should have 36–40 croissants.

RISING AND BAKING

1. Beat two eggs until smooth and paint each croissant with the egg wash.

2. Let rise for 2–3 hours in a warm place.

3. Halfway through the rising, paint the croissants with the egg wash a second time, if possible. (No worries if you have to skip this step due to sleeping.)

4. Bake at 350 degrees F. for 20 minutes.

5. Allow to sit for 20 minutes before serving with butter and jam.

NOTES:

The croissant dough, once it has been rolled three times, is very versatile. It can be used for any number of other French delights. You can cut the dough into small rectangles 3 inches x 5 inches and, placing a bar of semi-sweet chocolate at one end, roll it up to make "*pain au chocolat.*" You can also use this dough to make "*pain aux raisins,*" but that requires making a rum custard, and perhaps we should leave that idea for another adventure. It also works as a pastry on which to cook a dessert pizza (very fancy), and you can even use it sliced in long strips, painted with egg wash, and rolled in cheese to make cheese sticks.

5

How and Why Did the Meal Change?

Most people, including ourselves, live in a world of relative ignorance. We are even comfortable with that ignorance, because it is all we know. When we first start facing truth, the process may be frightening, and many people run back to their old lives. But if you continue to seek truth, you will eventually be able to handle it better. In fact, you want more! It's true that many people around you now may think you are weird or even a danger to society, but you don't care. Once you've tasted the truth, you won't ever want to go back to being ignorant.

. . . SOCRATES

WHAT DO THE COMPLAINTS TELL US?

On my writing desk I have laminated a quote from Reinhold Niebuhr. In his book, *The Irony of American History*,[1] he writes:

> No virtuous act is quite as virtuous from the standpoint of our friend or foe as it is from our standpoint. Therefore we must be saved by the final form of love which is forgiveness.

I first read that quote thirty years ago, when I was a graduate student, but, like baking croissants, some ideas require time to mature, working them

1. Niebuhr, 63.

in different directions before they make sense. In this case, I focused more on the phrase "the final form of love." It seemed so romantic. But now, the entire quote reminds me of two important facts of life: First, we are none of us as virtuous as we would like to be—and so the necessity of forgiveness, and second, as I said in the previous chapter, we all can learn from the commentary of both friends and foes. Our naysayers know, often better than we do ourselves, how we have fallen short or been blind to our own shortcomings. Put another way, we can be taught as much from our enemies as from our friends, sometimes more.

In the case of Jesus, what generalizations can we draw from his critics and the complaints outlined in the last chapter?

First, the "who" of his detractors is quite revealing. They are usually "named" individuals. People with positions of respect: scribes, chief priests, Pharisees, Sadducees, teachers of the law, and synagogue rulers. Apart from the anonymous "evil spirits," who seem to know Jesus and want to reveal his true identity, all his other critics are people with titles and responsibility. They are "somebodies." One might draw from this that the gospel writers prefer to mention the important people in Jesus' life. The common peasant doesn't attract attention or deserve notice. Or it could be that, given the necessities of the oral traditions which produced material which was eventually written down, people were given a title to make memorization a bit easier and the story a tad richer.

There may be other complex reasons for the fact that only "important" people criticize Jesus, but I would argue that there's a simple explanation. Jesus' detractors are individuals with status and power. They are the ones in charge. Somehow, whatever Jesus is doing, he's irritating or undermining, ridiculing or belittling systems of domination and control. His base of support is the crowd (as is mentioned often in Mark),[2] and that's intimidating to those who *think* they have power—both Romans and Judeans alike. It is this power play that gets Jesus executed.

Recognizing that most gospels never claim[3] to be historically accurate—at least not as modern, secular audiences might wish to describe historicity—it is important to recall that both the complaints and critics of

2. See Mark 12:12 and Mark 14: 1–2.

3. The one exception is the two-volume Gospel of Luke/Acts of the Apostles which begins with a claim of careful recounting of the events "handed down to us" concerning Jesus. Luke 1:1–5: "*1 Many have undertaken to draw up an account of the things that have been fulfilled among us, 2 just as they were handed down to us by those who from the first were eyewitnesses and servants of the word. 3 With this in mind, since I myself have carefully investigated everything from the beginning, I too decided to write an orderly account for you, most excellent Theophilus, 4 so that you may know the certainty of the things you have been taught.*"

Jesus change over time. At first, in Mark's gospel, they seem to be centered largely around the temple mount, with chief priests and scholars arguing about Jesus' authority and posing questions which point to his serious lack of credibility. That makes good sense, since a large popular movement arriving in or growing out of Jerusalem might well intimidate the priestly caste, who believed they controlled the holy city and its temple administration.

As time passes and we move from Mark to Matthew, the emphasis shifts from a priestly class to the Pharisees. (We've come down several notches with respect to wealth and privilege.) And as the Pharisees take over the central role of Jesus' critics, there seems to be a heightened level of resentment, focused to a large degree on Jesus' eating fellowship. That trajectory continues with Luke. If we take as an example the shift outlined in the previous chapter with respect to the anointing story at a meal with Simon, Luke moves the critical issue from messiahship to hospitality. The meal becomes the battleground for a clash of basic ethical and spiritual values. How do we want to structure our world: according to the elitist, imperial principles of merit and power or according to the sabbath values of equality and forgiveness? That's Luke's question.

As mentioned above, the chief complaints of all the gospels represent more precisely the grievances and grumblings that were active and pressing, when the particular gospel itself was being written. So, by in large, we are dealing with the phenomenon of third (Mark) and then fourth (Matthew) or even fifth (Luke) generation followers of Jesus. Their version of the "good news" is a response to what they were hearing from the other side, at the time of writing, and how they were trying to counter what Jesus' detractors were saying about him and about his movement.

That being said, we can make a generalization, which, like all such descriptions, may fall short on details but is helpful in broad terms—to give us a general direction. It is possible that the first followers of Jesus were focused on asserting his validity as the long-awaited messiah—what the devout believed and hoped. Hence, we have complaints directed at his authority—complaints which give the gospel writer a perfect opportunity to refute such criticisms. The temple mount discourses in Mark portray Jesus as the brilliant teacher, who proves his messiahship through wit and wisdom.

Credibility and authority are at issue initially because Jesus' followers are claiming he is the long-awaited messiah. A messiah, according to the legends and dreams surrounding a renewed Davidic Kingdom, must be, by necessity, alive. Dead kings can't rule anything—except faintly through nostalgia or sentimentality. His questionable birth, lack of "Kingly" pedigree, and low social status are easy targets. His death is quite literally the nail in the coffin of his credentials. And to confront these issues, as mentioned above, Matthew, Luke, and John give a prologue to the core of the Jesus canon to counter criticisms of his right to be called a "lord" or "prince."

His credibility as a messiah was the first hurdle for the evangelists: asserting that a crucified messiah made sense—both theologically and pro-grammatically.[4] Passages referring to the "suffering" servant of God, taken from the prophet Isaiah, are used to make the case that a "weak" or "humili-ated" messiah is the one we should expect.[5] Likewise, Mark uses Psalm 22 as the structure on which he hangs (quite literally) the final moments of Jesus' life—giving a holy and redeemable coloring to the crucifixion of the long-awaited messiah.

Over the first century, the dead messiah is transformed into the soon-to-return triumphant messiah. Taking the Christian canon as a whole, we begin in Mark with a discerning, non-violent, but not entirely centered, Jesus of Nazareth—an itinerant preacher and healer—and we end with the Book of Revelation, in which Jesus is the victorious, triumphant Savior from on high, who returns back to earth to conquer the forces of evil through violence and power. Quite the shift, but one that has been the dominant pat-tern of Christology ever since. Jesus is lifted out of his humanity and deified. So, today, as always, our challenge as believers is to reassert his humanity.

The Christological debates of the first few centuries of the Christian era are well-known and need no further elaboration here. A quick review of the early creeds illustrates how the primary focus was on the balance of Jesus' humanity and divinity. What has been overlooked was the way in which, at the same time as his two natures were being elaborated, a shift in his central strategic tool—the common meal—was also changing. If the Kingdom of God is incarnated in a shared loaf of bread,[6] how this special meal fellowship begins and where it travels is very important.

A second generalization. As the years pass, the chief concern of those on the Jesus Way[7] became the need to defend and clarify his/their eating practices. Put another way, once his unique messiahship was established as a theological affirmation, the style and content of the celebration of Je-sus' meal and the issue of who is able to participate became more pressing

---

4. Paul is focused on this question in his first letter to the church in Corinth. (See 1 Corinthians 2:1–10.)

5. Compare Matthew 8:16 and Matthew 27:38–44 with Isaiah 53:4–6.

6. See Luke 24:34, the Easter story in which two travellers proclaim: "It is true! The Lord has risen and has appeared to Simon." 35 Then the two told what had happened on the way and how Jesus was recognized by them when he broke the bread."

7. I have will put the word "Way" in quotes, because the author of Acts of the Apostles repeats "the Way" several times as the name given the followers of Jesus. See: Acts 9:2; 19:9, 19: 23; 22:4; 24:14, 24:22.

matters. Hence, we have more questions about his eating practices put into the mouths of his critics, the Pharisees. And this in turn gives Matthew and Luke a chance to have Jesus himself refute false claims. Set the record straight. Let's look at that, closely.

THE MEALS OF JESUS

I can't spell. Anyone who knows me will attest to the fact that, even after 60 years of training, I confuse "angel" and "angle." So, you might think the subtitle above is a typo. Isn't there just one Jesus "meal," not "meals?" Right?

Again, we are entering into a hallowed academic realm of historic conjecture (that's a polite way of admitting we are guessing), but it does appear that there are at least two types of meals mentioned in conjunction with Jesus and his followers. First, it seems clear that Jesus ate an ordinary meal, often with his disciples and with other named individuals. To mention a few, there's Simon the Leper in Mark 14 or Simon the Pharisee found at Luke 7. Zacchaeus the tax collector eats with Jesus, according to Luke 19, and Jesus celebrates the calling of the disciple Levi (Matthew), a tax collector by eating with him—cited in Matthew 9.

This common shared dinner is happening before the Maundy Thursday/crucifixion event. Examples are abundant: at the house of Levi, with Simon's mother-in-law, at the feeding of the multitudes. And if food is mentioned at all before the last trip to Jerusalem, it's the pedestrian diet of bread and fish. Even after the Easter event, Jesus meets with his disciples to eat, and again the meal consists of bread and fish.[8]

The participants in this first meal are varied. Beginning with the huge crowds of the feeding stories to the one-on-one meetings between Jesus and a single sinner, Jesus seems to make no distinctions around table etiquette. He eats with any who will have him. He's invited to Pharisees' homes and into the household of wealthy men. And if his detractors are right, Jesus also shares bread often with tax collectors, or prostitutes, women or men, unwelcome, unspecified sinners or lepers. He does it often enough that it becomes a common slur.

And it may well be that this complaint was voiced during Jesus' own lifetime by more than his enemies. The gospels all record how, at least once, an unnamed and unwanted woman breaks into the common Jesus meal to minister to him, massaging his feet or, in one case, anointing his head

---

8. See Luke 24: 34 . . . shared bread reveals who Jesus is, and in Luke 24:42, fish is used to prove he is "corporal" and not a ghost. In John's gospel, when the post-resurrection Jesus greets his disciples, they are having a meal of bread and fish (John 21:13).

with oil. Then comes the pushback from his own people. Even Jesus' own disciples are disturbed by her. They criticize the waste of expensive perfume (Mark 14:4–5), but it may well be that it was easier to point out this failing, than to reject her outright as a disreputable person. Because it's not very flattering, I can't imagine Mark including this bit of resistance coming from Jesus' disciples, unless he felt he needed to do so for accuracy's sake.[9]

Clearly the "who" of the common meal caused consternation among many groups in Jesus' circle, even his own followers. How can he include unwanted sinners, women, and traitors in common, shared meals? And so, because of his inclusion of outcasts in his first meal, there arises what will become a common critique of Jesus and the generations of his followers: "He eats with publicans and sinners" (Luke 5:27–32, Mark 2:14–17, Matthew 9:9–13). In modern terms we'd say: "This guy has no class. He'll drag us all down into the gutter."

So, before we go on to the second meal, the Eucharist, let's underline this single truth. Jesus is criticized for the company he keeps when he eats. In the common meal of bread and fish, everyone is welcome, especially the unwelcome, unrighteous, and undeserving. And that's the real problem. Yes, there's some consternation over the fact that Jesus and disciples break the rules at their meals by eating without clean hands (Mark 7:1–5, Luke 11:37, Matthew 15:1–9), but the main deal, the big deal, is the "who" of his dinners.

Of course, there is a second meal of Jesus. It is the Passover supper shared on the night before Jesus was betrayed. It is mentioned explicitly in all three synoptic gospels. It is not found in John, a point that we will outline further down.[10] This second meal becomes the basis for the ritual we now call by many names: "The Eucharist," "Holy Communion," "The Mass," "The Lord's Supper."

This second meal is still a regular supper—food is served, people eat according to the etiquette we explained in the last chapter, but it has ritualized elements. It's a celebration of God's once achieved and soon-again-to-be-fulfilled liberation of the people of Israel. It's a dinner to announce

9. It may well be that Mark is also wanting to send a message to the members of the Jesus community, who complained about or betrayed the "Way" during the war, which happened while he was writing. In that case, this portrayal of church leaders as being doubters themselves is a pastoral response of forgiveness underlining how even the disciples didn't understand what Jesus was about.

10. In John, the gospel writer makes it quite clear that, when Jesus meets on Thursday night before his crucifixion, the Passover is still one night away, at least. John 13:1 "It was just before the Passover Festival. Jesus knew that the hour had come for him to leave this world and go to the Father. Having loved his own who were in the world, he loved them to the end."

immanent freedom from oppression.[11] So, there would have been readings from scripture (more than likely they would have been recited by heart rather than read). Blessings over the food would be required, and likewise, there would have been some prayers of thanksgiving. No doubt, some memories of past Passover celebrations would have been shared.

The food of a Passover meal is prescribed. Because a lamb's blood was used for marking the door posts of the Israelites, so that God's spirit would "pass over" their homes when it came to smite the first born of the Egyptians,[12] roast lamb was the most desired main dish for any Passover dinner. Lamb would not always be possible, given the cost, so poorer people sacrificed doves or pigeons.[13]

The foods mentioned in the gospels are bread and wine. These elements would have been present as regular food, but also as pieces of a ritual practice. The bread would be the unleavened bread outlined in Exodus (Exodus 12:8) and bitter herbs. Perhaps during Jesus' time there was a prescribed pattern with respect to the wine. In later times, the Seder involves at least four glasses of wine, one of which is left until the very end of the celebration.

The gospels do not mention how Jesus got his meal organized, who did the necessary preparations, or who cooked it. Presumably, it was the women mentioned elsewhere[14] as helpers and financiers. None of the gospels mentions the actual dinner help,[15] the servers. Were they absent or of no consequence?

Unlike the first meal of Jesus, this Passover celebration, second meal, comes with a distinct, set-apartness. It was a "sacred" moment—rich in memories and fueled by hopes. One can imagine that everyone approaching the event would have their own expectations. Certainly, for the circle of

11. Christians often overlook the fact that the meal on which their communion is based is a celebration of God's immanent liberation of the people, a return to the reign of God, when justice and grace will hold sway, when all will enjoy freedom and peace.

12. See Exodus 12:1–15

13. A note on sacrificial animals: The custom was to bring a live animal—lamb, dove, pigeon to be sacrificed at the altar of the temple. We can picture blood being poured over a stone or burned on a brazier; but given the thousands of animals slaughtered each day in the temple, one has to ask what happened to all the dead carcasses? Was there a smelly trash heap of dead animals out behind the holy courtyards? Of course not. You brought your animal to the priests to be butchered (much as we still do when we send our farm animals to an abattoir), and then you get the animal back. It has been made "holy" by this process and is now ready to be part of the holy meal of Passover. After all, the sacrifice is made so that, symbolically, we could have "dinner with God."

14. See Mark 15:40–41, Mark 16:1, Luke 8:3.

15. In John's gospel (John 13:2), Jesus washes his disciples' feet, a lowly, humble service relegated to women. Does that mean John assumes no women were present to undertake this basic bit of hospitality?

Jesus, it looked like their plans were coming to fruition. Up to that point, Jesus had bested all the critics on the temple mount. They had been widely received for poking fun at the Romans. Hallelujah was in the air. People were getting excited. Surely, this Passover was the one for which they had all been waiting. So, on that night, the meal had richer food and the symbolic bread and wine. It has the flavor of tradition, a foundation of revered history. But it also contains hints of a new time and overtones of a utopian community yet to be.

This second meal is characterized by ritual gestures and palpable hope. But there is also an undercurrent of betrayal. One of the twelve will sell Jesus out, and Peter, the leader of the twelve, will deny him. Laughter and tears mingled together. At this meal there is no mention of women or outcasts. That's not to say they were not present. Either they were absent, or the gospel writer took it as a given that they would be part of the generic designation of "the twelve."

It is the first, common meal which is the focus of the complaints directed at Jesus. His naysayers never comment about his Passover meal. It is not scrutinized by religious authorities or given as evidence for their concern about Jesus' table etiquette. Granted, this special meal takes place just before the end of the story, and the exigencies of plot development might mean we can't have any outsiders involved. Nevertheless, the Lord's Supper is never mentioned, even by the false witnesses, as problematic. The second meal appears to be unassailable.

Returning to the first meal, as already stated, we know that Jesus' detractors had two problems, one minor and one major. There was a rather nit-picking question of the impurity of his preparations—his disciples didn't wash their hands before eating (Mark 7:1–5), or a similar small issue that they picked their own ingredients on the sabbath (Mark 2:23). The major complaint, one that is consistent throughout the gospels, is the "who" of his meals. Jesus lets anyone in. How can he be a spiritual leader, if he doesn't restrict his encounters with sinners?

If the messiahship of Jesus raises the issue of power, the eating practice of Jesus is all about propriety. And while we might want to discount this, let us never underestimate the emotional depth of resistance created by what appears to be a superficial problem.

CHURCH FIGHTS

When I taught theological students, there would come a time in our lectures on practical theology (usually mid-term) when we would have to set aside a class for what I called, gently, "church fights." All our Christian grace and goodwill notwithstanding, the community of faith is filled with real people who bring their "realness" to the pew every Sunday. That means we have differences of opinions and moments of crisis.[16]

I can recall how we would all claim, from student novice to ordained professional, that we would stick to the lessons of forbearance and forgiveness. Being kind and patient was the "right" answer to every question about church fights. But, of course, theoretical "fights" are much easier to resolve than real ones. When push comes to shove, Christian congregations can be uniquely vicious—gossip and slander, name calling, and backbiting being the primary means of communication. And people will suppress or ignore the real reasons for disagreement and focus on peripheral issues, often choosing the ones where there seems to be a clear "right" answer. So, we don't talk about how that homeless person makes me feel guilty and helpless; we complain about their smell. No one says the minister's sermons make me work too hard; they complain about how she looks too often at the choir. We don't speak of our own feelings of regret and resentment at getting older, we criticize the student minster, because he leaves the church kitchen in a mess after the youth group meeting. Incidentals become the safe harbor, when our deeper fears threaten to drown us. We hide our deep concerns behind the question marks of propriety.

With respect to the complaints about Jesus, is it possible we have that same dynamic operating? His open table, where food is shared with all, no matter who they are, threatens our sense of security. We know how the world works. Power and control, exploitation and domination are systems that have shaped us. We may not like it, but we have accommodated our lives and loves, our work and our dreams, to fit in and survive. So, we work to produce food to eat or to barter for the things we need. We don't question the "why" of things, at least not overtly. We expect to be taxed and burdened by the system of domination which controls us. Again, we don't like it, but that's the way the world works. Tough though it may be, this structure of our daily lives gives us the assurance of knowing. If we follow the rules, adapt ourselves to society's dominant values, we'll be able to make it . . . just.

16. You don't understand 1 Corinthians 13 . . . Paul's ode to loving, if you do not put it into the context of the entire letter. 1 Corinthians is a very carefully worded response to a church fight between people who demanded that true believers speak in tongues and those who were willing to see it as merely optional. Of course, Paul deals with many issues: marital relationships, eating practices, often beginning his advice with "And now concerning . . . " But the letter is like a spiral, circling round and round until it hits the bull's-eye in chapter 12:1 "Now concerning spiritual gifts . . . " Chapter 13, is an ode to the triumph of love over animosity and how it is most important, precisely when we are fighting each other.

When Jesus comes to town, he serves food in a way that ignores all those unwritten little rules that we have developed to survive in the system of domination. In the real world, you pay (somehow) for what you get, and he gives it away from free! In like manner, we structure our eating along power/status lines, just as our social world dictates. There's a pecking order. In our society, pyramids are the prescribed form of human interaction. And this Jesus works with circles where all are equal.

Reclining with Jesus, I'm set adrift. It feels freeing on one level to have food shared equally and abundantly, but there's an underlying anxiety. Sure, this feels much like what the prophets might have called God's banquet, where all are filled and none is afraid (Micah 4:4), but that's very disquieting. I know what Jesus is doing is running contrary to all my instincts about surviving in the real world. He's ignoring the consequences of bucking the system. He asks me to join him in God's Kingdom, but we all know we live in Caesar's realm. There's no going back to that holy time in the wilderness, when as a people, we had faith in God alone to provide. Now it's the sweat of our brow that saves us, and reclining with Jesus is nothing more than wishful thinking.

If I want to complain, I am probably not going to speak to Jesus of my inner foreboding, how what the meal practice is living out is essentially an affront to and an attack on the system of domination. Rather, I'll attack the incidentals. The simplest way to push back against Jesus is to disparage the company he keeps. How can his meal be credible, when he lets in "those people"?!

I would credit Jesus' detractors with the same amount of intelligence and insight as modern audiences. So, when religious authorities of all stripes, be they synagogue rulers, Sadducees, Herodians, Chief Priests or Pharisees, complain about Jesus, they know what they are doing. They are attacking him on issues of propriety. It's the easiest way to deal with our objections. I form a prejudice against the externals. Our deepest fears hide behind these superficial complaints. We cannot live with that foundational fear about existence and acceptance. I will not survive—at least not in a manner I enjoy—if I trust in God's ways. To use contemporary vocabulary, Jesus is asking me to step outside my comfort zone. And that's too much.

And here's the rub. We know in our hearts that Jesus is right. Having been groomed by dreams of the wilderness, when God ruled our hearts and met all our needs, we are attuned to his vision. And while the pilgrimage in the desert may seem like a distant and impossible utopia, the laws about the sabbath are not. We know very well that God demands that all beings, animals, and even the earth itself need to be free of exploitation . . . at least periodically. We know that economic exploitation is a fact of life, but we also know about a sacred day of rest. And from that foundational "sabbath" principle, we can extrapolate to other values: that economics should not rule human interactions, that hospitality to strangers is a key element of God's household, and that bread liberates the soul when it is shared without restrictions.

So, on the surface we complain that Jesus eats and drinks with tax collectors and sinners. And that accusation is powered by a virulence born of our underlying and usually unacknowledged sense of guilt. We can't follow in Jesus' footsteps. His call to discipleship is the right thing for us, too, but the cost of this discipleship[17] is too steep.

I've just described an emotional state, but let's never lose sight of the fact that this "church fight" also has some very clear political dimensions. Jesus may never overtly protest against the Romans. He never attacks the system of domination. Nevertheless, his alternate style of living and eating is an affront to the powers and principalities. And they are smart enough to see it. People who eat as if they are living in God's reign put Caesar's kingdom in jeopardy. At best, Jesus' followers are mocking the system, and at worst they are revealing it for what it is: a means by which a very small group of rich and powerful people lord it over the masses. And when you don't play by the game, the ones who set up the game in the first place get very belligerent. Jesus didn't have to call out the Roman empire directly. His meal practice was enough to put him on a collision course with the cross.

CHANGE HAPPENS FOR THE BEST OF INTENTIONS

No one changes because they want things to get worse. I wouldn't adjust my diet or eating habits, travel plans or career goals, in order to not get what I want. As humans, we change to achieve something: better life-style, easier workload, more money, emotional fulfillment, bigger house, spiritual enrichment. Our choice for change may be impetuous or well-planned; either way we bolster our choices with justifications that "it's for the better," or "it's what I always wanted."

If the meal practices of the followers of Jesus changed from his original design, and I believe they did, dramatically, then no doubt there were many good reasons. It may have been an issue of ecclesiastical necessity . . . bigger crowds means small-time rituals and encounters have to adapt themselves to take into account the need for crowd control. It could be about crisis management. Conflicts over dietary differences are solved or

---

17. In this vein one should have a copy of Bonhoeffer's *The Cost of Discipleship* at hand as a guide to following Jesus. Bonhoeffer, as a modern Christian martyr, knows what it means to resist the domination system of fascism.

at least avoided, if we adapt our eating style to suit different expectations. Then again, the shift in the way food was handled may have its roots in practical considerations. A regular meal requires many hands. And perhaps there were fewer people available to prepare and serve a common meal or attend to the details involved in dishing up a dinner for an eclectic crowd of disciples. Too many chefs and not enough dishwashers, so to speak. We'll go into more detail, below, into the reasons why change happened to the meal fellowship of Jesus. At this stage, I just wanted to point out that the shift would have happened with good intentions. It seemed the right thing to do at the time. Since I am going to be critical of where this change had led us, I wanted to preface my remarks with the acknowledgment that the shift in the Jesus meal fellowship was not necessary, but it may have seemed inevitable at the time.

So, we begin with two meals: the bread and fish fellowship circle and the bread and wine Passover ritual. Each involves a real meal. This is an essential fact to be acknowledged.

Given the sacrament of communion Christians now celebrate, we might forget that the second, ritualized meal was not easily reduced to symbolism. For Jesus and his followers, indeed for the Jewish tradition in general, the Passover celebration could and would not happen without a shared banquet of some kind. Just reading the prescribed words, reciting the required prayers, is not enough. Even adding some broken matzah and cups of wine would not do it. A Passover celebration *is* a meal, since the meal, no matter how meagre, is an embodiment of God's message of salvation. Freedom from slavery begins with real food.

Likewise, the first meal of Jesus accentuates community through use of actual food. It's a circle where bread is passed hand to hand, where all are fed and none is left out. It is the incarnation of Jesus' proclamation of the Kingdom of God. Dominic Crossan often explains[18] the basic program and mission of Jesus by picturing God as the ultimate householder. The earth and its inhabitants are his family. Can you picture the householder coming home to find that some members of the family are overeating, taking food from weaker ones? What would an honest patriarch think, if some children were banished from the table altogether because of their skin color? How about if there were rooms filled with people who were banished from eating anything at all? The householder will judge us, not by what we say or don't say, but by whom we include and whom we feed freely. Who gets enough clean water, and who gets included at the great family banquets? The first

18. I first heard Crossan speak in this manner at a conference at the Ecumenical Theological Seminary in Matanzas Cuba, April 2008.

meal fellowship of Jesus was the very practical and very tangible enactment of living in a world where God is our householder.

And when we take away the food from this first meal practice and simply speak about it in theoretical or metaphorical terms, it loses almost all of its concrete, miraculous capacity.

After the crucifixion/Easter event, the first meal continued. People gathered and did what Jesus did, and in a spiritual way, they could continue to say that they were eating with Jesus. And it appears that the meal practice continued including the world's rejects: women, slaves, outcasts. Certainly, the experiment in communal living in Jerusalem was a logical extension of this first meal (Acts 4:32). As cooperative experiments go, it had some shortcomings. It seemed to be in financial difficulty quite quickly after having been established—hence Paul is bent upon taking up an offering for what he calls the "poor in Jerusalem" (Romans 16:26). And it appears that this common meal was more conservative than the original Jesus meal of equals. Reading between the lines, this Jerusalem circle centered around James, the brother of Jesus, and was more restrictive in its eating habits and whom it includes at its common meal. Paul and Peter are at odds over "eating with gentiles," and the Jesus community in Jerusalem appears not to have been open to gentiles, especially at mealtime.

Perhaps one of the earliest allusions to the continuing presence of the first communal meal of Jesus is made by Paul, in his first letter to the church in Corinth—a fascinating letter that reads like a shopping list of complaints and questions addressed to Paul, the apostle and church leader. Chapter by chapter, he runs down the issues beginning with the phrase "now concerning . . . " And he hits on issues of leadership and humility (chapters 1–5), sexuality, immorality, and litigation among church members (chapter 6). There's a need to address the strategies around marital compatibility (chapter 7), and then we get to food. Of the sixteen chapters of this letter, Paul uses four to sort out how people should eat together, deal with meat sacrificed to idols, the sticky problems of appropriate meal service, hospitality across cultural divides, and how to gather honestly to share in the common meal.

If Paul is writing to the Corinthians approximately two decades after the original mission and ministry of Jesus, then it is noteworthy that the "hows" and "whys" of the common meal are being questioned. Cracks are beginning to show in the foundations of Jesus' Kingdom movement. A circle sharing food, where there are no distinctions of class or gender, is beginning to unravel. Paul has to remind the community, in several different ways, that humility and not pride is the sign of discipleship, that no one should boast of being more righteous or worthy, that the wealthy do not have a special place at the table. I think it would be safe to say that the shared-food program of mutual vulnerability and cooperation is faltering badly, a mere twenty years after the original events.

This initial communal impulse of Christianity is largely lost to modern believers. The Catholic monastic movement, a few initial Protestant reform churches, and several Anabaptist sects[19] have taken "all things in common" as their guiding principle. But apart from church socials and potluck dinners, the mainstream Christian world shelved the communal meal as *the* cornerstone of its on-going practice.

Indeed, even with Paul, it seems that the common meal is being supplanted by the celebration of the Lord's Supper, which in Corinth was still a full meal fellowship. It would be logical to assume that the communal meal project shifted away from a stand-alone activity and was incorporated into the sacramental meal, within the first generation of Jesus followers. That being the case, we can assume that the dominant form of gathering to eat as a community was the second meal, the ritual we now call the "Eucharist" or "Lord's Supper."

We have no way of knowing what actually was the motivation for the early followers of Jesus to drop his first communal meal. It might have been the most practical approach—working people can't take too much time away from their labors. It might have been spiritual. The ritual of the breaking of bread and the pouring of wine are more meaningful than the sharing of bread and fish. It could be a question of ecclesiastical control. Anyone can catch a fish, bake it, and dish it up. But only certain people can make and serve wine. Wine requires forethought and careful attention to detail. It's labor-intensive and available only to those who have the means and the property to produce it. Poor Christians would be at a disadvantage, having to purchase wine. Did Church leaders prefer the bread and wine, because it put boundaries around who could and should preside over the Lord's meals?

No matter the reason, the communal meal was taken into the Passover ritual meal, but this second meal was still a real supper. Food was served, and if we can trust Paul, it was enough to feed everyone at the end of their work day. The apostle complains[20] that some who do not have to work are coming early to the meal and eating too much, so that the ones who come later are left out and hungry. So, the meal is not peripheral. The ritual of bread and wine is still integrated into a common meal. Jesus is present with us as a guest, albeit spiritual, at our table.

---

19. Hutterites, Mennonites, Shakers.

20. 1 Corinthians 11:17–22.

THREE WAYS WE GET TO "WHY?"

So, then the question becomes, why did the second actual meal get dropped so that the Christian community became synonymous with symbolic, ritualized "eating and drinking?" How could it happen? Of course, there is the argument from divine providence. What happened was pre-ordained, so there's no merit in questioning it. And while that may satisfy those who simply want to believe in the triumph of Christ's church, I would like to understand why a community of faith, based on the stories of Jesus, would depart so dramatically from the impulse and direction of those very stories. Why did we stop eating together as a community? I can think of three possible reasons for this shift—none very complementary to the growth and development of the church: practicality, accommodation, and power.

First, there is the mundane issue of getting along—the path of least resistance. It just is more practical to avoid creating conflict about food practices that differ widely across many cultures. What we know from Paul's letters and from the Acts of the Apostles, the meal fellowship of Jesus was a flash point for conflict. Strict Jewish purity codes did not sit well with Hellenistic largesse, and when new, gentile converts joined the essentially Jewish Jesus movement, tensions arose almost immediately. Gentiles were unclean, by virtue of their lifestyle and diet. The righteous Jews would ask, "How do we let these contaminated people put their hands in our common bowl?" They eat meat that has been sacrificed to idols—a betrayal of God's commandments—for as Paul states (1 Corinthians 10:20): this meat is sacrificed to demonic forces, not to God.

In the Acts of the Apostles, the author takes great pains to show how eating across cultures caused the first and fundamental rift within the company of Jesus. As a righteous Jew, Peter believes the "uncircumcised" are unclean. How can a devout believer in the God of Israel extend the good news of Jesus to the gentile community? But then the central leader of the church is portrayed as having an epiphany (Acts 10 and 11), in which the Spirit reveals to him that his prejudice about eating with gentiles is unfounded. Soon after, he is invited to the home of a Roman, and they predictably eat together. This convinces Peter that there is a mission, embodied in the common, shared meal, to the unclean, gentile converts to Christ's Way. But Peter's "conversion" is short-lived. Paul relates, in his letter to the church in Galatia (Galatians 2:12), how Peter did an about-face. He may be open to sharing a meal with gentiles, when no one is watching, but when leaders from the Jerusalem church are present, he backtracks. Paul is obviously dismayed and disappointed that Peter, who had previously had no trouble eating with the "uncircumcised," drew away from them (Galatians 2:11–13).

In what Paul calls a "hypocritical" stance, Peter also influences other community members to leave the circle of the gentiles and eat separately.

Initially, this problem of Jew and Gentile (Galatians 3:28) eating together was solved by separation. We may love our gentile brothers and sisters in Christ. They may be strange to us and we are not sure they can be full members of the Kingdom company, but for the time being, we allow them to be present in our company. However, don't confuse tolerance with acceptance. We see them as they are—different from righteous Jews, and we don't have to eat with them! If need be, they can eat their food separately from us. Hospitality does not stretch endlessly. There have to be some limits.

Hence after some deliberation, the church council in Jerusalem separated the evangelistic missions of the Apostles. Peter and others were to preach to the Jews, while Paul was the missionary to the gentile community (Romans 15:16).

That separation may have worked for a time, throughout Paul's life, perhaps. But I can imagine that a simpler compromise was possible. If we separate the actual eating from the sacrament of the Lord's Supper, we avoid so many headaches. And why not have a ritual that only talks about eating together, but doesn't insist on doing it? Everyone can then participate fully. No one is looking over their shoulder, so to speak. We can all rest a bit easier. No meal, no fuss. Makes sense to me. And you can see how this perfectly practical solution to a thorny problem is made for the best of intentions: to bring peace to a community of faith. The consequences of that practical solution, however, can be dramatic, as we will explain in our next chapter.

Second, as I mentioned, I am conflict-averse. Ask anyone. I'll go out of my way to avoid trouble. That being the case, I like to fit in. Doesn't everyone have that desire? On a fundamental level, our primal fear is that we'll be left out, left behind, or left alone. The anxiety of isolation is not new. All humans feel it, and so it would not be a stretch to assume that the first followers of Jesus would know the pressure to accommodate themselves to the culture in which they lived. If I was part of the Jesus circle in southern Galilee, that might not be very difficult. After all, our eating and drinking with Jesus was an entirely acceptable resistance to the imposition of Roman ways on traditions. We eat as Jesus taught us, because that's how we retain our identity.

But as we move beyond Palestine, the pattern of open hospitality and eating with outcasts marks us as different. Once we change our ways and adopt Jesus' eating practices, our gentile neighbors look at us differently. They may begin to grumble that we're gluttons or secretive. We are no longer trustworthy. They'll start to be suspicious, when we refuse to go to the temple or eat meat from Roman altars. They'll suspect our gatherings of being nefarious or even seditious—which of course they are, in some respects, since we pray to a God who wants us to live in a realm that is in serious contradistinction to Rome. A first-century Roman senator and historian, Tacitus, gives voice to this argument, when he says of those who followed the crucified Jesus that they are "a class hated for their abominations, called Christians by the populace."[21]

Being despised and considered a contagion[22] may be a badge of courage for the first generation of those who attend the Jesus circle and enjoy the open hospitality of food fellowship. They knew the truth of what they did. But over time, the resentment and suspicion of neighbors weighs upon us. Their sporadic outburst of hatred and then the later, more organized, acts of persecution frighten us. As Socrates said in the quote from the start of this chapter: "When we first start facing truth, the process may be frightening, and many people run back to their old lives." Naturally, being frightened, we start to search for ways to appease the unrest that our gatherings have caused.

When we ate with Jesus, we enjoyed a circle of acceptance where all are welcome: Jew, gentile, slave, free, man, and woman (Galatians 3:28). He was our guest, even after the cross, and we welcomed all in his name. Our shared bread underlined that principle. None was left out. But that openness is not easy to maintain. Given external and internal pressures and values, we can feel our hospitality growing some conditions. We start to say to ourselves that not all are equal. Even in the early church in Corinth, Paul criticizes a widening gap between the economically well-off and those who labor (1 Corinthians 11:21). Wealthy people eat too much and poor workers go hungry. And what if the social divide only gets worse? We can see in the New Testament, itself, that there is a steady decline in the participation of women in leadership roles[23] and an increasing intolerance to allowing slaves and their masters to gather and eat as equals.[24] And the argument for accommodation becomes reasonable.

---

21. Tacitus, *Annals*, 15:44.

22. Tacitus later alludes to Christianity breaking "out not only in Judæa, the first source of the evil, but even in Rome, where all things hideous and shameful from every part of the world find their center and become popular (*Annals* 14:44)."

23. A simple contrast of how women are treated is evident, when comparing Paul's letter to the Galatians 3:28, in which men and women are equal, to 1 Timothy 2:11, in which women are told to be totally submissive. Likewise, one can compare the authentic Pauline letter to Philemon, in which Paul indicates that a Christian cannot own another Christian, as a slave, to the clearly non-Pauline letter of 1 Timothy. In chapter 6, verse 1, slavery is not only accepted, but slaves are also admonished to obey their masters.

24. For a comprehensive analysis of this process of accommodation evident in the gospels themselves, I would direct you to Crossan, *Render unto Caesar*. Examine closely his chapters on Luke as the gospel writer who wants to accommodate Christianity to imperial ways. Part Two: Culture Accepted and Canonized, chapters 6–10.

If the mission of the church is to preach the good news to the whole world, then it goes without saying that we will have to shape our message, rituals, and theologies to accommodate the values and principles of the world we are converting. Acculturation is natural, and given the arguments made above concerning the human need to fit in, one might say it is inevitable.

And so, as the fellowship of Jesus tries to shape itself judiciously to accommodate, but not capitulate to, imperial values, the open meal is problematic. As we have seen, the sharing of bread without condition is the embodiment of the potent message underlying Jesus' add "Kingdom o" so the phrase reads "Kingdom of God"Kingdom of God. All people are equal. However, if we want to ingratiate ourselves to those who think differently, it's an easy, we could even argue, a face-saving, step to dispense with the meal. If we let the common meal go by the wayside, we have fewer points of disagreement, there's less explanation required, and we can speak of ourselves as a loving and open community, without having to prove it by eating together. And the cynic in me says that we might even add to these arguments for accommodation the patronizing additive that even the poor and dispossessed prefer it. Otherwise, if we had to eat together, they would feel even greater shame at their condition. So goes the argument from privilege.

And that brings us to the third and final reason the meal may have been dropped from the celebration of the Lord's Supper: power. Anyone who has eaten with their hands will know that it's a messy business, a bit chaotic. Bread and fish is a greasy meal. It's hard to be discrete and stay clean. Bread and wine is a bit better. There's less chaos; but still a meal is a pretty free-wheeling enterprise. By its very nature, everyone has to participate in a common meal. And while a host can impose some control over the participants, still everyone has the freedom to eat, to talk and debate, to laugh and cry. Having Jesus for dinner is a spectator sport, since a shared meal spells community, especially one that is held in a close circle with everyone dipping a hand in a common dish. And community implies participation, perhaps innovation and inspiration.

As any teacher will tell you, class lessons take twice as long, if you let students participate. You have much more control over time and indeed over content, if you keep them quiet while you talk.

Now, if I am a leader of a Jesus circle—I'm the one who has the wine press for instance—then I may want to impose some order over the chaos of our shared meal. It might begin with assigning certain people respected tasks: offering the opening prayer, reciting the blessings and thanksgivings, breaking the bread. From that place, I might add a rule of silence. Some Jesus meals are shared in the peace of meditation—no debating. It is not hard to argue, from the altruistic point of view, that order is important. It allows us to achieve a better sense of Jesus' presence with us as we eat. And so, we add more and more stipulations to coordinate and eventually corral the gathering community.

Of course, power is enticing. The more I get to be in control, the more I enjoy it. It inflates my ego, makes me feel important. It goes without saying that I am not going to admit that publicly. I'll couch my position of privilege in terms of its benefits to the wider circle. I'll call myself a servant and initially give orders from that humble place. And it works! With order comes respect, and with respect comes peace. When I am in charge, loudmouthed extroverts are silenced, and harmful extravagances are curbed.

The point is that power seeks to control, and meals are, by their very nature, uncontrollable. It's not difficult to imagine that community leaders would argue against too much eating together, because it causes doctrinal confusion, enables unwanted disputes, and disrupts our spiritual journey. Who can disagree! The meal gets dropped to suit the need for ecclesiastical control.

There may be other reasons for separating the meal from the ritual. Perhaps there was a historical event or scandalous incident that inspired the elimination of the common meal. We don't know. But what we do know is that the elimination of the common meal happened more or less at the same time as a shift in theological sensitivities. When we are sharing a common meal in the first century, even one that contains ritual elements, it is quite easy to assume that a deceased friend or family is still present. We would eat in their honor; we would toast their memory. It was common practice, and still is even today. Take away the actual eating and the shared food, and this honored guest is harder to celebrate.

Did the elimination of the shared food result in a greater concentration on the elements of the ritual? Did those who led worship find it easier to literalize the words of institution found in the story of the Lord's Supper, to turn bread and wine into body and blood? Was this shift an accommodation to Roman precepts? Did the need for control result in a deification of bread and wine? Somehow, Jesus the guest became Jesus the meal itself. Questions for the next chapter.

Tourtière

Tourtière is the quintessentiel Québécois dish. It looks like an exotic pie and contains beef and pork, in equal measure, and is baked in a regular pie pastry; but those who know it and enjoy it would say that *tourtière* is not a meat pie. It lives in a world by itself. It's that special delight reserved for the traditional Christmas Eve celebration called "*le réveillon.*" French Canadian families everywhere will meet late at night on Christmas Eve; maybe they go to the midnight mass at the local Roman Catholic parish or they stay home and listen to folk stories. Either way, in the wee small hours of Christmas morning, there's a feast—to celebrate Christ's birth. *Tourtière* is the first dish of that banquet. It was designed to deliver maximum protein and fat to a people trapped in an unrelenting snowstorm of winter. But it also had to have a cheery, almost other worldly, flavor, given the "Joy to the World" it was helping to announce. So, this meat dish is heavily spiced with what bakers call "sweet" spices: cinnamon, nutmeg, ground cloves.

THE RECIPE

Here's the *tourtière* recipe that I use to make what I sell at my bake stand. It makes four 9-inch pies.

PASTRY

1. Mix 6 cups of all-purpose flour with ½ teaspoon of salt.
2. Cut in 1 pound of "Tenderflake" lard (it's real lard, not vegetable based . . . any pastry maker will tell you it makes the best pastry).
3. Mix 2 eggs with ½ teaspoon of vinegar and 1 ¾ cup warm water.
4. Mix the eggs with the flour/lard mixture, but be careful not to mix it too thoroughly. We don't want the gluten to start forming. It's the flakes in a pastry that matter. We don't want either bread dough or

pastry powder. We should have a crumbly mix. I know this is a tough thing to explain. The dough sticks together a bit, but it also has plenty of flour flakes. Practice and time will help you achieve the real crust you need.

5. Flour a rolling surface, shape 8 equal sized balls and roll out each to a 12 inch diameter pastry shell. Line four 9 inch pie plates with one pastry shell each. To save time, you can shape these bottom shells and them wrap them and keep them in the fridge until you are ready—the next day—in time for Christmas Eve dinner.

THE FILLING

1. Finely chop 8 small onions and 4 cloves of garlic and fry them in 2 Tablespoons of olive oil until tender.

2. Peel and chop 16 potatoes into bite size pieces, place in water, and boil until *al dente*.

3. While potatoes are boiling, mix together 4 pounds of lean ground beef and 4 pounds of pork into the onion/garlic mixture and cook until well done.

4. Pour off grease and liquid from this mixture.

5. Mix potatoes with meat mixture.

6. To the meat mixture add: 4 teaspoons of cinnamon, 2 teaspoons each of ground cloves and ground nutmeg, 1 teaspoon each of freshly ground pepper and powdered mustard. (You can test taste the meat mixture at this point. It should have a pungent flavor, given the cinnamon and nutmeg—no worries, this will bake off slightly in the oven.)

7. Once mixed well, divide up the meat mixture into four equal parts and place in the pie shells.

8. Roll out 4 more pie shells and cover the pie-filled meat mixture with a top, crimping the edges so they are sealed.

9. Using an egg wash, paint the top pastry of the pie. If you like, you can add a design at this point. Using left over scraps of pastry, you can shape a design that sits on the top crust, held in place by the egg wash. I like pine trees or stars, given the festive season of the year.

THE BAKING

This unbaked *tourtière* can sit in the fridge for a day, if you need to prepare it in advance. Everything, apart from the pastry, is already cooked, beforehand. I wouldn't leave it much past 12 hours—the pastry could get soggy.

Bake at 350 degrees F. for 45–55 minutes. Serve while hot with plum chutney, sweet chili sauce, ketchup, or hot salsa, depending on your tastes. You can add a steamed vegetable or salad if you like, but traditional *tourtière* is not intended to be a meal unto itself. It is usually followed by other Quebecois Christmas delights: *ragout aux boulette, ragout pats de cochon,* and for dessert, *tarte aux sucre.* But we'll save those dishes for another time.

Enjoy.

6

Imperialism and the Shift from Community to Cannibalism

Conformity is the jailer of freedom and the enemy of growth.

. . . JOHN F. KENNEDY

WHAT IF?

When we grow up with a specific diet, we don't question it, not seriously. It just is what it is . . . like the *Tourtière* I describe just before this chapter. Live in Montreal, and you assume that's all there is for that unique, late-night celebration of Christ's birth. I grew up in an English Protestant world. No Quebecois dishes in sight. Rather, we had hot oyster soup on Christmas Eve. Didn't everyone? Ellen, my partner, remembers a Christmas tradition from her father's home, a Norwegian dish called *lutefisk:* take some salt cod fish, cure it in lye, and then rehydrate it for several days before baking. The result: a gelatinous, white, jellied fish. Norwegians swear by it.[1] No one questions why *lutefisk* got the way it is. No doubt it has a good deal to do with preserving fish for the long winter nights, when the fjord is too cold or frozen for fishing. So, we accept what is put before us at times of celebration, believing it has always been that way.

---

1. There's a recent film spoofing all things Norwegian called "The Lutefisk Wars," and the subtext is what describes this dish for me . . . "before this is over, somebody's gonna eat it. Ya betcha."

Hence, the 1800-year-old habit, of taking a thin slip of bread and a thimble full of wine and calling it the body and blood of Christ, is not doubted. It's in the bible, right? We've always done it this way. We were told this is how it began. From that very first Maundy Thursday Passover meal until today, the Eucharist was a holy moment, when we ate the gifts of salvation.

"Body and blood of Christ, given for you." How many times did I say that, while serving communion as a minister? As Protestants, we meant the words to be symbolic. The bread and wine were *like* Christ's body and blood. The Roman Catholic world still takes them literally, believing in the transubstantiation of the bread and cup—they become the body and blood of Christ. Lutherans, several Orthodox variants of Christianity, and some Anglicans believe in the "consubstantiation" of the elements. The bread and wine remain bread and wine, but there exists the presence of the divine in them at the same time.[2] This presence can be real or mystical. The point is that finite objects, like bread and wine, are capable also of displaying, containing, or embodying that which is beyond our predetermined understanding.

But whether as transubstantiation, consubstantiation, or metaphorically symbolic, the "meal" we enjoy as the Lord's Supper is now a small piece of wheat (matzah-like cracker, wafer, host, or cube of ordinary bread) and a drop or two of wine (it will be grape juice for many reformed traditions). It's a sacred moment when we consume these elements, because Jesus said they were a memorial of his death—his body broken and his blood poured out. Whether symbolically or literally, we are feasting on Jesus. And that's just the way it is. You could reduce our stance on the eucharist to what could easily be a bumper sticker: "Jesus said, I believe it, that does it."

What if we got it wrong? What if the meal Jesus shared with his disciples on the night before he was betrayed was never intended to be an act of consuming Jesus, our host? What if Jesus had another meaning in mind, when he broke bread and lifted the cup?

I have several reasons for suggesting that we misunderstood the meaning of this last meal.

First, the notion that Jesus was inviting his followers to consume bread, that was either symbolically or literally his body, would be an anathema

---

2. Luther's phrase for this coexistence was "*finitum copax infinitum*" (translated as: the finite is capable or contains the infinite), and on a mystical level, he may be right. Even though a post-enlightenment mind is not tuned to see mysteries behind reality, who can argue with the romantic affirmation that "the heart has reason that the reason cannot tell."—Blaise Pascal, 278.

to Jesus. He was, by all accounts, a righteous, devout Jew.[3] In this world, no one would imagine eating human flesh and drinking human blood.[4] Moreover, the theological explanations we now give to this ritual are at best third-century arguments. They use vocabulary and categories that are more Hellenistic than Hebraic: that Christ has two natures— human and divine, and that he is speaking in this last encounter with his disciples before his death, as one who bridges heaven and earth. Such distinctions would make no sense to a first-century Jew.

Our problem as moderns is that we misunderstand the notion of "sacrifice." Some conservative evangelicals associate it with the requirement that something must be killed to appease or ingratiate oneself to God. And we use the Jerusalem temple as evidence. They regularly poured the blood of innocent creatures on the altar seat in the Holy of Holies, didn't they? But we have to recall that this temple cult was established not because its founders believed God required or even liked blood sacrifices. We bring our best to God—not because death is desirable, but because we want God to eat with us. Our gift of an animal, which as I stated above is not wasted slaughter but sanctified meat, is intended as the first step in hosting our Creator at our festive meal. It's a sacred butchering, undertaken by priests, so that my sacrifice, "my gift," will be acceptable to the real guest at my table: God. The sacrifice never becomes God, and as a temple worshipper I would never imagine I was eating God, when I cut into the pascal lamb. That would be idolatry!

The key notion of sacrifice is found in the prophet Micah (6:8), who redirects the devout and their thinking. We come to God wanting to offer many gifts, hoping that our sacrifices will bring us closer to our Creator. And through the prophet, God responds: *He has shown you, O mortal, what is good. And what does the Lord require of you? To act justly and to love mercy and to walk humbly with your God.*

In the Hebraic world, sacrifice is not about killing. To make something "sacred," which is the root[5] of the notion of sacrifice, is to achieve justice. Or to put this thinking in the right order: "doing justice while loving mercy is all the sacrificial action God expects or desires."

So, when Jesus breaks bread and holds up a cup and asks his disciples to "remember this," he may have had another, entirely different, meaning in

3. Matthew would even paint Jesus as a hyperorthodox Jew, who followed the law and added even more strict interpretations to it. See Matthew 5:17—7:29.

4. See the prohibition against worshipping "Molech," a god who desired the sacrifice of human babies (Leviticus 18). And God further forbids human sacrifice as a means of atonement (Exodus 32:19–33).

5. The English word "sacrifice" comes from the two Latin words: *sacra facet . . .* to make sacred or holy.

his mind. What if we didn't focus on the elements but the circle of those who joined him. As bread passes from one to another, as all are fed and sustained with wine, then we have Jesus in our midst. It's the community of justice that is key, not the two examples of bread or wine that Jesus uses.

Let's examine the first interpretation of the Lord's Supper given by Paul in his first letter to the Corinthians (11:23–26). Is it possible that we have been putting the emphasis in the wrong place?

> For I received from the Lord what I also passed on to you: The Lord Jesus, on the night he was betrayed, took bread,24 and when he had given thanks, he broke it and said, "This is my body, which is for you; do this in remembrance of me."25 In the same way, after supper he took the cup, saying, "This cup is the new covenant in my blood; do this, whenever you drink it, in remembrance of me." 26 For whenever you eat this bread and drink this cup, you proclaim the Lord's death until he comes.

There are two points that I will explore in greater depth in the next chapter as avenues for developing a new "Lord's meal." First, Paul explains this as a real meal, separating the bread and the wine with a "supper." He may have done this so that people didn't come to the actual dinner, eat everything, and leave before the ritual sacrament. Whatever his motivation, the two symbols are joined by the communal meal where all are fed. Second, eating and drinking are not only an act of remembrance to "do this in memory of me." They are also affirmations of hope "until he [Jesus] comes."

What strikes me as essential, when reviewing Paul's explanation, is to think as a first-century Jew. I would not immediately go to the literal meaning that we are now eating Jesus body and drinking his blood. Rather, in the context of a Passover meal, we would see the bread and wine as sign posts, mundane items which have symbolic meaning, just as the matzah and the roast lamb, the cups of wine, etc., are the vehicles for remembering God's salvific acts in bringing us out of slavery. So, Jesus reasserts and interprets slightly the meaning behind the bread and wine. What would make the most sense to his gathered company is that Jesus has laid down a new, perhaps more inspiring, layer of meaning on an ancient meal of memory and hope.

Is it possible that Jesus wanted his followers to focus on the Kingdom of God way of eating and drinking? Whenever, you take bread or raise a cup, remember me, Jesus, who always served people in such a way that all are fed and that none is left out. It's the community of just distribution that is holy and not the two symbolic elements used for achieving it.

Nevertheless, the community that followed Jesus opted for the more literal interpretation of the Lord's Supper. Below, as we explore some of the consequences of that choice, we may uncover some of the reasons it happened. At this point, we can simply note that it is a very bizarre direction. It might have precedents in "Showbread," which the priests in the temple were allowed to eat. Every week, this special bread was placed on the altar as an embodiment of the message of God's historic salvation.[6] But showbread did not contain God. As the priests ate it, they no doubt remembered God's salvation in the wilderness, the free gift of bread from heaven, and by extension, they renewed their trust in their Creator. But make no mistake, God is not consumed.

Nevertheless, showbread shows us that, in the Hebraic word, holiness can be eaten. That may have been a precedent-setting idea behind the practice of consuming elements construed to be Jesus' body and blood.

Blood has always been a very suggestive and powerful symbol. It is the source and sustainer of all life. Hence, it features in religious ceremonies, either literally as blood of an animal or human, or symbolically as wine. In the gentile culture surrounding Palestine, consuming blood was a practice deemed medicinal. People drank Gladiator blood to receive their strength and courage, and it was also believed to cure diseases like epilepsy. So, there is a spiritual or socially predictable precedent—call it a free-floating idea— that by consuming a "special person's" blood, one would manifest that person's qualities. The cult of Mithras, which some say has many comparisons to Christianity, featured a common feast, the consuming of the elements of a sacrificed bull in the expectation that one would receive and exhibit bull-like qualities of endurance and power. For that reason, it was favored by soldiers and legionnaires.

But I have failed to uncover any clear precedents of ritual consumption of the deity being worshipped. And if we think about it, this should not be a surprise, since the consumption of the one who is revered as God would either make that God unnecessary or finite. Not a good start for a religious tradition.

The lack of clear precedents for the transformation of bread and wine into body and blood and the Jewish repugnance in consuming blood lead me to surmise that the shift from communal meal to ritualized consumption of Jesus comes from a source or sources we have not yet uncovered. Perhaps it is a natural, and largely unconscious, step in the progression of Christian spirituality. Once the real meal fellowship is relegated to secondary place, the mind is freed to wander.

---

6. See Leviticus 24:5–9. "Showbread" is the English translation of a Hebrew phrase which is "bread of many faces."

On another level, one might say that the shift away from common, shared eating to a metaphorical ritual meal may be evidence that the Christian story is seeking to conform to the expectations of the world in which it is growing. Leaving behind the messy business of a common meal, and the more thorny question of distributive justice, we spiritually domesticate the Way of Jesus so that it is more accessible and acceptable to empire.

EVERY IDEA HAS A CONSEQUENCE

At this point, you might be wanting to say, "So what?" So what if Jesus didn't mean the Last Supper the way we have interpreted it? Or what if he did? Either way, "what's the big deal," as my grandson might now respond. Is there anything intrinsically wrong with using the bread and wine as spiritual or literal allusions to Jesus?

I have been shaping this book with the explicit purpose of questioning the logic of moving from the common meal to a sacrificial ritual. Something is lost, or perhaps we could say, something has been introduced into the Jesus story, when this shift happens. And it is to these consequences that we'll now turn our attention. There are at least four: 1) the diminishment of the mission of Jesus; 2) the erosion of service and elevation of power; 3) the loss of the feminine within the Jesus movement; and 4) the emphasis on elitism. Let's examine each of these consequences in turn.

LOSS OF JESUS' MISSION

The most obvious result, of the decline and then eventual elimination of, first, the communal shared meal and, then, second, the Last Supper meal practice of Jesus in favor of a ritualized "supper," is the reorientation of the entire Christian program. When we focus on the second meal of Jesus and interpret his words as the institution of a sacrifice, we are taken up by a momentum of ritualism. The Maundy Thursday actions of this Jesus become stylized, sanctified, and eventually reified. Everything that comes before is seen as derivative or foreshadowing of the cross, the sacrifice to which the Lord's Supper, as body and blood of Christ, is pointing.

I am not making this up. The modern understanding of the "Eucharist" is the lasting proof of this impetus to lift up an ordinary meal and turn it into an eternal sacrifice. It then becomes possible, as has been done by so many sects and denominations ever since, to turn the purpose of Jesus' life on earth to be his death. He comes down from heaven in order to die.

We begin to see everything before Jerusalem as a pretext for this final sacrifice. And all the seaside, miracle stories are used as a foreshadowing of his crucifixion.

In that case, the importance of the ministry of Jesus is certainly diminished, if not relegated, to the status of a backstory. The central project that Jesus himself is preaching—the Kingdom of God—is lost or spiritualized. If modern believers think of it at all, it's as an other-worldly realm we attain, because of Jesus' death and resurrection. Or it's an impossible utopia beyond our reach. The healing and eating miracles in Galilee are then transformed into foreshadowing examples, subsumed under the weight of Christ's triumph over death. In this respect, there's no real need even to know what Jesus said or did. His death and resurrection are all in all.

Consequently, Jesus' sacrifice on the cross becomes a lens through which to understand other key principles. Take resurrection as an example. For most western Christians (Roman Catholics, Protestants, Anabaptists), the cross is a price paid to achieve salvation for true believers. And Christ's resurrection is a triumph over death and the promise that true believers will enjoy freedom from sin and eternal life. That's why Ignatius of Antioch called the feeding on Christ's body and blood "the medicine of immortality."[7]

John's gospel is an early example of this transformation of the primary Christian focus away from the mission and miracles of Jesus' ministry to his predestined and all-important death. It has been called the "converting" gospel, because it most effectively portrays Jesus as the glorious son of God.[8] His ministry is merely a revelatory platform from which his final victory over the grave will certainly rise and shine.

It is noteworthy that the most quoted line of the Christian scriptures comes from John. You'll see it on everything from coffee cups to screen

---

7. For a deeper exploration of this topic of resurrection and how the West lost its original meaning, I would direct the reader to Crossan, *Resurrecting Easter*. In summary, his argument goes that the Eastern churches retained the more original meaning of Easter. In the West, we portray resurrection as an individual act—showing Jesus rising into heaven by himself. It's what our Savior does by himself, so that we, as individuals, can enjoy a similar freedom from the chains of death. It's all about getting my soul into heaven (a very Stoic idea, I might add.). The Eastern Christians (Orthodox) have a slightly different perspective on resurrection. The resurrection of Jesus is the starting point for a renewal of the earth. Think of Paul's "first fruits" of the great harvest (described in 1 Corinthians 15:20). Resurrection first signals the start of the restoration of those righteous people who have been lost in hell. Their freedom is the necessary precursor to the recreation of the earth. Resurrection, in this Eastern frame of reference, becomes a corporate act and one that is focused primarily on the renewal of the earth's peoples.

8. See footnote 2, in chapter 2 above, for the complete list of the seven signs which point to Christ's triumph and around which John builds his gospel.

savers. John 3:16 *For God so loved the world that he gave his one and only Son, that whoever believes in him shall not perish but have eternal life.* A statement of the final purpose of Jesus' life on earth: his preordained and sacrificial death that saves all those who believe.

I have yet to see "Blessed are the poor" (Luke 6:20) as a popular slogan. No one quotes: ". . . he was known to them in the breaking of bread" (Luke 24:35). But I can't count the number of times I have been approached by a street evangelist who has said nothing more than the scripture citation: "John 3:16." They shout chapter and verse like a talisman or secret code. No one has ever preached on a street corner shouting out: "Matthew 5:42"[9] or "Luke 4:18."[10] No one knows those verses off by heart. John's Jesus preaches everlasting life, and it works. The rest of the good news is minor details.

You may have noticed above that I did not include John's gospel as a source for the Lord's Supper. There's a simple reason for that. It doesn't exist in John's gospel. There is a final meal between Jesus and his disciples, and it takes place on Thursday evening, but it is explicitly not a Passover dinner . . . since, according to John, that is a few days off. Likewise, there is no bread and wine distribution in John. Instead of a Eucharist, John depicts a sacrament of service in the washing of one another's feet (John 13:4–11). The obvious reason for John's departure from the plot laid out by Mark and copied by Matthew and Luke is that John wants Jesus not to eat the Passover lamb, but to *be* the pascal lamb. In like manner, earlier in his story, John has Jesus proclaim that he *is* the "bread of life" (John 6:35). So it is that the writer of the fourth gospel sets up his audience to see Jesus as the sacred meal. Jesus tells his followers, in what seems to be an invitation to ritualize this eating and drinking: *Whoever comes to me will never go hungry, and whoever believes in me will never be thirsty (John 6:35b).* In John, Jesus has already moved away from being the host to being the meal.

Over the history of the Christian community, the first consequence of turning Jesus into our meal, as John suggests, has been that "justice" is relegated to a second or third place of importance for believers. The ritual of salvation is primary, worship is central, and if there is time and inclination left over, we are freed to be charitable and merciful. And as I mentioned in

9. Matthew 4:42 contains the admonition to be selfless. Found in the Sermon on the Mount, Jesus tells his followers to give to all those who ask without condition. It's the conclusion of the famous passage about turning the other cheek.

10. Luke 4:18–19 is the passage, found only in Luke, in which Jesus quotes the prophet Isaiah 61:1 and portrays his ministry as one of liberation for the oppressed: "The Spirit of the Lord is on me, because he has anointed me to proclaim good news to the poor. He has sent me to proclaim freedom for the prisoners and recovery of sight for the blind, to set the oppressed free, to proclaim the year of the Lord's favor."

chapter 1, this state of affairs is not only theologically suspect, it's been one of the reasons the Christian message is no longer credible to a secular audience. We talk our talk very well, but rarely do we walk it. Rather than expending our best energy establishing a reign of God in our community that reflects sabbath principles Jesus embraced,[11] we bend our knees in prayer. Another goal has replaced the Kingdom of God as our mission: power.

EROSION OF SERVICE, ELEVATION OF POWER

In a seminal text on the ethics of violence viewed from a Christian perspective, Jacques Ellul makes a convincing argument that there are rules or guiding principles that govern how violence[12] is seen by others and how it operates for those who use it. Most people are aware of the argument that violence begets violence. That's a rule we can count on. Ellul goes on to suggest others, one of which is that violence always seeks to justify itself. A friend once said[13] it hides in the shadow of the cathedral. The same could be said of power.

The powerful are never at a loss for reasons explaining why they have power. For kings, it is divine right. For presidents, it is an electoral mandate. For dictators, it is the prevention of chaos. For popes, it is apostolic succession. For wife beaters, it is a biblical commandment. Bullies tell themselves they're better than all the rest. Executioners say they're just following orders. Power will always find respectable, even logical, reasons for it use and abuse.

This has been true in every empire, and alas, it is all too evident in the Christian church. Power has been centralized in the hands of a few, even though the movement began as a circle of equals. One of the consequences, of moving from a communal meal to the ritual in which Jesus becomes the meal, is that the importance of the egalitarian, all-accepting, community is buried under spiritual justifications about apostolic succession and priestly authority, the submissive role of the laity, and the basic sinfulness of all church goers.

Above, I mentioned that pursuit of power may have been one of the reasons why the ordinary communal meal was incorporated into the "Lord's Supper" meal and why the primary focus of piety shifted from bread and fish to bread and wine. We can imagine the one who has the means to

---

11. In Levan, *Prayer*, I show how the petitions of the Lord's Prayer focusing on daily bread and the forgiveness of debt are examples of his allusions to the jubilee/sabbath economics of his tradition

12. See Ellul, *Violence, Reflections from a Christian Perspective.*

13. In a conversation with Jim Cunningham, a reporter for the Calgary Herald.

produce and store wine might see himself (probably it wasn't a woman) as being important, if not essential, to the Jesus circle. Of course, he takes on this responsibility out of a sense of generosity and tells himself he is being the selfless disciple Christ has admonished his followers to be. Can you hear him, as his whispers to his friends: "Supplying the wine—which is a considerable cost to my household—is my 'cross to bear.'" From necessity grows influence, and with influence comes power. It is not a stretch to imagine that this same person might say to the company of Jesus that a real meal is troublesome. "It gets in the way of our prayers to Jesus. Why do the cleanup of all the fish flakes, bread crumbs, and the general mess of a common meal? Let's just stick with broken bread and a cup of wine. And since I have been pouring the wine all these years, I'll be in charge of the ritualized meal." And we would agree. This makes sense. It won't be long before we won't begin our prayer circle, until our wine pourer is present. We'll treat him like our fore-ordained presider, and pretty soon, that's what he'll be. And only those who have his approval can touch the wine. Do you see how power begins and takes over and how it has very reasonable justifications for doing so?

It's also not a coincidence that our church structure starts to resemble Caesar's world round about us. Is this the conformity that John Kennedy says becomes "our jailer?"[14] Partially, as a way to "fit in" and perhaps also to streamline invitations and explanations to new converts, the Jesus community adapts its levels of responsibility and leadership so that they mirror the empire. Power gets centralized, and it is so much easier to do, when there is a ritual over which to preside, as opposed to a common meal.

It's not long before power posits itself as necessary. To keep order and avoid unwanted heresies from corrupting the pure fellowship of Jesus (a fear that was very really, given the mushrooming of variants to the Jesus circle), the Christian church established that there would be the rulers (a very few) and the ruled (the vast majority). In order to make this situation palatable for those who seek power, and those who submit to it, we began to impute divine or transcendent status to the few who sit at the top of our organization. In the church world, it was called apostolic succession. We traced our leadership back to the first apostle: Peter. And those who followed after claimed his "authority," as if they, too, had the mandate and sanction enjoyed by eyewitnesses to the Jesus events. In some circumstances, with respect to the Pope for instance, this reverence for this principal church leader developed into the belief that his decisions and actions were beyond questioning.[15] In more pedestrian ways, churches singled out special people to

14. See the quote that begins this chapter.

15. While the Roman Catholic Church often esteemed the infallibility of the Pope

be "ordained," and only those individuals would preside over sacraments—a belief that holds true for almost all[16] Christian denominations.

Power also builds upon itself. What began as a simple designation, as one who presides over the special meal, turned into a multi-layered pecking order or privilege, much like Caesar's court. The "gift" to host the sacred Lord's Supper was reserved for those who were deemed to be qualified and sanctified. And it then became a self-perpetuating hierarchy, where those in power "ordained" the next generation of church priests and presiders. That's when it became a men-only club of special presiders, who jealously guarded their right to be at the front of the community. Then as humans are wont to do, the church invented a hierarchy of these set-aside individuals. Priests, bishops, archbishops, cardinals, and finally, the Pope grew out of this momentum of power.

A cynic might suggest that the church developed as it did, along power lines, because the church leaders very quickly wanted to appear like imperial officials. They matched their organization to that of the empire to curry favor with the real Roman authorities. And that was certainly the case for first- and second-century church leaders. However, in the first few generations of the Jesus movement, I suspect that the centralization of power was less Machiavellian and more a result of natural human ambitions to serve.

The communal meal implies that everyone has a place and everyone is accepted. It's a circle. It may not always operate on an equal basis, but the potential and principle are present at every gathering. When that communality is lost and the meal is eliminated, then the circle becomes a pyramid. And those at the top tell themselves that their job is to control the proceedings, so that no false teaching or misguided behavior disrupts the sacred ritual of the Lord's meal.

A modern example—a review of the curriculum of theological colleges—makes this point clearly. Our emphasis has been on worship and preaching. I have been part of designing the style and content of degree programs in ministry training, and we gave four-fifths of our energy to biblical training and theological awareness. That is so the final fifth of our energies can be used wisely in the shaping of our technical skills in worship leadership and preaching. That's the chief focus of what we imagine Protestant minsters must do. We train them for power, to be the ordained minister or priest, who is set aside to preside over and be in control of the sacred rites and rituals. If we touch on strategies for social ministry, or best

---

in matters of doctrine when he was speaking *ex cathedra,* the actual doctrine was enshrined and defined more recently: in the First Vatican Council (1869–1870).

16. The Society of Friends (Quakers) might be one exception to the rule of ordained presiders.

practices in the feeding the hungry, well, these studies are seen as derivative areas. They're a subset of Christian ministry skills we might call "diaconal ministry"—what you do if you have time and interest for such tertiary aspects of ministry.

The abuses of the church, whether they are the promotion of slavery, the slaughter of innocents, the oppression of First Nations, the subjugation of women, or the condemnation of alternate sexual orientations, result from this primary reorientation of the ministry of Jesus away from mission (embodied in a common meal) and towards ritual (made manifest in the sacrament of the Eucharist). The one who controls the wine now sees his primary function as the administration of a holy sacrament that gives participants a taste of eternity. Hospitality for the dispossessed is forgotten, as is the inclusion of the outcast.

The last century was called "the Christian Century," because we were going to convert the whole world to Christ in 100 years. Our goal was to convert, not to host. We wanted to convince all people that Jesus was "Lord and Savior" and not to spread open hospitality as the means to achieving lasting peace and justice.

Alas, our adaptation of our faith and theology to suit systems of power has perverted our sense of purpose. Ironically, much of what we currently claim is real church work runs contrary to the project Jesus purported to have championed in his ministry in Galilee: a household of the humble, who give space for everyone and offer bread for all who are hungry.

Seemingly without regard for the outcomes, the Jesus community accommodated itself to the structures and exigencies of imperial power, effectively negating the very goal of living in an alternate world governed by God's sabbath principles.

It goes without saying that the acquiescence to the Roman empire and its values favored male power. So, when the disciples let go of a shared, egalitarian meal mutuality, they also eliminated the feminine from the foundations of our fellowship.

THE LOSS OF THE FEMININE

If you ask a secular crowd about Mary of Magdala[17] (called "Magdalene"), there isn't much our culture knows beyond this: she's a prostitute. The generation that grew up with the song "I Don't Know How to Love Him,"

---

17. A woman from Magdala, a fishing village south of Capernaum on the west shore of the Sea of Galilee, was called "Magdalene."

featuring the Mary made famous by Andrew Lloyd Webber,[18] will also claim that she fell in love with Jesus. We might go one step further to suggest that Jesus "healed" her, perhaps freed her from the sex trade of her day. You may have heard of or read a number of recent books and articles[19] that claim there is now historical evidence that Mary Magdalene might have been Jesus' wife or at least an intimate partner. The idea of Jesus being married is still in a tough sell. Christians have a resistance to acknowledging that human side of Jesus. He can't be a sexual being like us. Elaine, a colleague and pastor from Cuba, once told me that we want Jesus from the neck up.

So, Mary's marital status may be a question mark, but her profession is not. We know she's a woman of the night. The bible says so.

And indeed, as was evident when we examined the story of the un-named woman anointing Jesus' feet (Luke 7:36–50), he did associate with prostitutes. Unfortunately, the story of Jesus forgiving this unknown prostitute, in Luke chapter 7, is followed immediately, in Luke chapter 8, with a list of the women who bankrolled the mission of Jesus.[20] Three women are named; presumably they had financial means. It's a fair bet that, Joanna, who is married to a steward in Herod Antipas' court, certainly had access to the financial resources needed to finance Jesus' itinerant mission band. A second woman, Susanna, is listed without any other information about her status. But the first name cited by Luke is Mary of Magdala. She is described only as one from whom seven demons were exorcized.

There is no reason to associate any of the women mentioned, in Luke chapter 8, with the prostitute found at the conclusion of Luke chapter 7. Luke makes no literary allusions that could be construed in that fashion. Nevertheless, as early as 591 CE, Pope Gregory 1, conflates the verses,[21]

18. Andrew Lloyd Webber wrote "Jesus Christ Superstar," a fabulous Broadway musical, which features all the disciples but gives Mary Magdalene a key role. Portrayed as a prostitute, this Mary sings the heart-wrenching melody: "I Don't Know how to Love Him," igniting all kinds of speculation about a love relationship between Jesus of Nazareth and Mary of Magdala.

19. See Wilson, *Was Jesus Married?* See also Lumpkin, *Jesus and Mary—Husband and Wife.* Further, there is Jacobovici, *Jesus' Marriage to* Mary, January 26, 2015. They marry, but she's not simply "Mrs. Jesus." She is a partner in redemption referred to as the "Daughter of God" and "The Bride of God."

20. Luke 8:1–3: "After this, Jesus traveled about from one town and village to an-other, proclaiming the good news of the kingdom of God. The Twelve were with him, 2 and also some women who had been cured of evil spirits and diseases: Mary (called Magdalene) from whom seven demons had come out; 3 Joanna the wife of Chuza, the manager of Herod's household; Susanna; and many others. These women were helping to support them out of their own means."

21. Pope Gregory 1 (some call him "Great") gave a sermon, in which he stated: "She whom Luke calls the sinful woman, whom John calls Mary, we believe to be the Mary

making an explicit connection between Mary of Magdala and prostitution. He assumed the prostitute, who is forgiven, in Luke chapter 7, must also be the first woman named, in Luke chapter 8; an understandable, if regrettable, error in judgment.

Once this mistake in reading scripture was accepted as fact, many traditions were shaped to justify associating Mary of Magdala with prostitution. Some suggest that early believers liked to associate Mary of Magdala with sexual promiscuity, because her story illustrates the depth of God's forgiveness. Her gifts of anointing give witness to her conversion. She left the trade behind to follow Jesus. Like Zacchaeus, Mary become a perfect example of the triumph of morality. Some recent scholars[22] maintain that the connection between Mary of Magdala and the sex trade is a, not so subtle, form of character assassination. Mary of Magdala is mentioned more times in the gospel record than any other woman, save Mary the mother of Jesus. The Magdalene is featured along with Jesus' mother as being one of the women watching at the cross and attending to him after his death. In John's gospel, she is even portrayed as the first person to meet Jesus after the resurrection (John 19:11–18). We have already noted that this Mary contributed to the ongoing costs of the mission. It would be a reasonable assessment to suggest that the gospel record portrays Mary of Magdala as a leader, one close to Jesus, and in a similar position to that of Peter. So, if this Mary is central to the Jesus mission, what better way to discredit her, and by extension the place of women in the church, than to label her as a woman of night?

The gospel of Mary,[23] a non-canonical early gnostic text, portrays her as more of a leader than a servant. Even some traditional Catholic websites are now suggesting[24] she might be considered "an apostle to the apostles." So, she might have been seen as unwanted competition for an increasingly male-dominated community—hence the slurs.

This is speculation, of course. We have no evidence to assume that the early Jesus circle intentionally maligned one woman, Mary (Magdala)— the contemporary leader along with Peter, who embodied a different Jesus

---

from whom seven devils were ejected according to Mark." Gregory said in his 23rd homily. "And what did these seven devils signify, if not all the vices? . . . It is clear, brothers, that the woman previously used the unguent to perfume her flesh in forbidden acts . . ." Pearse, "Homily of Gregory," 1.

22. Schüssler Fiorenza, "Feminist Theology," 625. Christine E. McCarthy, "Imitation of Mary Magdalene," July 22, 2014.

23. The Gospel of Mary is a non-canonical text discovered in 1896, in a fifth-century papyrus codex written in Sahidic Coptic. There are many translations now available. I prefer the one found in Miller, *The Complete Gospels*.

24. See Kun, "Mary Magdalene, Apostle to the Apostles."

circle—and exalted a different Mary—the mother of Jesus, who incarnated traditional values and patriarchal family structures. There's no biblical or archeological evidence to suggest that the dynamic of attacking one Mary, while worshiping the other, was consciously at play in the early church. However, that is certainly what happened. While Mary of Magdala has her own feast day in the Roman Catholic church (July 22), there is no question that the worship of Mary, the meek and mild mother of Jesus, was, and still is, the dominant picture of the feminine with the Christian community.

It is easy to fall into caricatures. Mary, the mother of Jesus, does not need to be the always supportive, never demanding mother we all want to adore. But there is certainly plenty of evidence to show that the veneration of Mary never becomes a critique of unjust structures of social and political power. She loves, forgives us, and restores us. Hardly ever does she chastise us for acquiescing to the domination systems of civilization. There is no implicit critique of a male-dominated church or the pyramid design of ecclesiastical power. No question, our tradition suggests that Mary, the mother of Jesus, offers peace and healing[25] that are remarkable.

In sharp contrast to this gentle Mary venerated around the world, the Mary mother-to-be we meet in Luke's gospel is a revolutionary, who speaks out against wealth and oppression. It is important to note that, in scripture, Mary the mother of Jesus has no voice other than the one found in Luke 1:46–55— "the Magnificat." And that poem/prayer features a declaration that the world's values of riches and power will be overturned. The hungry will be fed, while the wealthy are turned away. The mighty will be pulled down from their thrones, just as the meek are lifted up.

This is not the kind and gentle voice of an adoring mother. And it is certainly not the basis for the portrait of Mary (*Theotokos*),[26] which the world has come to know and love. The history of Christian liturgical traditions suggests that we have ignored—certainly spiritually—or trivialized this disruptive, prophetic side of Mary. In its place we have a Saint of peace and tranquility.

Is it possible that the world in general, and the Christian community in particular, diminished and demeaned Mary Magdalene, who challenged Peter's role as sole church leader? Instead, did we lift up and venerate a

25. The veneration of Mary at Loudres in France is an excellent example of the power of her worship to bring about healing of body and spirit. I visited Lourdes, prepared to be scandalized by the religious superstition, and instead, it was a mystical experience in which the outcast and the sick were welcomed and included.

26. The council of Ephesus in 431 declared that Mary, the Mother of Jesus, was to be known as "Theotokos" roughly translated as "the Mother of God."

fabricated, inoffensive, benevolent, and benign Mary, the mother of Jesus, who does not challenge power and its many configurations?

The church's critics would quickly point to the quest for power as the reason for the diminishment of women's influences with the Christian church. And there is considerable historical evidence to make that argument. But I would also want to suggest that the loss of the feminine within our tradition is a consequence of the Lord's Supper becoming nothing more than ritual. If we return to our meal with Jesus, you will recall that much of the preparation work: grinding wheat into flour, preparation of protein and vegetables, is woman's work. Cooking and serving the food is what they do. That's their part in our meal. Apart from the on-the-water fishing, itself, done by the men, the rest of producing a common meal of bread and fish is carried out by the women. They would be present and active in the meal, and if accounts of those meals are accurate, Jesus would be inviting them not just to serve, but to stay and eat. You will also recall that wine making is a man's job. So, when wine becomes a more central aspect of the Jesus gathering, the role and necessity of male leadership become understandable, if not required.

In addition, the creation of a circle, the closing of the gap between differences, the seeking out and sustaining common ground . . . these are the gifts of women in many cultures. And as my mother taught me, this happens best through shared food.

As a child, I recall the many dinner parties my mother hosted as her part in the family business. My dad was the minister, and he did the talking, in the church, at its meetings, and in our home. And a superficial analysis might suggest that he was the key to good communication. It was only much later, when my mom and dad spoke of their strategies for community building, that they both admitted how shared food was actually the key element as the way to begin establishing healthy relationships. My mother would coax a compromise from warring factions in churches, where she was serving as co-minister, with a platter of egg salad sandwiches. Hours of debate had nothing on common food, passed hand-to-hand.

And when the practice of breaking bread together is turned into a ritual and then further transformed into a symbolic gesture, the "Communion" loses much of its power to heal—a power exercised by women. With the meal taken out of the Lord's Supper, it is only sentimentality and nostalgia that make it feel special. What is lost is the ability to be vulnerable to each other. Spiritual ecstasy replaces human intimacy.

Moreover, a real meal introduces into our living a sense of contingency that reminds us of our roots. Bluntly, if our rituals only point us heavenward, how can they be of any earthly use? When we lost the feminine influences in our discipleship, we confused spiritual stature with achieving, solving, producing, and winning. In that world "Truth" is an either/or proposition. There is little space in our current practice for the inclusion of humility and weakness as goals, or for the use of compromise and tolerance as community building tools. Have we not been taught by women in our midst that true wisdom is a both/and truth rather than either/or proposition?

One final consequence of the loss of an actual meal in our Eucharistic practice is the rising validation of boundaries and distinctions.

RISE OF ELITISM

"Why are there so many different churches?" A serious question raised at the end of a delightful meal.

It was a very well-known question. How often have I tried to answer it? My questioner is a wise woman, who has seen the world. Growing up in a secular household, she was only introduced to religion in any serious way as a backdrop to other people's weddings and funerals. One summer, as a child, her dad took her to the some of the sanctuaries in her home city in California: Catholic, Methodist, Episcopal, Pentecostal, Presbyterian, United, Alliance. They didn't linger. It was mostly a way for a tired father to entertain a curious child. As an adult, it became a question mark for her. "Why are there so many different churches?" she asked. It's one of the consequences of being a minster of religion that you are asked about the divisions in a spiritual community that claim to honor and desire "unity of faith." So, I've had some practice in answering.

Having studied the history of Christian thought, one might answer such inquiries with a rundown on religious sectarianism—how theological differences divide communities. You could answer with an explanation about heresies and the corrupting power of religious fantasies. However, at its roots, Christian denominationalism arises out of social and ecclesiastical elitism.

We divide ourselves in factions, because we confuse the retention of high standards with faith. Unassailable boundaries are evidence of our faithfulness. The logic works in this fashion: faith is the elimination of doubt. If I believe Jesus as my messiah or Lord or Savior, the more sure I am; the deeper is my belief. If I give myself entirely to this idea, if I am able to ban any doubt or qualification from my heart and mind, I am a saint. Those who think and act like I do are likewise virtuous. But if you have an alternate view, and if you sow seeds of doubt about my position, then you are of the devil. It's best not to keep company with those who would contaminate your uprightness. Separation is, therefore, the only solution.

If faith, as I suggested above, is turned into an either/or proposition, then the building of boundaries is essential to delineate who is in and who is out. There's a right way (the one I am following), or there is a path to perdition. Hence, to be considered a serious disciple, one keeps to one's narrow discipline.

In this case, boundaries and borders may only be an invention of the mind,[27] but they act as sign posts of theological integrity and moral superiority. Rather than being evidence of our failure in basic unity, our divisions, as Christians, have been built on the high ground of unswerving faithfulness to Jesus and his path. Of course, every generation has its own interpretation of the Way. Mark extols patience and forgiveness. Matthew's Way is a revitalizing return to the traditions of Israel. Luke's path is the itinerant's journey of hospitality that will convert Rome. And John's Way is the mystical, labyrinthine journey into understanding. And those are just the first four possibilities. Over two thousand years, countless strategies and tactics have been elevated to eternal status as *the only* Way to Jesus.

And every Way posits its own importance over the others. I don't believe the followers of Jesus began with an exclusivist approach to the profession of their faith. They were reformers and zealous disciples, but they didn't claim elite status, any more than any other variants of Judaism. However, given the resistance of Pharisaic Judaism, it's natural that Christian Judaism, and then Christianity itself, proclaimed its right-headedness and then its righteousness, by claiming, as Paul did,[28] that it knew only the crucified Christ. The wisdom of the world was mistaken. Only in the weakness of the cross do we comprehend the purposes of God. The first apostle starts to separate himself from others, using an often-forgotten notion of God's weakness, a weakness that arise from love. So, even with Paul, there is a tendency to use "us and them" categories; to set himself apart from the wider world.

My point is that separation is the evangelistic tool needed to declare victory over earthly temptations or capitulation to the world's values. However, a common meal makes separation very challenging. As we noted above, it was the common meal that posed the greatest problem for keeping the unity of the Christian church. When we eat with strangers who have different ways and who eat unclean things, we cannot also be "separate" from them. Reclining together, we are tainted by all those who are in our circle.

---

27. Thor Heyerdahl, the adventurer who built and sailed the Kon-Tiki, a raft of balsa wood logs, across the Pacific Ocean in 1947, said, "Borders? I have never seen one. But I have heard they exist in the minds of some people."

28. See 1 Corinthians 2:2–3: "For I resolved to know nothing while I was with you except Jesus Christ and him crucified. 3 I came to you in weakness with great fear and trembling."

Whether the need for separation came first, or the decline of meal practice was its necessary precedent, it is obvious that the rise in an elitist attitude of Christians[29] is established as a *sine qua non*[30] of discipleship. The more fervently you seek unqualified allegiance to Jesus (and the minutiae of discipleship as any group might define them), the closer you are to God.

And in what seems to be the exact opposite of Jesus and his eating fellowship, disciples of the Way begin to distinguish themselves by raising boundaries around the common table. Only those who think and act in the right manner are welcome. The Jesus Way gets punctuated by gates. You can't walk freely. We create confessions of faith, like the Apostles Creed, and we demand that new adherents accept and follow the implications of its precepts. Only those who forsake old ways, the licentious habits learned in the outside world, are welcomed into the sanctity of our circle. Soon, even those inside the camp must undergo regular rituals to renew their acceptable status (confession, for instance). The elements of the meal are elevated to such a degree that only special people (priests) can touch them. So it is that the ritual of the Lord's Supper has the highest walls built around it. What we do, and think, and say about the Eucharist become the ultimate in boundaries.[31]

Hence, many denominations—each one claiming ultimate truth and stacking their claim on the rigidity with which they protect their boundaries. And lest the liberals in our midst become too self-righteous, there is currently a trend toward what one friend[32] called "closed-minded liberalism"—a phrase that meant that everyone *must* be open. Behind the seeming

---

29. Immediately after the great affirmation of John 3:16 that the world is so loved by God that God sent God's only son to die so that everyone could enjoy eternal life, the gospel writer adds the line that condemns those who do not believe. Verse 17: "Whoever believes in him is not condemned, but whoever does not believe stands condemned already because they have not believed in the name of God's one and only Son."

30. *Sine qua non* a Latin phrase which translated literally means "without which not" and in English is used to designate something without which something else could not be or exist or happen.

31. The Marburg Colloquy, Oct 1–4, 1529, brought Martin Luther and Ullrich Zwingli together to debate the basis for their respective reformations of the Roman Catholic tradition. It was a meeting of both theological and political importance, a chance to unite the reformers' movement against a very powerful church based in Rome. In the end, the two leaders could agree upon 14 principles, but the Colloquy failed, because they could not find common ground on the question of Christ's presence in the eucharist. Neither side would capitulate. Zwingli went home wishing "There are no people on earth with whom I would rather be at one than the [Lutheran] Wittenbergers." While Luther initially refused to consider Zwinglians as Christians.

32. George Tuttle, the 27th Moderator of the United Church of Canada, used this phrase in a personal conversation in 1999.

easygoing nature of some liberal denominations is the imperative that the lack of strict doctrinal boundaries was the sign of correct discipleship.

My point is that the Christian church has traveled a long distance from the dusty, side of road, and much maligned gathering of Jesus, where the rejects and outcasts ate with this carpenter from Nazareth, while the "good people" stood at a distance, gripping and gossiping. I am not suggesting that a real common meal, if it had persisted as the central liturgical practice of Christ's followers, would have been able to resist the creation of borders and boundaries. My point is that the loss of that meal practice had the consequence of removing any resistance to the creation of an elitist form of piety and practice.

THE COMMUNITY OF DOING

The original sign of following Jesus was an act, be it the common meal, or the feeding of the outcast, or the healing of the sick. Christians were doers. As time passed and the meal was forgotten and healing was rendered a spiritual gift, we became a circle of believers. Recently, Robin Meyers made this observation about the shift in the Christian vocation:

> Consider this remarkable fact: in the sermon on the mount, there is not a single word about what to believe, only words about what to do and how to be. By the time the Nicene Creed is written, only three centuries later, there is not a single word in it about what to do and how to be—only words about what to believe.[33]

For this reason, I believe it is entirely reasonable to claim that the original common meal of unlikely companions was one, if not *the,* central tool in the strategies of Jesus to inaugurate the Kingdom of God. It was more than talk about belief; it was faith in action. And as a meal that was given without price and distinction, it stood in contrast to the meal practices of the empire and the elite.

Those who joined Jesus for a shared meal understood immediately that they had left the "normalcy of civilization" (Crossan) behind. In Jesus' circle, food was shared without condition; abundance reigned. Money was not an issue. Everyone was served.

The meal was Jesus' way to break down barriers of class and gender, race and righteousness. His common meal repeated the lessons of sabbath and distributive justice. But as the generations of disciples of the Way came

33. Meyers, *Saving God from Religion*, 102.

and went, the meal changed, as noted above. As the glory and majesty of the person, Jesus, rose, the importance of a real meal declined. As I speculated above, moderating and then eliminating a shared food fellowship made the Christian Way more accessible to others and reduced the barriers to social acceptance. We accommodated ourselves to what was perceived as "normal." Dominic Crossan puts it well in his recent book on Jesus and Caesar. He describes the process of conformity.

> . . . the conscious or unconscious submission to the drag of normalcy, the lure of conformity, the curse of careerism that can— under certain leaders, in certain circumstances, at certain times and place—turn some of us into monsters, many of us into liars, and most of us into cowards.[34]

Whether intentional or accidental, the shift from real meal to symbolic ritual had the effect of relegating questions of justice to tertiary place which also made the Christian Way easier to embrace. Acquiescence to normalcy, or injustice, and violence was the price we paid for joining mainstream with imperial values.

To use a mercantile metaphor, Christianity needed to fit in or accommodate itself to empire. So, a deal was struck. Wittingly, or more than likely unwittingly, disciples of Jesus dropped the justice questions implicit in shared eating and elevated God-worship; a change that made sense to an imperial audience that had been paying tribute to a god-man (Caesar) for many years.

I recognize that this chapter has been one speculative idea after another: alleyways of potential meaning that need to be explored in greater depth. No doubt, there are cohorts of doctoral students wanting to do just that. For the present, we conclude with the simple affirmation that the Christian church is not where the Jesus movement began and, in many ways, is traveling in precisely the opposite direction from his original vision. Through the shifting of our meal practice, Christianity has evolved into a Kingdom of Caesar, all the while pretending it is the Kingdom of God.

One question remains. Can Christians reset the table for a new expression of Jesus' "holy" meal? One that might open our tradition to a renewed energy to approximate God's reign here on earth?

---

34. Crossan, *Render unto Caesar*, p.276.

Bannock

Regular Bread, whether it is made from sourdough or yeast, assumes an establishment of sorts. You can't change locations and bake it, at least, not easily. Most often, you have to spend a day letting it rise enough to bake. And then you need some form of constant heat, preferably on the top and bottom of a loaf, as is provided by an oven or cast iron pot with a lid. That takes some organizing. For most people, to bake is to stay put.

On the other hand, Bannock is a travelling bread. It is designed to be cooked on the run, at the end of a day's walk or over the morning fire before the journey begins. You can bake it, fry it, roast it on a stick, or grill it. If you have heat you can make Bannock,

Keep your Bannock mixture dry, and it will last for months. Then add a little water, and it's fresh and flavorful. And depending on where you are traveling, you can add blueberries or raspberries into the dry mixture, before you add the liquid, to get a fruit bread. After it's baked or roasted, Bannock works well with cheese or jam. If you make a pancake Bannock, you might use maple syrup and butter to jazz it up. It can also be a sandwich bread or dipped in yogurt for dessert.

Bannock has roots in the Scottish Highlands, where the harsh climate requires an easy source of energy, and is also an indigenous staple among First Nations, who used it as an ideal diet during seasonal migration. Hence, there's an argument to be made that Bannock is one bridge, among many emerging possibilities, for finding common ground between peoples in the U.S. and Canada.[1]

I have used the following recipe for everything: overnight canoes trips, youth group weekends, national church celebrations.[2] It's a versatile and easy bread to share. It's filling and fun.

---

1. See Saul, *Comeback.*

2. In 2010, I helped organize a nationwide celebration of the United Church of Canada and its 85th anniversary. After receiving flour from all parts of the country, a local congregation in Fredericton, New Brunswick (Wilmot United), organized teams of volunteers to put together Bannock packets like the one described in this recipe. We made over 3000 Bannock bags—all from the same flour—a symbol of unity. Then these

BANNOCK MIX

In a plastic bag combine and mix thoroughly (it will keep like this for months—you can do multiples of these amounts to make more Bannock mixture):

>   1 cup white flour
>   1 teaspoon baking powder
>   1/2 teaspoon salt
>   1 Tablespoon sugar

Take 1 ¼ cups of this Bannock mixture and follow the steps below:

- For pancake Bannock, stir in 1 cup water or milk. Pancake Bannock will be much runnier than baking/frying Bannock.

- For frying Bannock into a biscuit, add ½ cup water. To fry your Bannock in a pan, fry each side until golden brown.

- For baking Bannock add 1/3 cup water. Work the dough for a few minutes, until it sticks together, and then bake it. Put it on a baking sheet in the oven at 350 degrees F. for 15–20 minutes.

Bannock packages were sent to every congregation in the country. On the anniversary Sunday, it was therefore possible for each local church to make a common bread (Bannock) to share.

7

Resetting the Table for a Twenty-First-Century Meal

Without leaps of imagination or dreaming, we lose the excitement of possibilities. Dreaming, after all is a form of planning. Gloria Steinem

YOU CAN'T GET THERE FROM HERE

When I was young and foolish, I would take my children on weeklong bike trips. I remember them fondly, but my daughter now tells me they were not quite as exciting as I imagined them to be. Their protests notwithstanding, we would look at a map, calculate how far we could get each day, and make a plan. When they were teens, I chose a tough route . . . something to ensure they were too tired at the end of a day to protest an early bedtime. With three kids, two friends, a borrowed bike, and a tandem, we took off for our first destination—marking the passing kilometers by regular stops at ice cream stands to enjoy milkshakes.[1] We were exploring southern New Brunswick. My idea was to visit the islands: Grand Manan, Deer Island, and end on Campobello, the Canadian island, where Franklin Roosevelt and his family spent their summer vacations.

I thought I had studied the route carefully. One of the advantages of biking is that you never go very fast. There are frequent stops to verify

1. It is a strange quirk of long bike rides that the best way to quench one's thirst is a cold milkshake . . . sugar energy and a nonacidic calming liquid. Perfect. We would keep a running tally of the best milkshakes of the trip.

the road ahead. So usually, any errors in planning can be corrected. I saw the lines of ferry routes leading onto Deer Island and assumed it was large enough to host a grocery store, maybe a couple of campgrounds, a restaurant, if my band of teenagers needed chips and a coke. "And, look," I said pointing to the map. "It's so close to Eastport, Maine. I figure we can set up camp and then spend a few hours walking the streets of a quaint fishing village." Nods all around the circle. We had a plan.

Alas, when we got to Deer Island, we discovered it was a cottage resort destination. No stores for food. A convenience shop with candy was the best we could do. I didn't know how I would feed the hungry teenagers, who had been complaining for a few miles that they were tired and done for the day. I had to scramble eggs on the side of the road to give them some energy to make the last push to our campsite. A bit refreshed, we set out on our final leg to the very end of the Island. Just as we were setting up our tents, we discovered that there was no ferry, no bridge, not even a water taxi between Deer Island and Eastport. (Did I mention I was young and foolish? A bit shortsighted too!) We stood on the last point of land overlooking the cheery lights of that village, not more than 200 yards of water away, and realized that we couldn't get there from here. It was a sorry night.

In many ways that's how I feel, having taken you, my patient reader, through the twists and turns of our church's treatment of the meal fellowship of Jesus and the ritual of the Lord's Supper. Are we at a dead end? My critique has been quite harsh, and I know there are many for whom the Eucharist is a still a deeply meaningful tradition. Christmas Eve Midnight mass at St. Peter's Basilica? Can it get any better? And not all the problems facing the church can be laid at the feet of the drift from a shared communal meal to a "holy" ritual.

Nevertheless, there seems little doubt in my mind that we have backed ourselves into a corner as a community of faith. Riding on the momentum of a Christendom model of faithfulness, which assumes constant growth in membership, revered social status, and widespread public acceptance, if not reverence, the church never contemplated that it would be abandoned and that its definition of truth would be ridiculed, worse yet . . . ignored. Our humiliation as an institution was never in the cards.

Certainly, the model used by the historic, northern, Protestant churches is done. It's at a dead end. It can't get us where we want to go. Sure, there will be some churches, which for specific demographic or financial reasons are able to hang on, even thrive. But for the vast majority of historic churches, this glorious trip of two thousand years, ends here.

The institution may not have lost all its energy, but the place we thought we had in society is certainly gone. No one turns to the church any longer for advice. We used to joke that the Prime Minister no longer has the United Church Moderator's phone number on speed dial.[2] Actually, that's not true. It may well be the PMO[3] is in touch with the church often these days. But more than likely, it is to consult and complain of our role in residential schools and the suppression of indigenous culture and rights.[4] Alas, if the Christian church is acknowledged at all within the media, it is for past abuses and criminal negligence of defenseless children given into our care. Another instance of the church's shame.

Indeed, our humiliation as a social institution is hard to ignore. Travelers no longer stop at one of our local congregations, when they are on holidays. They're out of the habit of churchgoing. Kids don't get taken to Sunday School, whether they like it or not. Sunday schools are an endangered species. Parents are too busy to sit on church boards or volunteer on property committees. Add to our social irrelevance plummeting memberships with the burdens of real estate mentioned in chapter 1, and the direction we are headed seems clear: Institutional demise.[5]

And if, as believers, we tell ourselves that we are to' be the world-transforming movement of faith of which Jesus spoke—then, unfortunately, I don't think we can get there from this place. The current model of church, that imitates social structures of power and is built on the assumptions of mass appeal, is an empty and failed experiment. Counting our faithfulness by the numbers of people in the pews on a Sunday morning is a loser's gamble.

Likewise, we can no longer claim exclusivity. The community of faith that considers its version of spirituality as the singular gift of revered truth for members is delusional. There are many more enticing versions of truth and wholeness sold across the Internet—most don't require that you leave

2. There was a time when the Moderator of the United Church of Canada, being the leader of the country's largest Protestant denomination, would have reason to be consulted by political leaders.

3. PMO is a short form for "Prime Minister's Office" and is used in the media to be synonymous with government policy.

4. In the lead up Pope Francis' visit to Canada in July 2022, the PMO (Prime Minister's Office) was frequently urging the church to apologize for decades of abuses of indigenous children in their care in residential schools. While the United Church apologized for its part in the prejudice against First Nations and made reparations, as did many other denominations, we are still viewed, by the secular world, as responsible for and still unresponsive to the question of indigenous injuries and oppression.

5. At one point in my career, this kind of statement would sound like an overstatement, melodramatic rhetoric. No longer. Allow me a recent example. East of Toronto lies Oshawa, population 170,000. Where once there were half a dozen thriving United churches in Oshawa and environs, the expectation is that only a couple will survive beyond 2023.

the comfort of your computer screen or iPhone. There's everything from hot yoga, zoomed live to your living room, to weekly-guided, New Age meditations sent directly to your inbox. Why leave home to go to a one-dimensional church, when you've got four dimensions right here at home?

Returning to the conclusion of the last chapter, if Christians focus almost exclusively on worship, they miss the central principle of their tradition. If we do justice work as if it is a tertiary, optional diversion from the main event which is Sunday morning, we will never find our way back to Jesus' Kingdom of God.

My question for this final chapter: Is it possible to move from that "established" institution to an itinerant movement? We can't reverse the tide of events that has brought us to this point. What's done is done. And that raises a strategic question: Can we relinquish power and status—not just have it taken away by virtue of our irrelevance—but actually give it away meaningfully? Is there a humble seat at the back of the bus with our name on it . . . a place from which to serve rather than preach? Are there ways to salvage the kernels of truth that still exist in our church culture: volunteerism, non-violence, common sharing, resistance to injustice? Is there a path forward that will make the "old, old story,"[6] we sang about in the heyday of our church, sound like "good news" again, as this church model dwindles and declines?

That's the challenge. I have several glimpses of what might be a "new meal" within our tradition, but first I begin with the bad news. Some things may have to die completely, before there can be rebirth. Lest we despair, this is not a novel idea. Resurrection is about new life coming from real death. We do not worship resuscitation, as if all we need to do is breathe some extra energy into our unfortunate soul that is existing on life support. No. Things must die.

RESURRECTION: A PHOENIX LIKE EVENT

Take the lodgepole pine as an example. It needs fire to prosper.

Recent years have seen a dramatic rise in our awareness of devasting forest fires in the western United States and Canada. Whole cities and towns have been destroyed, when winds swept these conflagrations in the wrong

---

6. The hymn "Tell me the Old, Old Story," was written by Kate Hankey. She was a member of the Clapham "sect" of Anglicanism associated with William Wilberforce. Hence, she acts as a symbol of hope for our current explorations. That group was instrumental in the abolition of the slave trade, the promotion of public health, and popular education. An example: Hankey used the proceeds from her compositions to support local missions.

direction.[7] Horrendous events! And their frequency and severity seem to be increasing. Our attempts at fire suppression appear to be counterproductive. It's become so bad that some people are deciding to move from their home states, to avoid what they see as the inevitable fire destruction of their houses and livelihoods.[8]

Ecologists and environmentalists are now pointing out that, since the turn of the last century, our strategy has been the suppression of potential forest fires. But what appears to be happening because of global warming is that our regular fires are turning into massive conflagrations that cannot be controlled in the ways previously thought possible.

What has been overlooked in our approach to forest fires is the fact that many species of trees and some ground cover plants have adapted to, and even require, regular fires to prosper. Enter the lowly lodgepole pine and its serotinous cones. Lodgepole pine trees are ubiquitous across the western United States and Canada. The seeds for replanting new lodgepole pines are locked (actually glued shut by pitch) inside their cones. They hang in the branches waiting, waiting for a forest fire. It requires the intense heat of a fire to melt the sap and unleash the seeds. No fire, no new pines. Jack pines and Table Mountain pines have the same system for regeneration. Living examples of the Greek myth of a phoenix rising from the ashes. Death is not an end, but the means for new life.

One wants to be very careful to avoid the mistake of turning suffering into something it is not. Fire burns. End of story. A forest fire is devastating. It destroys homes and sweeps away prosperity, property, and people—not to mention wildlife and natural habitats. Nevertheless, environmentalists tell us that it is a natural occurrence. Forests go through cycles, and as one colleague once said to me, "A beautiful mature forest is a forest fire waiting to happen."

To transfer the metaphor to the church, it may be necessary that the institution goes through a similar cycle of fire, so that rebirth can happen. I believe that the current humiliation of our institution must be followed to its very conclusion, before we can achieve any real renewal. Given the seductive appeal of a Christendom church with growth in membership and

7. In 2016, a forest fire in northern Alberta destroyed large parts of the city of Fort McMurray, destroying over 300 buildings and costing over 9 billion dollars in damages. A smaller fire, but equally devasting, took the village of Lytton, British Columbia, in 2021, killing two people and wiping out 90% of the buildings in the village.

8. In some parts of California, house insurers have issued nonrenewal notices, forcing governments to step in and offer partial coverage. But the fear of fires and the lack of protection have led people to leave California to avoid personal and devasting loss to forest fires.

status as an institution, this process of death and rebirth will not be easy nor appreciated. Most church leaders will feel like failures, and the remaining church members will take no joy in the death of their congregations.

No institution embraces its own demise with any sense of relish or celebration. We dig in and hold out for a variety of reasons: resentment, pretense, sadness, grief, and weakness. Each aspect of this resistance deserves some clarity.

RESENTMENT

Do you recall Bob Dylan's famous melody about the changing world: "The Times They Are A- Changin"? He wrote it in 1963 and sang it first in New York, a month before John F. Kennedy was assassinated. The lyrics have a haunting, prosaic quality. Everything was in flux. Old ways were dying and not useful. New ways were coming. I recall singing it on the beach around a campfire, putting special emphasis on the verse about our parents and how their values are "rapidly aging" and they need to clear out of our way if they can't change. As kids, we knew we were right, and we would change the world for the better, correct the mistakes of our parents, and build a new road to prosperity and peace. Echoing the slogans of the civil rights movement and borrowing a good deal of their spiritual power, we would march onto this new road with pride and determination.

Predictably, our parents' generation reacted with anger and resentment. How dare we characterize their way as the "old road!" Sure, it was "aging," but they had just fought through a world war to preserve it, and they were going to hang on to their way of living for as long as possible. No doubt, some of our mothers and fathers used the famous slogan of church resistance to change: "We have never done it that way before." How often has that phrase been bandied about congregational board meetings to forestall new ideas?

As young people, we derided these "old" people (anyone over 30) and what looked like their unthinking pigheadedness. Perhaps if we had seen it for what it was—resentment over being left behind and fear over not mattering any longer —we might have been kinder and more understanding.

Now that am I "old" (can there be life after 69?), I understand this resentment over change. I have given my life to building a religious institution,[9] and it irks me greatly to see it leave all those good efforts be-

---

9. I would often joke with my students that I have never received a regular pay check from anything other than an institution related to the United Church of Canada. I had some part-time contracts with CBC and a few speaking gigs, but regular pay:

hind in search of some "newer, better road." Did I not matter? Was there no merit in what we tried to accomplish? Change calls into question antecedent movements and ideals, and that's hard to take if I was integral to building those, now, "old roads."

PRETENSE

I use the word "humiliation" advisedly, when I speak of the decline of the church. It's a very tough picture to contemplate. A once noble and important social and religious establishment is crumbling. And no one wants to admit it—especially those who still believe in it. But our decline is embarrassing. So, we expend a lot of energy keeping up the façade of health and prosperity.

On the coast of Gaspé, Quebec, at the beginning of the last century, before ubiquitous travel made possible by airlines, local fishing communities stayed put. There was very little commerce with the outside world beyond the next harbor. That being the case, high holidays were local affairs. Come the Christmas season, homemakers would spend their free afternoons baking cookies and cakes in preparation for the onslaught of visitors during Christmas and New Year festivities.

There would be a few children who made their way home for the holidays, but most of the visitors were locals. Folks didn't have much to give each other, apart from warm hospitality. But everyone visited each other. Coffee, tea (homemade hooch if you were so inclined), fruitcakes, and shortbread were on offer. Hospitality was the gift neighbors gave to one another. When I arrived in the late 1970s, to serve a local congregation on that coast, the old crowd still baked their Christmas treats, but no one came to call. Families had drifted away, and neighbors were busy with their own plans. How often did I go for tea during Advent, only to discover a full table laden with goodies—for one person. At that point, my hosts were mostly widows, matrons of the days gone by, and they couldn't bear not to bake— even though they knew no one would be coming. It was partly habit, but it was mostly pretense. Christmas baking is what you must do. The show must go on, no matter that it is a largely forgotten tradition.

I would sit and drink tea, nibble on a cookie, and feel the weight of a dying proposition. My host and I would exchange stories and rehearse fond memories of times past, telling ourselves that more visitors would no doubt appear. Next day, next year. They never came.

---

it was the church always, even though I have worked in everything from university administration to welfare rights.

I had the same sinking feeling, when I attended a graduation ceremony for one of my favorite seminaries. In the past, their convocations had been grand affairs, daring to push the limits of academic excellence, inviting into the circle many who would otherwise have given the church a wide berth: social agitators fresh from a stint in jail, movie directors of *avant-garde* films. What a party! Crowds of celebrations. But that was back then. At this particular ceremony, my good friend and I sat in a 1000-seat church sanctuary. I counted twelve other audience members. The academic procession was slightly larger than those in attendance. Now we could have laughed at our numbers and retired for a more informal gathering, something small but meaningful, to toast the graduates. No. We went through the entire formal service: speeches from board members and faculty, a student valedictorian (there were only three graduates) bidding us all to move into ministry with hope, the offering of an honorary doctorate, with attendant acclamations of excellence, and a closing triumphant hymn. It was a litany of pretense. We went through the motions, as if we were a great ship of state, embarking on another glorious voyage of discovery. Just like my hosts on the Gaspé coast, no one wanted to admit that the party was over. No one is coming.

So, we resist the demise of the church, because it feels embarrassing. Once we were important, now we are not—worse—we are irrelevant. Not just dead, but forgotten.

And since no one wants to be humiliated, as church leaders we see every new face as a chance for renewal. That young person, who wandered into the Sunday service (maybe thinking it was cute or charming!), is evidence that the church ain't over yet. There is still hope. And so, rather than planning our ending in a sincere manner, we hold onto false pictures of renewal.

GRIEF

And there's a great deal of sadness mixed in with our decline as a church. Last month, I sat in the small Anglican church down the road from my house on Salt Spring Island. St Mark's is a quaint chapel, sitting quietly on a hill overlooking the road. Unassuming, but very dignified. It has been in existence since Queen Victoria sat on the throne. The stained glass window at the back of the nave was installed in her honor. Looking across to the west wall, I saw several brass plaques: one giving testimony to the dedication and generosity of a founding family, another bearing witness to the sacrifices of young men from the congregation who had gone off to the "Great War" and never returned. What happens to all these sacrifices? Humble folk had given their lives, some quite literally, to St. Mark's and, by extension, to the Anglican Church of Canada. And now that that building was closed and the community of faith disbanded, what can be said of past efforts to raise the cross of Christ on this country lane? Was it all a farce? Did it matter? Is there any redeeming aspect to this church closure? The decommissioning service had ended it all. The building would be sold. No doubt, it would end up as a redeveloped monster home with unusual stained glass windows overlooking a hot tub and pottery studio.

While I had never worshiped at St Mark's, I grieved for all the lost dreams, the forgotten acts of generosity, the heartfelt prayers, the many hours of dedication and hope spent on that little chapel. Its death felt like a failure and a very sad commentary on human frailty. No wonder we want to resist the closing down of the church project. It hurts too much.

Those who have walked with friends and family out to the graveyard know that the heaviest burden we bear is grief. The sorrow over what has been lost, when someone dies, is tremendous. But grieving is more than sadness. It also has overtones of regret, a deep desire to be forgiven or to forgive. Grief brings us to the edge. All our weakness and frailties become visible, and more importantly, we see them more clearly and recognize that there isn't time or opportunity to make them right.

Grief makes us do funny things. Like Ms. Havisham,[10] we refuse to admit "the times they are a-changin'," and we are determined to stop the clock at the moment of our loss. We pretend it's not over. We complain about anyone who tries to get us to move from our nostalgic picture of past events and lash out at suggestions we are out of touch.

I can't help my own grief. When I began ministry, churches were booming. Yes, the place where I began my preaching career had small numbers—ten on a good Sunday. But I told myself that it was a rural parish and it was all a matter of time before things turned around. Half a century later, I still preach to ten people, but now it's in one of the major congregations in the center of Canada's largest city.

How can we have sunk so low?

Not only does the current situation seem unreal, and a bit farcical, there's a deep sadness, as I think back to my childhood church when the pews were full, twice a Sunday, and when the local newspaper came to the minister's house to take pictures of the annual Christmas party. We thought we were somebodies. The Christian church was on the rise. And I have to

---

10. Miss Havisham is a character in Charles Dickens' novel, *Great Expectations*. Miss Havisham was jilted at the alter and wears her wedding dress for the rest of her days, living in a slowly dilapidating mansion, trapped by her own grief. Her wedding cake still sits on the dining room table, a decaying, disgusting reminder of her lost hope.

admit that I wish I could get back to the time when my dad's sermons would be quoted in editorials and discussed in city council chambers and when our Nativity pageant drew hundreds. There was a sense of purpose in our mission and importance in our choices—both personal and professional.

Now it feels like a bad joke.

WEAKNESS

And that brings us to one final problem with facing change in our rituals and religious gatherings. I'm tired and more than a bit jaded. And so, I resist having to contemplate trying, yet again, to make the gospel story make sense. Binging on Netflix is easier and certainly more entertaining.

As I was about to retire, I served a community that had been the source of countless, justice-based initiatives. It began the homeless shelter and spearheaded community dinners, including a still-operating Christmas day meal for hundreds. In addition to these charitable acts, they wrote letters of resistance to torture used by foreign dictatorships, asked governments to cease racism policies regarding indigenous peoples, and stood up for women's rights. In its prime, this community of faith exemplified the best of our Christian tradition.

But age takes its toll. As we grow older, our psychological energy and emotional elasticity are tested. What was once quite doable and desirable became, in time, irritating and impossible. Once we fed the homeless and had them sleeping in our basement. Now they frighten us, and we want them to go somewhere else. At one time, the fact of homelessness was an affront to questions of justice. Now it's an irritating embarrassment. We'd like to be more open, welcoming of differences, but we're not able to think beyond the boundaries of our own security. Our hearts and minds are not endlessly elastic. We're done. "It's just beyond us," we mumble with regret.

And alas, this may be the epitaph written on our church's tombstone. If we resent and grieve, pretend and resist too long, our end will come before we are able to do anything more creative than close doors.

One of the saddest days of my ministry was helping a group of people close their church. We sat in the "boardroom" of a 1960s building. On the painted, cinder block walls were the mementos of a great beginning: a chrome-plated shovel from the first days of construction and a hammer fixed to a plaque, which also had a photo of cheering participants. The faces are filled with hope, as they built their dream. Alas, some of people sitting around the table discussing how to close their church down were the very same ones as those in that inaugural portrait. They'd tried everything, rented every space of the building they could not use themselves, cut staff, trimmed lighting bills. Still, the envelop offerings continued to drop well below the annual expenses. Time to call it quits! Last one out, turn off the lights.

But we had waited too long.

Faithful though they were, those folk didn't have the energy left for creativity. Lots of courage, but precious little foresight. So, we debated how to disperse the resources gained from the sale of the building and church assets. Most would go to a central, anonymous church fund. Some would follow the few members still standing who would join another congregation. And that's the tragedy. All the plans and hopes of that initial group of disciples are lost. Their unique mission, nurtured by the gift of their context and geography, winds down to a bill of sale. I tried to persuade them to use their final decision to transfer resources to a project that might continue a Christian ministry in their name, reincarnate their special spirit in another place. But we had waited too long. There wasn't sufficient energy to think outside the box.

And that's the current challenge. When communities of faith shrink and the dreams of a thriving church seem impossible to achieve, we often wait too long to make a decision about our demise. Like so many individuals, we do not want to contemplate our own death and so we come ill-prepared to our end times. Often what happens in urban settings is that congregations amalgamate—joining one dying community to another. We don't change the basic model, and so it becomes a game of musical chairs. Some church communities thrive as they receive an influx of resources and new members from neighboring churches that have closed. The names of buildings get hyphenated to reflect the new union of congregations, but the approach remains the same. Eventually, the music stops, and that newly amalgamated entity closes down to join a church that still has a seat in the game and the energy to continue this ill-fated dance. So, it goes.

This is not the forest fire phenomenon. There is no new life springing from the dispersal of seeds falling from freshly opened pinecones. To switch metaphors: there is no phoenix rising from the ashes of the old church. It's just black soot and cinders.

DYING WITH DIGNITY

There once was a dying church that had the foresight and courage to see its end and to plan for a death with dignity. They could have done the traditional thing: batten down the hatches, cut staff, and hold on 'til the well runs dry. Instead, they chose to die. They would not squirrel away their remaining trust funds, postponing the inevitable for as long as possible. No. Showing considerable nerve and audacity, they gave themselves three years. They planned their dying carefully. Being a congregation built in the heart of a large Canadian city, they had many options. They could use their final years to develop and nurture a ministry to their neighboring corporate community, one that had lost its soul—becoming a chaplain to industry, so to speak. They could have transformed themselves into a mission band, preaching the "good news" on the street corners surrounding their old building (it took up an entire city block). How about a soup kitchen? Heaven knows, the city had far too many hapless, hopeless, hungry citizens. In the end, they chose to offer programs that explored the artistic edges in the expression of faith. They decided they would put all their energies into a creative dialogue between ancient Christian theological principles and modern artistic expressions of truth.

Of course, I have given you the romanticized, rationalized version of the story. I am sure that no one saw the steps they were taking with exactly that kind of clarity. As we all know, when church motions get seconded, and amended, and revised, the guiding vision is often maddeningly blurred or obscured. But the basic idea stands. Planning a dignified death allows for the possibility of new life. No pretense or prevarication.

Speaking to the wider community of faith, I would invite us to think strategically about the use of what resources in people power and economic assets still remain available to us. Is there a way to plan for our demise that would maximize the possibility of new life emerging from our death as an institution?

Working as a volunteer with the Royal Canadian Marine Search and Rescue, we often speak of the "1–10–1" principle of survival in the deadly cold waters of the Salish Sea that surrounds the island where I live. This principle is all about survival and priorities. Once you fall in the water, you have "one" minute to stabilize your breathing. Most drownings happen in that first minute of immersion, because people swallow water rather than air in their desperate attempt to live. Then you have "ten" minutes within which your fingers and limbs will be useful in performing whatever you need them to accomplish. After that time of physical ability, you have "one" hour as your body slowly is unable to respond to minimal calls for movement, until finally you lose all consciousness. That's the formula, and since we know that it does not vary much from person to person, the wise ones will take the ten minutes of relative physical flexibility and mental acuity to plan how they can survive, when both these things are gone.

We've got those "ten" minutes as a church.

In that spirit, and recognizing what the previous chapters have in-
dicated about the original strategy of Jesus, when he was proclaiming the
Kingdom of God, I would conclude with one general principle and several
signs of hope . . . hints of what could be. Here's how Christians might reset
the table for a new expression of Jesus' "holy" meal.

A GUIDING PRINCIPLE

If I take my search and rescue example as a helpful metaphor, the guiding
principle in our efforts should be to maximize the survival of the "good
news," so to speak, by limiting any distracting options. There's no time to
waste on useless illusions of immediate rescue—dreams of a benevolent
boat crew coming by just in time to pluck us from the water. Likewise, we
can forget the valiant attempt to make for that distant shore. They won't
come, and we won't make it.

It's time to think very quickly, carefully, to sort through what is actually possible. We can't be distracted by the luxuries that came into the water
with us—luxuries we have to let go: the sports watch, the cell phone, a wallet, or car keys. None of them can help us now. Let them go, for no good will
come, if we focus on their loss.

We don't have time to grieve or pretend.

If something like the wisdom and truth of Jesus of Nazareth is to survive beyond this lamentable though certain death of the Christian church,
we should take this brief time to focus on what will help the gospel stay
afloat, so to speak, until new models of the community can arise.

If I was a church leader, I would be trying to focus resources on those
few communities that are showing signs of vibrancy and which have solid
ministries of justice and peace. I would be looking for the creative edge of
the faith and thinking of ways to sustain it—fund it well, so that it is freed
to do ministry.

Since I have worked in theological education a great deal, I have some
sense of what could and perhaps should happen in this concentration of
resources, when it comes to training for ministry. I would be looking to
sustain serious training programs for laity, oriented by the need to sustain
faith communities that are very small, house-church size. Ministry training
would be reorganized to assume that there would be no paid profession as
such. It would be training in leadership models that focus on service and
prepare individuals to discern the moving of the Spirit in a secular world.

Ministry would be unpaid. Leadership would have to be trained
to do "church work," after their day job is finished. This would mean the

development of educational models that would allow people to earn a living, while studying. It would assume that the empowerment of laity was a central skill to be developed.

And as happened in the Middle Ages, it would be helpful to concentrate sufficient resources in one or two intentional communities, whose purpose was exploration and research—institutions that might sustain the wisdom of the tradition, while exploring new forms of expression. They could house our libraries and be the reservoir of traditions and wisdom. They'd be tasked with preserving and saving what is helpful from our past, while waiting to see how our uncertain present and future possibilities unfold.

This sounds so terribly melodramatic: survival tactics. But without such strategic decisions, we will watch the church of Christ sink into obscurity, and the story will be lost.

In the meantime, there are a few signs of hope that give me a sense of how the Christian Way might continue.

SIGNS OF HOPE

It happens around the world. Christians cook food and give it away. It's perhaps a natural instinct. When things go badly, I quite naturally head to the kitchen and start to prepare something to eat . . . shared food makes troubles more bearable, somehow. Don't we do the same with our church kitchens? Lacking better ideas, we offer food to our communities. There are so many examples, it would be impossible to note them all.

In the U.S. and Canada, there are many churches that have a once-weekly meal for the destitute in their neighborhood. Perhaps it is associated with a food bank, or maybe it stems from a local bakery. Sometimes, it's the work of a men's breakfast group or the outcome of a woman's reading circle. In almost all cases, it is the work of volunteers, who gain nothing for their labors but goodwill and comradery.

In my own experience, we partnered with a pub that provided free Saturday night dinners for the homeless, in exchange for using some of our parking lot as a summer patio. On another street corner, a church congregation offered free pizza every month—a welcome alternative to mission meals that tend to be wholesome, but uninspiring. Pizza day was a party, an excuse for celebration. It was a treat that some could ill afford. "Eat as much as you like," we said. "It's pizza day!" And yet another example in a local church basement—we served a weekly breakfast, given free to the folks who had no permanent home and who spent their days in the park by the church.

One congregation took a day a month to make bread—giving it away free for any and all. Everyone from medical doctors to university students gathered at 7:00 am and mixed the dough to make hundreds of rounds of buns. A full-day deal. Once baked, we took bread to shut-ins as a gesture that people are not forgotten, gave away rounds of buns to anyone off the street, and even supplied fresh bread to two sides of a labor dispute (we'd like to think we contributed to its resolution).

Two key aspects of all this work: the food is given away and it's available on a regular basis—something you could count on. There are minimal restrictions on how much or who could take this food. I know it is common for churches to hold sales of cookies and pies—fundraisers. Yard sales and bazaars are often accompanied by a café-style lunch room. In contrast, this ministry is about "giving away" without distinction. No one is asked if they really need free bread or if they will use it wisely.

The first objection that is often raised, when I suggest we give food away, is that it will get abused. People will hoard it, taking more than their share. Or they will abuse it—take one bite and throw the rest away. But let's face it. Every kind of gift in the North American world can be converted into addiction money. All our food bank restrictive efforts notwithstanding, those who need money will find a way to take what we offer them and use it to buy illicit substances. And my response has always been that I would rather not spend good energy playing "food police." It's better to give without distinction, so that those who are sincere are given what they need with the greatest amount of dignity and goodwill possible. After all, the point of any shared bread is to create community.

I call this work apron theology. It grows out of the notion that the circle of Jesus, each day, prays for daily bread. Like the manna from heaven.

In our modern context, as we see our community of faith dwindling, I would head to the kitchen. With what energy is left—in people power and bank account alike—I would dedicate my efforts to giving away free food. Open the doors and welcome people in to eat . . . who knows what will happen and whom we will meet? It's not a clever strategy with achievable goals or long-term objectives. It's a journey that we start, not knowing how it will end. At this stage, it is just an initiative based on intuition. But in the "ten" minutes that our church has left, I would focus most of our good energy on food and feeding.

The beauty of this apron theology is that you don't need prior experience. No university degree or college course is necessary. We all eat, and we all know about kitchens. We all can imagine hunger, even if we haven't already experienced it, and we recognize the basic need. And it need not be bread. Someone in your circle will have a special food they can cook in quantity. And I would imagine there are enough aprons to go around.

There's no predicting where our aprons will take us. But there are surprises waiting for us . . . that is certain. An example: I recall one instance, when the director of medicine in our town had her hands in the dishwater with an ex-chef, who lived with a serious addiction. It was this community's special Christmas dinner, cooked by volunteers from all walks of life. These two were chatting away about the best way to make turkey gravy. In what other world would they ever meet? They left the kitchen that night, on a first-name basis, and sought each other out in subsequent gatherings.

The hope is to break down the barriers that divide us. Over shared food, our distinctions get lost, and we can find an avenue for communication, perhaps even genuine community. So, in all our feeding, can we find ways that the line between those who serve and those who are served is blurred and eventually wiped out?

Like all forms of ministry, apron theology requires commitment and time. It is not easy to sustain. There is usually lots of goodwill at the beginning, but then, as the months pass and the same people keep coming back because they still need food, people can get discouraged. Volunteers find other outlets for their time. Best to start with what is manageable and to offer ongoing encouragement and training for those who are preparing food, while building up the goodwill and grace among those who eat it. Eventually, the hope is we all share bread together.

CONVERTING OUR SANCTUARIES INTO FOOD STANDS

Aside from those congregations that feed their neighborhoods, there are some instances of churches giving their space over to alternate purposes to share food. There are experiments where sanctuaries become local shopping malls or eateries. In Maryland, there is a Black Church Food Security Network[11] that is matching local congregations with farmers, using church property and other spaces to grow food and hosting mini-farmers markets in local church buildings to coordinate with worship times. They call it "soil to sanctuary."

In San Francisco, there is an Episcopal church that turns its sanctuary into a vegetable stand.[12] It's a joyous celebration of food and sustenance, as

11. For more information regarding this innovative program, see their web-site: https://blackchurchfoodsecurity.net/about-us/

12. See St, Gregory of Nyssa Episcopal Church: https://www.saintgregorys.org/the-food-pantry.html

the crowds gather to be served from the selection of fresh vegetables, breads, and dried goods. The location of their weekly prayers is also the foundation of their food ministry.

SABBATH POTLUCK COMMUNIONS

While there are many examples of feeding missions and church markets, there are fewer well-known integrations of real food and the Lord's Supper. Many congregations reenact the Last Supper on Maundy Thursday, but this is a special event. Regular masses or Eucharist services allow the ritual to stand alone.

There is one example that stands as a sign post of what might be possible. When I attended a communion at Hillhurst United Church in Calgary, the table was spread with finger food. There was a loaf of bread and chalice of wine, but arranged with these central elements were platters of cheese and vegetables. The congregation was invited to help themselves to whatever was available, whenever they wanted. And some people did just that. Taking a cue from this practice, I began to introduce the same practice at the church where I served at the time. A communion Sunday was a time when the table was laid with enough food that anyone could make their lunch from the common table.

I watched as the choir proceeded up the aisle, and some members felt comfortable enough to snag a bit of food, as they processed by the table on the way to choir stalls. Some parishioners thought it was novel. They stayed awake during the sacrament. And after the service, all the luncheon type food was eaten. No problem for hungry people. But there was precious little integration. The sacramental morsels of bread and wine are so imbedded in our psyches, that the extra food sitting on the table was seen as something entirely separate. Nice, but not spiritually significant. If there was a reaction at all to this experiment, it was a bit of frustration. "Too much to take in all at once," was the response. "I didn't get it!"

Next, I introduced more food at all services. There was a "lunch table" sitting in the center of the sanctuary (our pews had a lovely division that allowed for tables to be set up halfway down the aisle). It was always laden with easy to handle fresh fruit, cheese squares, and bread. There was enough to make a lunch, and some of our guests from the street would attend church and help themselves. With time, that might have tipped the balance toward a shared meal as a sacrament, but we never got that far. Resistance to "those" people was so great that I had to leave.

Perhaps this is an instance when we have to allow the church as it now stands to wither away, before something new can be created. The architecture was against this kind of innovation. It was built for large crowds and assumed a speaker/audience relationship. Introducing a participatory, informal circle into this environment is always clumsy. Pews are fixed to the floor; people are used to sitting in relative isolation facing forward. Sharing bread and conversation is a tough sell, when the building is telling everyone to sit still and listen.

In a similar manner, the centuries of training in sacramental piety make it difficult to break through to a new understanding of our holy meal. It's meant to be a revelatory moment, an other-worldly pause in the business of living. Introducing a bit of domestic chaos—a real meal is always chaotic in a good sense—is not welcome. Asking people to share more than the simple elements of the Eucharist felt a bit like I was a food-pusher. No one understood or appreciated what they felt was a cumbersome intrusion in their otherwise simple spiritual practice.

Using a real meal for a sacramental understanding of the Jesus story worked, when it was separated from Sunday worship. Everyone likes to eat, and hosting a potluck is not a difficult ask. When the preconceived expectations of public worship are removed, I found participants much more willing to experiment with new ideas and alternate interpretations of our Jesus movement. However, these "feasts" were never seen as a substitute for worship or the foundation for a new understanding of community. They were educational events, informative, even inspiring, but marginal to the faith journey.

So, I conclude this text with nothing more than hints. There are several living examples of alternate religious communities—intentional, deeply spiritual circles. Taizé[13] in France is an example of an a-denominational, intentional community of prayer and peace. Iona[14] in Scotland is a similar example. There are countless other, smaller, less well-known, Christian communities and religious orders that live an alternative life. And perhaps this is where our hope lies for the future: in isolated small gatherings of believers, who share food and prayer with action and service.

While I can't see over the horizon to what might be, I do have a story that gives me hope that some form of Christian community will arise from our current decline.

13. For details on this community, see: https://www.taize.fr/en

14. For details on Iona, see: https://iona.org.uk/visit-and-stay/iona-abbey-centre/iona-abbey-programme-bookings/

Let's go back to the bread day, I mentioned above. A local congregation gathered once a month to make hundreds of rounds of buns. Nothing special. No fancy toppings or ingredients. Just regular, fresh-baked bread.

On one of those days, I had arranged for a local flour mill to send its portable pizza oven to our church parking lot. Fired by wood, this special oven could bake two dozen rounds of buns at a time. Not only was it an impressive kitchen aid, it had quite the visual presence in our little downtown. People could smell the bread from afar, and so we gathered some curious spectators. There were downtown, business types and a few folks who walked the streets asking for charity.

It so happened that, on that particular day, I had also invited some of my university students to volunteer. I was teaching a course on introduction to religion and told them to come and see how one faith tradition exercised its piety through action. We needed lots of hands to shape bread and to share it. One young woman, who had been clear from the beginning of the year that she was part of a Wiccan circle, agreed to help out. She was keen and open, and a real delight.

After several hours of mixing dough, we went outside to watch the outdoor oven. It had been fired and was ready to bake the rounds of buns that others had begun much earlier in the day. The oven baked 10 rounds in record time. We drew them out of the oven and set them on a table to cool. People gathered round, "Ooh's" and "Aah's" on their lips. After a few minutes, we broke one round open for tastes with butter and started giving the baked rounds away—to any and all. In the line was an older man in a suit—looked like he served in the bank next door. Behind him was a fellow who begged on the street corner outside that bank. Everyone took some bread. Each one waiting, while the oven did its thing, and then taking away a fresh round of buns until they were all gone.

The baking of our entire batch of bread took several hours, and we followed basically the same procedure. Some church members came by and picked up several rounds for their list of shut-ins. A few students from my class took some rounds back to their residences.

My Wiccan helper watched and, in the end, pulled me aside. "What kind of Christians are you people?" she asked. She was overwhelmed by the idea of giving food away without condition or distinction. "If I were to be a Christian, I would come here," she admitted.

The miracle of bread.

That's how the movement began. We did not convince people to join the Jesus Way with theology. It wasn't our doctrine that was inspiring. Passing bread—hand-to-hand—that was the message.

Perhaps it still is.

Conclusion

So What?

As I write this final chapter, I am surrounded by young students—part of a folk music program in Norway. They're delightful and sensitive. Much more creative than I can imagine I ever was. And while their world is taken up in rehearsing melodies passed down by oral tradition and mastering dance steps from centuries old traditions, they do ask me what I am doing. Curious perhaps, but also sincere. So, I try to do a summary of the thesis of this text. Alas, many have just a passing awareness of the church. There's a small, white chapel down by the lake that is open from time to time. But they never go in. They've heard of Jesus, and some know about the sacrament of Holy Communion. But like many of their generation, it's a faint awareness based more on caricatures drawn from movies than any personal experience.

So, at best, the issue of a revitalized, common Christian meal is a passing curiosity. They listen sincerely to what I explain is my purpose in writing, and then we go back to the difference between a violin and a hardanger fiddle.

"So what?" they might respond, if they were less generous with their sentiments. "Is there really anything important in this examination of Christian eating habits?"

On a purely academic level, I might argue that it is important to analyze critical transitions in history. Given the importance of the Christian church and its values within the evolution of Western thought and culture, the misappropriation of the Lord's Supper sacrament is important. From humble beginnings as a meal that is shared, it moved to become one of the levelers of power used by popes and princes to manipulate world events. Moreover, the way the sacrament was used and abused was the source of considerable political conflict that resulted, quite literally, in rewriting the map of Europe and eventually North America. Not a minor subject.

Speaking from a personal perspective, the Eucharist has been, for many centuries, the source of peace and forgiveness. It was our "Garden of Eden" paradise in the here and now. In a broken, finite world, we have only faint glimpses of what humanity could be. But the bread and wine ritual was an oasis of hope, a space where individual faults were wiped away and new beginnings of innocence were possible. So, a vehicle for personal hope and the source from which forgiveness might flow.

Indeed, there are good reasons to care about the Lord's Supper and how it changed. But they mostly point backwards to a past historical relevance, not forwards toward some future pertinence.

Moving from sharing food to ritualizing it, from community to cannibalism . . . the question remains: "What's the big deal?"

It requires an entirely separate book to answer that philosophical question of meaning, but as a conclusion, let's just note the simple fact that a modern culture, bereft of its religious underpinnings, is rudderless. The culture that promised us freedom from restraint and abundance of choice has not proven equal to the task of establishing lasting purpose to life. In a book examining the psychological effects of a self-directed and self-centered world, Anne Lembke suggests:

> . . . we've transformed the world from a place of scarcity to a place of overwhelming abundance: Drugs, food, news, gambling, shopping, gaming, texting, sexting, Facebooking, Instagramming, YouTubing, tweeting . . . the increased numbers and variety and potency of high rewarding stimuli today are staggering. The smartphone is the modern-day hypodermic needle, delivering digital dopamine 24/7 for a wired generation. If you haven't met your drug of choice yet, it's coming soon to a website near you.[1]

Instead of lasting world peace and personal harmony, the modern world has established the rule of addictions, freedom from moral restraint, and tribal exceptionalism. It is difficult to imagine a set of commonly accepted values and standards. Apart from the "rule of law," how do we call ourselves and others to account? Our world gets reduced to what and who we are . . . which admittedly is pretty short-sighted and small.

Further to the words of Niebuhr cited in Chapter 5:

---

1. Lembke, *Dopamine Nation*, 1.

Nothing worth doing can be achieved in our own lifetime, therefore we must be saved by hope. Nothing which is true or beautiful or good makes complete sense in any immediate context of history, therefore we must be saved by faith. Nothing we do, however virtuous, can be accomplished alone, therefore we are saved by love.[2]

Niebuhr makes three essential points about human civilization. First, we need more time than we have been given to do anything that is of lasting significance. Therefore, we need the hope of future generations. That's hard to achieve in a self-oriented world. Hence, a spiritual or communal identity is required. Second, our dreams have to stretch beyond our own vision. Any significant ambition points beyond the horizon. It is other-focused. Not a heaven-bound vision, good spirituality always directs people back to this earth and its welfare. No escape. That being the case, we require faith in something beyond ourselves: God, human goodness, global justice. Finally, apart from Mozart and Einstein, perhaps human beings need one another for lasting inspiration and security.

While there are many pathways to enlightenment, I consider the Christian approach to truth to be the most satisfying, at least the most familiar to me. And I believe that a redevelopment of the Lord's meal, as outlined above, would be the sound foundation on which a new Christianity might grow.

2. Niebuhr, *Irony of American History,* 63.

Appendix

The List of Complaints about Jesus

The following is a comprehensive listing of the complaints leveled at Jesus, taken from the three synoptic gospels. As a graph, you can follow not simply the content of the complaint but who made it.

	Complaint	Text	Complainants
	Food / Meal Practice		
1	Disciples don't fast	Mk 2:18, Mt 9:14–15, Lk 5:23	Pharisees' scholars
2	Disciples strip corn (work) on sabbath	Mk 2:23, Mt 12:1–8, Lk 6:1–5	Pharisees
3	Eating with defiled hands	Mk 7:1–5, Mt 15:1–9,	Pharisees
4	Touching sinner woman at a meal	Lk 7:36–50	Simon the Pharisee
5	No washing hands before eating	Lk 11:37, Lk 7:36, Lk 14:1	A Pharisee
6	Eating with tax collectors and sinners	Lk 5:27–32, Mk 2:14–17, Mt 9:9–13	Pharisees and their scholars
7	Eating with Chief Tax Collector: Zacchaeus	Lk 19: 1–10	The unnamed crowd surrounding Jesus
8	Wasting ointment on Jesus while he was eating	Mk 14:1–9, Mt 26:2–5, Lk 21:1–2	Disciples
9	Healing on the sabbath at dinner	Lk 14:1–6	A prominent Pharisee

10	Jesus was eating and out of his mind	Mk 3:20–21	Jesus' relatives
	Authority of Jesus		
1	By what authority does he do what he does in the temple precinct	Mk 11:29, Mt 21:23–27, Lk 20:1–8	Ranking priests and scholars
2	Are you the one with real authority (the messiah)	Mk 14:58, Mk 14:61	Chief priest
3	Jesus blasphemes because he forgives sins	Mk 2:1–12, Mt 9:1–2, Lk 5:17–26	Scholars
4	Only the head demon has the authority to command evil spirits	Mt 12:24, Mk 3:27	Pharisees, scholars from Jerusalem
	Miscellaneous Complaints		
1	Healing on the sabbath	Lk 13:14, Lk 6:6–10, Lk14:1–6, Mk 3:6, Mt 12:19	Leader of the synagogue, Pharisee and Herodians
2	Jesus has no regard for social order and the importance of class and money	Lk 16:14	Pharisees
3	Crowd/mob leader	Mk 14:1–2	Ranking priests and scholars
4	Knows the true nature of evil spirits	Mk 1:24, Mk 1:34 Mk 2:3	Evil spirits
5	Unwanted healer	Mk 5:17	Townspeople near the region of the Gerasenes
6	Isn't this just a carpenter's son	Mk 6:2–3, Mt 13:53–57	Jesus' hometown crowd
7	Jesus questions hometown virtue	Lk 4:28	Jesus' hometown crowd
8	Jesus' prejudice against gentiles	Mk 7:24–30, Mt 15:21–28	A gentile, Syrophoenician woman

Bibliography

Bonhoeffer, Dietrich. *The Cost of Discipleship*. New York: Simon & Schuster, 1993.

Borg, Marcus. *Meeting Jesus Again for the First Time*. New York: HarperCollins, 2015.

Brown, Raymond. *The Birth of the Messiah: A Commentary on the Infancy Narratives in the Gospels of Matthew and Luke*. New York: Doubleday, 1993.

Brueggemann, Walter. *The Prophetic Imagination*. 2nd ed. Minneapolis: Fortress, 2001.

Clarke, Brian, and Stuart Macdonald. *Leaving Christianity: Changing Allegiances in Canada since 1945*. Montreal: McGill-Queens University Press, 2019.

Cox, Harvey. *The Future of Faith*. New York: HarperOne, 2009.

Crossan, John Dominic. *God and Empire*. New York: HarperOne, 2007.

———. *Render unto Caesar: The Struggle over Christ and Culture in the New Testament*. New York: HarperOne, 2022.

———. *Resurrecting Easter: How the West Lost and the East Kept the Original Easter Vision*. New York: HarperCollins, 2017.

Ellul, Jacques. *Violence: Reflections from a Christian Perspective*. Eugene, OR: Wipf & Stock, 2007.

Funk, Robert. *Honest to Jesus*. New York: HarperSanFrancisco, 1996.

Ghandi, Mahatma, and Thomas Merton. *Gandhi on Non-Violence*. Cambridge, MA: New Directions, 1965.

Hall, Douglas John. *The Reality of the Gospel and the Unreality of the Churches*. Philadelphia: Augsberg Fortress, 1975.

———. *What Christianity Is Not: An Exercise in "Negative" Theology*. Eugene, OR: Cascade, 2013.

Heyerdahl, Thor. *Kon-Tiki*. London: Allen & Unwin, 1950.

Jacobovici, Simcha. "Jesus' Marriage to Mary the Magdalene Is Fact, Not Fiction." *HuffPost*, January 26, 2015. https://www.huffpost.com/entry/jesus-marriage-to-mary-th_b_6225826.

Josephus, Flavius. *The Antiquities of the Jews*. Translated by William Whiston. Denmark: Titan Read, 2010.

Kitamori, Kazoh. *Theology of the Pain of God*. Eugene, OR: Wipf & Stock, 2005.

Kun, Jeanne. "Mary Magdalene, Apostle to the Apostles: Mary Followed Jesus in Faith and Constancy." *The Word among Us*, n.d. https://wau.org/resources/article/re_mary_magdalene_apostle_to_the_apostles_1/.

Lembke, Anna. *Dopamine Nation: Finding the Balance in the Age of Indulgence*. New York: Dutton, 2021.

Levan, Christopher. *Healing Death: Finding the Healing to Live Well into Our Dying*. Eugene, OR: Cascade, 2020.

———. *The Prayer: 68 Words That Changed the World*. Eugene, OR: Cascade, 2018.

Lindsey, Hal. *The Late Great Planet Earth*. Grand Rapids, MI: Zondervan, 1970.

Lumpkin, Joseph. *Jesus and Mary-Husband and Wife: Who Were They and What Was Their Relationship?* Blountsville, AL: Fifth Estate, 2012.

"Mahmoud Abbas: Haunted by Ghost of Yesser Arafat." *The Telegraph*, September 22, 2011. https://www.telegraph.co.uk/news/worldnews/middleeast/palestinianauthority/8784000/Mahmoud-Abbas-haunted-by-ghost-of-Yasser-Arafat.html.

McCarthy, Christine E. "The Imitation of Mary Magdalene: Apostle to the Apostles." *Daily Theology Podcast*, July 22, 2014. https://dailytheology.org/2014/07/22/the-imitation-of-mary-magdalene-apostle-to-the-apostles/.

Meyers, Robin. *Saving God from Religion: A Minister's Search for Faith in a Skeptical Age*. New York: Convergent, 2020.

Miller, Robert, ed. *The Complete Gospels*. Sonoma, CA: Polebridge, 1994.

Niebuhr, Reinhold. *The Irony of American History*. New York: Scribner's, 1952.

Origen of Alexandria. "Contra Celsum." In *The Complete Works of Origen*, 248. Toronto: Public Domain, 2016.

Pearse, Roger. "A Homily of Gregory the Great and Mary Magdalene." *Roger Pearse* (blog), October 12, 2020. https://www.roger-pearse.com/weblog/2020/10/12/a-homily-of-gregory-the-great-and-mary-magdalene/.

Pascal, Blaise. "Pensées." In *Collected Works of Blaise Pascal*, n.p. Hastings, UK: Delphi Classics, 2020.

Reed, Jonathan, and John Dominic Crossan. *Excavating Jesus: Beneath the Stones, Behind the Texts*. Revised and updated edition. New York: HarperCollins, 2009.

Saul, John Rolston. *The Comeback: How Aboriginals are Reclaiming Power and Influence*. Toronto: Penguin Books, 2015.

Schüssler Fiorenza, Elizabeth. "Feminist Theology as a Critical Theology of Liberation." *Theological Studies* 36 (1975) 605–26.

———*In Memory of Her: Feminist Theologica Reconstruction of Christian Origins*. Tenth anniversary edition. New York: Crossroad, 1994.

Schweitzer, Albert. *The Quest for the Historical Jesus*. London: A. & C. Black, 1926.

Spong, John Shelby. *The Fourth Gospel: Tales of a Jewish Mystic*. Toronto: HarperCollins, 2013.

———. *The Sins of Scripture: Exposing the Bible's Texts of Hate to Reveal the God of Love*. New York: HarperSanFrancisco, 2005.

Tacitus, Cornelius. "Annals IV and XV." In *Complete Works of Tacitus*, translated by John Jackson, 109. Hastings, UK: Delphi Classics, 2014.

Tertullian, Quintus Septimus Florens. "On Baptism." In *The Complete Works of Tertullian*, 155–220. Toronto: Public Domain, 2016.

Vosper, Gretta. *With or without God*. Toronto: HarperCollins, 2008.

Wilson, Lee. *Was Jesus Married? The Case from the New Testament*. USA: Grace Centered, 2022.